Thanks

This book has only been made possible with the help and enthusiastic support of many organisations and individuals and our thanks go to:

BTCV, Butterfly Conservation, Campaign to Protect Rural England, Forum for the Future, Friends of the Earth, Friends Provident, *Geographical* magazine, Natural Collection, Solartwin, The Body Shop, The *Ecologist*, The Ramblers' Association, The Soil Association, The Wildlife Trusts, Unit[e], WRVS, Zac Goldsmith, John Humphrys, Tony Juniper, Jonathon Porritt, Harry Ram and John Vidal.

We would also like to thank all of our advertisers who have supported this book.

Contents

go make a difference

OVER 500 DAILY WAYS TO SAVE THE PLANET

First published 2003 by Think Books an imprint of Pan Macmillan Ltd
Pan Macmillan, 20 New Wharf Road, London N1 9RR
Basingstoke and Oxford
Associated companies throughout the world
www.panmacmillan.com
www.think-books.com

ISBN: 978-1-84525-056-0

Editors: Joanna Bourne, Emma Jones and Sonja Patel
Editorial team: Tania Adams, Camilla Doodson,
Clare Mendes, Malcolm Tait and Marion Thompson
Design: Sally Laver and Lou Millward Tait
Illustration: Thomas Boivin

1 3 5 7 9 8 6 4 2

A CIP catalogue record for this book is available from the British Library.

Printed and Bound in Italy by Printer Trento

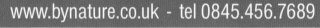

Why go make a difference?

There is only one world, and we all have a role in looking after it. But what can we as individuals really do to make a difference? Well, the answers are here in this little book. In the pages that follow are the details that will enable every one of us to tread more lightly on the planet that sustains us.

Whether the challenge is protecting local green spaces or fighting global climate change, the fact is that the most important force for change is you and me. If we don't do anything, then probably nothing much will happen. Small actions, by contrast, can have a vast impact. Simple deeds like writing letters, recycling waste, saving energy and being thoughtful about what we buy can have quite an awesome influence on the world we live in.

What's better still is that we can all choose how much to do and how to make our individual actions fit with our busy lives. That is why *Go Make a Difference* is so powerful. The hundreds of actions set out here provide everyone with the means to make a difference.

The greatest threat to our planet is people believing that the decline of our common environment is inevitable. Nothing could be further from the truth. If we all play a small part, big change is possible. Go on, Go Make a Difference.

Tony Juniper
Executive Director
Friends of the Earth

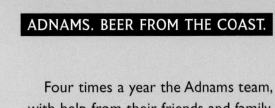

The future starts here

It's often said that the failure of people to adopt a green lifestyle is a reflection of our basic selfishness. The assumption is the kind of society that stands a chance of lasting beyond the next generation is one that only a monk could tolerate.

But that couldn't be further from the truth. The most damaging aspects of modern industrial society are not things that we would miss were they to be replaced. Who would mourn the end of pesticides or a reduction in packaging in supermarkets? Who would feel oppressed if, instead of promoting low-grade industrial food production, our taxes were spent on support for local organic produce?

There are any number of ways in which we can make a difference. For some people it is easier than others. It's hard for many to buy local organic produce when local shops have been bankrupted by politically advantaged out-of-town supermarkets. It's hard to unhook oneself from cars when the transport infrastructure so favours them. Without systemic or political change, our own individual actions are somewhat crippled. But we are also part of an economy that responds to consumer stimulation. When enough people choose to power their homes with renewable energy we will see a snowball effect and before long, Britain will be carbon neutral. After all, the consumer persuaded supermarkets to abandon GM foods, and it is working mothers in New Zealand who are responsible for the initiation of a 'zero-waste' strategy.

Go Make a Difference is primarily a guide to ecological living. But it is also a guide to ecological renewal, with vital information on how we can all get involved in pushing for change at the policy level. Combined, this process is irresistible.

Zac Goldsmith
Editor, the *Ecologist*

How to use this book

The tips in this book have been compiled and updated using information from over 300 leading environmental sources and organisations, from global charities to individual suppliers of environmentally friendly products.

The 14 chapters cover all aspects of life – from birth to death via shopping, holidays, DIY and petcare – for there is nothing we do as human beings that doesn't touch the wider world. Each tip highlights a small, practical, positive way that can help you make a difference to the world around you. They fall into three types: things you can do in order to make a difference, things you shouldn't do in order to make a difference and ways for you to make a difference by joining or helping an organisation and getting more involved. Websites and telephone numbers are given wherever possible so you can find out more; full contact details are in the directory on page 238.

Help us with the next edition

We have taken every care to make sure the information in *Go Make a Difference* is correct at the time of going to press, but things do change. If the contact details given don't work, or you'd simply like to comment on a particular tip, email us at editorial@thinkpublishing.co.uk or write to:

Go Make a Difference
Think Publishing Ltd,
The Pall Mall Deposit,
124-128 Barlby Road,
London W10 6BL

To find out how you can contribute to the next edition, please turn to page 237.

And help yourself

You can also use this book to raise funds for your organisation. Call Tilly at Think Publishing on 020 8962 3020 to find out more.

protect our future
Start with the Washing-Up!
Ecover ecological products have powerful formulas which are based on plant and natural mineral ingredients.
This gives Ecover products the Power of Nature - brilliant cleaning power - minimum impact on the environment - no unnecessary chemicals.
So to protect your environment for the future - start with the Washing-Up.
Brilliant cleaning
Minimum impact on aquatic life
Only natural colours & fragrances
Info pack 08451 302230 website www.ecover.com.
ECOLOGICAL
WASHING-UP LIQUID
WITH CAMOMILE AND MARIGOLD
ECOVER
NATURALLY MILD ON YOUR HANDS
for people who care

Home sweet home

Helping the environment begins at home. Whether you're decorating, buying furniture, gardening or simply cleaning, you can make a difference by using tools, materials and products that have less impact on your surroundings. Fortunately, we've never been better informed – visit the Greenpeace site for ways to create a toxic-free future at **www.greenpeace.org.uk/toxics**. Advice includes eliminating non eco-friendly chemicals from the home and looking at environmentally friendly electronic alternatives. If you're building, or even making simple repairs, the Centre for Alternative Technology (CAT) at **www.cat.org.uk** supplies a whole range of factsheets on everything from cobbing (building with earth) to sheep's wool insulation. Think though, before you go 'changing rooms' or re-landscaping the garden – do you really need to do it in the first place? The kindest solution for the environment is often that which has the lowest impact. Sometimes it's better to do nothing, sit back and let the grass grow.

...next to godliness

THERE'S NOTHING CLEAN ABOUT CHEMICALS When you're cleaning your house you're often doing the opposite to the environment and also to your health. Our lifestyles have never been so full of chemicals – by the 1980s, the world chemical output was 500 times greater than in 1940. There are now 60,000-70,000 synthetic chemicals in regular daily use. Increasingly, the link is being made between the chemicals we use and the rise in certain diseases – in the 30-year period from 1975 to 2004, the incidence rate for cancer has increased in Great Britain by 25%. More than 400 toxic chemicals – some of which are used in the home – have been discovered in human blood. For more information on these and other harmful chemicals visit the *Ecologist* website at www.theecologist.org and the World Wildlife Fund at www.wwf.org.uk/chemicals/glossary.asp.

HOW MANY CHEMICALS ARE THERE IN YOUR BODY? When Elizabeth Salter-Green, director of WWF UK's toxic programme, volunteered for a fat-cell test to establish the presence of chemicals in her body, she found that levels of contamination were far above normal. More worryingly were the traces of DDT and PCBs that were found – chemicals that have already been banned in the UK. The results spurred her into making some lifestyle changes – she now eats only organic non-processed food, avoids bleach and pesticides in her home, never dry-cleans her clothes and avoids parks and farms where spraying takes place. Tests showed that her contamination levels have significantly reduced as a result. Visit **www.wwf.org.uk/chemicals/feature.asp** to find out more.

USE OXYGEN-ENHANCING PRODUCTS TO CLEAN YOUR CLOTHES Phosphates are used as water softeners, and when they're discharged into the water supply they stimulate excessive algal growth. These 'algal blooms' starve water of oxygen, killing plant and fish life, and disrupt the sewage treatment process.

For every litre of washing powder you use, 20,000 litres of water are required to treat it until it can re-enter our water system safely. And it's not the detergent that cleans the clothes anyway – it's the water. All detergents do is separate the oxygen molecules to generate a 'wetter' water to penetrate the fabric deeper and thus remove most dirt. Alternatives to detergents do exist – Safewash's T-wave laundry discs (**www.safewash.com**) and Eco-balls (**www.ecozone.co.uk**) offer clean, inexpensive, chemical-free cleaning. Visit **www.naturalcollection.com** or call Ecozone on 0845 230 4200.

AVOID PRODUCTS CONTAINING CHLORINE Chlorine is highly corrosive, capable of damaging the skin, eyes and other membranes. It can also irritate the skin, eyes and lungs, and research has linked exposure to chlorine with birth defects and cancer. If mixed with other cleaning solutions it can produce deadly gases. Detergents transfer their chlorine into the air through a process called volatilisation – when you open the dishwasher the steamy mist that comes out is full of chlorine. Chlorine concentrations in the upper atmosphere have quadrupled over the past 25 years. Each chlorine atom released is capable of destroying tens of thousands of ozone molecules. Other chlorine-containing products to avoid are chlorine bleach, chlorinated disinfectant cleaners, mildew removers and toilet bowl cleaners. Find ecological alternatives at Earth Friendly Products (**www.greenbrands.co.uk**).

BEWARE OF CARPET CLEANERS
Perchlorethylene is used in many carpet and upholstery cleaners. It's a known carcinogen, which may be responsible for anaemia, damage to the liver, kidneys and nervous system. Carpet and upholstery cleaners that contain ammonium hydroxide should be avoided, too – they're corrosive and can irritate the eyes, skin and respiratory passages.

USE FRAGRANCE-FREE CLEANERS Avoid cleaners that use synthetic musk fragrances. They are potential hormone disrupters and have been found in human body fat, breast milk, fish, mussels and other wildlife. Use products with citronella instead or open the windows and create a homely fragrance by boiling some cinnamon.

USE BAKING SODA TO CLEAR YOUR DRAINS Many commercial drain cleaners contain corrosive and toxic products such as sodium or potassium hydroxide, hydrochloric acid and petroleum distillates that kill aquatic life and make water even more expensive to treat – there's no need for them! Flushing drains with a foaming solution of boiling water, baking soda, table salt and vinegar, then using a plunger will work just as well. And never flush harmful cleaning products down the drain, they can corrode water pipes and kill sewage-eating bacteria.

AVOID COMMERCIAL FURNITURE POLISHES Furniture polishes are petroleum distillates, which are flammable and have been linked with skin and lung cancer. They also contain nitrobenzene, a chemical that is highly toxic and easily absorbed through the skin. Natural Collection has alternatives, visit **www.naturalcollection.com**, or call 0845 367 7001.

USE BORAX AS A CLEANER INSTEAD Borax is a naturally occurring mineral made of sodium, boron, oxygen and water that has been used as a cleaner for decades. It is effective as a natural antibacterial, cleaning, fungicidal and bleaching agent. You can use it to clean your fridge, wash your laundry and to remove stains from your rugs. Local hardware stores and chemists sell borax – if you can't see it, ask for it.

AVOID PRODUCTS CONTAINING TRICLOSAN Triclosan is an antibacterial chemical used widely in the home to make germ-free utensils such as chopping boards. The ever-increasing use of antibiotics has been linked to the appearance of 'superbugs' – resistant bugs for which there is no treatment. Triclosan has been found in human breast milk and it may lower the body's immune system and ability to fight off other bugs.

MAKE YOUR OWN CLEANING PRODUCTS It doesn't take much effort to make cleaning products yourself. For washing powder, mix one cup of finely grated soap, one cup of washing soda, and two teaspoons of lavender oil. To remove oil on clothing, rub white chalk into the stain before laundering. Use bicarbonate of soda to clean sinks and baths, vinegar to clean windows, washing soda crystals in water to clean floors, a paste of baking soda and water to clean ovens and microwaves, three parts olive oil to one part vinegar to polish furniture and soda paste to polish silver.

READER TIP – MELANIE CLARE

USE ESSENTIAL OILS AND ALCOHOL FOR CLEANING TOO! Essential oils have such a wide range of practical uses around the home. Use pine oil as a bathroom cleaner – a tiny drop freshens the loo and plug hole. A refreshing antibacterial room spray can be made out of vodka, water and two drops each of lemongrass, lavender and tea tree oil. And to ward off insects in summer and generally freshen the air, use lemon oil or citronella.

AVOID WASHING CLOTHES AT 50°C No textiles need to be washed at 50°C. By changing all 50°C labels on clothing to 40°C, a clothing company can cut energy used during the lifecycle of its clothes by 10%. Marks & Spencer did this, saving customers the energy equivalent of running all its UK stores for four months. They also found that 70% of their clothes can be washed at 30°C and now include a 'Think climate – wash at 30°C' label. This could save around 40% of energy used in each laundry cycle.

DON'T USE COMMERCIAL MOTHBALLS Common mothball crystals contain nitrophenols, paradichlorobenzene (para-DCB) and napthalene vapour, giving them their smell. However, these are all toxic chemicals which hang around a long time in the environment. Para-DCB is a known carcinogen and repeated exposure at high levels can damage the nervous system and lungs. High levels of napthalene can lead to headaches, fatigue, confusion, nausea and vomiting. Make sure you store your woollens in air-tight storage containers or use natural alternatives: cedar wood or a mixed herb bag including dried rosemary, lavender, cinnamon, cardamom seed, cloves, tansy, wormwood, southern wood and pyrethrum (chrysanthemum family) flowers.

JUST BECAUSE IT'S ON THE FLOOR... Don't automatically toss anything that has been worn once or ended up on the floor into the laundry bin. Is it truly dirty? You could cut the number of loads you wash by half by airing clothes and putting them back in the wardrobe if they aren't dirty.

READER TIP – AGNES BODDINGTON

CLEANER CLEANING CLOTHS Invest in Microtex cloths to clean every area of your house. Microtex fabric is made up of thousands of tiny microfibres that attract dirt using only a little plain warm water. No cleaners, detergents or sprays are needed, so your cleaning will help the environment, too. Look out for the cloths in your local hardware shops.

BECOME A TOXIC EXPERT Brands of cleaning products you've used for years may be highly toxic or polluting your home – but their manufacturers will keep on making them as long as people buy them. The World Wildlife Fund's 'Chemicals and Health' campaign against toxins is a mine of information on how chemicals affect our lives, our environment and our wildlife. At **www.wwf.org.uk/chemicals/home.asp** they show you how to avoid hazardous chemicals in your home with a room-by-room guide. There's also a glossary of toxic chemicals – including PCBs, phthalates and brominated flame retardants – and a handy quiz to help find out how exposed to them you are.

READER TIP – NICK SMITH

DON'T LET WIRE COAT HANGERS BREED

Take wire coat hangers back to the dry-cleaners' rather than allowing them to accumulate in your wardrobe. You'll save space, and the shop will be grateful, too.

Home improvements

WHAT ARE YOU REALLY DOING WHEN YOU DO IT YOURSELF? The back-to-back home improvement TV programmes may inspire you to give your house a makeover. But often the products and methods they promote are designed to look good, without considering the harm they can do to your health and the environment. In terms of energy and toxicity, buildings and construction are among the most wasteful and polluting areas of modern life. But there are ecological alternatives. Visit The Association of Environment Conscious Building (www.aecb.net, 0845 456 9773) or the Green Building Store (www.greenbuildingstore.co.uk or call 01484 461705) to help you choose which products to buy and which to avoid. In the end though, if you really want to be happy with the place in which you live, it's a state of mind, not a coat of paint that will make the difference. And as you anguish over which shade of buttermilk to paint the hall, remember those without homes – buy *The Big Issue*.

ESTIMATE THE COST OF YOUR DIY TO THE ENVIRONMENT All buildings affect the environment. How disruptive or harmonious they will be as time progresses depends on how you build and maintain them. Is your house well insulated and energy-efficient so that it emits low levels of CO_2? Have you harnessed the energy of the sun, water or wind power? Are your building materials recycled or do they come from sustainable sources? Do they have a minimal effect on the environment, and

will they need to be maintained often? Do you choose materials that don't damage the ozone layer or your health? Do you conserve as much water as possible when you build? And have you taken into account the wildlife living around your home? The choices you make – either in building, repairing or redecorating – all count.

SHARPEN YOUR TOOLS Buy a sharpening stone from a hardware store. It'll cost £2.50 or thereabouts, and save you pounds on the cost of new tools. Chisels, screwdrivers, garden shears, edge-cutting lawn tools and even saw blades can be restored to pristine condition with very little effort. Tools cost money to make, and use resources in their manufacture, so sharpen yours regularly and make them last for years.

READER TIP – IAN CARE

INFLUENCE DESIGN FOR THE BETTER

When you buy a new house or build an extension, you can influence the design. Make the best use of natural light and heat – it has a far greater effect than replacing bulbs with 'energy savers' – if you plan your windows carefully you may not need that extra light at all. Have you planned the angle of the roofline so that it can accommodate a solar heating device? This requires more thought than just accepting the standard or choosing between options presented but the positive effects make it worth it.

ONLY USE BORON-BASED WOOD PRESERVATIVES

Wood preservatives don't just kill the pests they're designed to, they're also killing the environment. The pesticides they contain are nerve poisons and their fungicides are toxins, which harm the environment during their production and after they've been applied. When buying a wood preservative, check the tin to ensure it's made from boron. Boron is a naturally-occurring mineral and preservatives made from it are less harmful. They're the only kind approved by the Association for Environment Conscious Building. Visit **www.aecb.net** (0845 456 9773) or Auro Organic Paint Supplies at **www.auroorganic.co.uk** (01452 772020).

CHECK THE LABELS AND AVOID SOLVENT-BASED PAINT
Modern gloss paints can contain up to 50% solvents and volatile organic compounds (VOCs) that enter the surrounding air throughout the paint's lifetime. If inhaled or absorbed through the skin VOCs may irritate the eyes, nose and throat, affect the nervous system and damage internal organs. The World Health Organisation says that decorators are faced with a 40% increased chance of lung cancer as a result of continued exposure to them. Solvent paints also have a high product-to-waste ratio – every tonne of synthetic paint produced results in 10 tonnes of waste, so use natural paints made from plant and mineral bases. Visit **www.ecosolutions.co.uk** (01934 844484); **www.auroorganic.co.uk** (01452 772020) or **www.greenshop.co.uk** (01452 770629).

DONATE YOUR LEFTOVER PAINT Did you know that of the 350 million litres of paint sold in the UK each year, 45 million litres remain unused? The Community Re-Paint scheme run by Save Waste and Prosper runs paint collection schemes – sorting out paint and redistributing it to community projects, housing associations and schools. Visit **www.communityrepaint.org.uk** for more information or call 0113 200 3959.

INSTALL A SOLAR WATER HEATER A solar water heater in an average-sized house can save up to 2.5 tonnes of CO_2 emissions a year. They do not need bright sunlight to work effectively – diffuse light is just as efficient. They needn't be expensive to install, either. The Low Impact Living Initiative will show you how. It runs courses on constructing a solar hot water tank, building compost toilets and green DIY. Visit **www.lowimpact.org**.

AVOID OZONE-DEPLETING CHEMICALS IN INSULATION
Insulation uses HCFCs – which are used as a replacement for the CFCs responsible for depleting the ozone layer. HCFCs are also harmful to the ozone, yet insulations that have low HCFCs may also contribute to global warming. Use cellulose, cork and foamed glass as alternatives. For more information visit **www.greenbuildingstore.co.uk**.

BUY WOOD FROM A SUSTAINABLE SOURCE There's a strong demand for sustainable wood, or wood from managed plantations, which has led some manufacturers to make claims about their wood that are dubious. The best way of making sure wood is from a sustainable source is by becoming an online member of the Timber Research Development Association (**www.trada.co.uk**) who have a comprehensive information service. The Forest Stewardship Council also provide information. Visit **www.fsc-uk.info**.

AVOID CHIPBOARD AND MDF Chipboard and medium density fibreboard (MDF) have a high formaldehyde content. Formaldehyde is a recognised carcinogen, which also irritates the lungs, throats and eyes. It can take two to three years before a product has finished releasing formaldehyde fumes. Instead, use softwood or European plywood, and for kitchen worktops choose conifer.

USE RECYCLED MATERIALS Look for reclaimed, vintage or antique building materials such as baths, radiators and wood floors. They are unusual, stylish, often less expensive and come with a history, too. Visit **www.salvo.co.uk** for suppliers and products.

RENT POWER TOOLS OR SHARE THEM WITH NEIGHBOURS That small cheap electric drill was probably made on the other side of the world, its production and transportation consuming unnecessary amounts of energy and causing pollution. Why not hire tools, or invest in more durable ones that can be pooled with neighbours? The Local Exchange Trading System (Letslink), a community sharing scheme, will help. Contact them at **www.letslinkuk.org**, or call 020 7607 7852.

CAMPAIGN FOR THE RE-USE OF EMPTY HOMES For every homeless person in England, there are seven empty homes. Across the UK there are over 700,000 empty homes – and 10% of these belong to local authorities. Unused housing puts unnecessary pressure for development on greenfield sites, wastes resources and creates ghost areas and crime hotspots in towns and cities. The Empty Houses Agency campaigns to raise awareness of the problem of empty properties and promote solutions to bring empty homes into use. In 2004/5 over 21,000 empty houses were filled. Join the Campaign on Empty Homes around your area, visit **www.emptyhomes.com** or call 020 7022 1870. Londoners can report any empty house they know of on a special hotline: 0870 901 6303.

DONATE UNUSED TOOLS TO CHARITIES Unused and unwanted tools can be given to Tools For Self-Reliance, a charity that refurbishes tools and sewing machines into kits to go to tradesmen from Africa. It ships goods worth more than £500,000 each year to people building communities in Tanzania, Zimbabwe, Uganda and Ghana. To find out how you can help visit their website at **www.tfsr.org.uk**.

READER TIP – ADRIEN LEGRIS
TOOLS FOR SOLIDARITY

Tools for Solidarity is based in Belfast and has similar aims to Tools For Self-Reliance. Readers in Northern Ireland can join the scheme by visiting its website **www.toolsforsolidarity.org.uk**.

THIS LAND IS OUR LAND More than 50% of the energy we use goes on constructing and maintaining buildings. The Land Is Ours is a group that campaigns for access to the land, its resources and the decision-making processes affecting them. The group occupies derelict land, builds environmentally friendly houses and gardens, and highlights the misuse of urban land and the lack of affordable housing. For more information see **www.tlio.org.uk**.

FIND AN ENVIRONMENTALLY CONSCIOUS BUILDER
For a list of environmentally friendly architects, earth builders, thatchers, wildlife consultants, insurance companies, housing associations and manufacturers contact the Association for Environment Conscious Builders, which promotes environmentally

sensitive building – visit their website at **www.aecb.net** for details. If you're doing it yourself, visit the Association's message board to get answers to your questions.

READER TIP – NEIL ALLDRED
HOME AUDIT

Visit **www.homecheck.co.uk** to get a detailed survey of your postcode and find out what's been happening in your area. The results include information on pollution, landslides, flooding and other hazards.

TOP TIP – BENFIELD ATT (TIMBER TECHNOLOGY)
BUILD YOUR OWN HOME!

Bricks-and-mortar homes have turned our planet into a huge concrete village… break the mould! According to the Timber Frame Association, one out of 10 new homes in the UK is self-build and nine out of 10 of these are now built from state-of-the-art timber technology. A timber home uses a tenth of the non-renewable energy used to construct a brick and mortar home, and saves you money because it is both energy efficient and is built within weeks. You can also use other eco-products such as slate-effect roof tiles made from recycled car tyres, or rock foundations instead of cement. For more information contact Benfield ATT, **www.adtimtec.com** (01291 437050).

Table talk

CUT DOWN ON CLUTTER It's easy to think another piece of furniture will help make the house more cosy, but sometimes the more clutter we fill the house with, the less space is left for ourselves! The furnishing business is a massive industry that doesn't always take into account that our home environment should be in harmony with our wider environment. When you're buying furniture, think about where it has come from and what process it has gone through to get to your home.

RECYCLE CURTAINS Curtains are resource-intensive in the amount of material they require – so don't leave them to fester in the garage or dump them in the rubbish. Find your nearest textile recycler at **www.wasteconnect.co.uk**, 0905 535 0940. Or get in touch with the Curtain Exchange at **www.thecurtainexchange.net**. And why don't you buy a pair of vintage recycled curtains from them rather than a new pair?

RECYCLE YOUR FURNITURE AND WOOD Every year over £13 million worth of furniture is recycled and distributed to people who can't afford to buy new furniture. But demand for cheap recycled furniture still outstrips supply by up to 50%. Don't throw away your unwanted furniture – recycle it and help someone else build up a home. For details of a recycling point near you contact The Furniture Re-use Network on **www.frn.org.uk**. Some local authorities also recycle wood – visit Reuze at **www.reuze.co.uk** or contact your local authority directly.

...AND BUY RECYCLED FURNITURE Whether it's a gorgeous antique, a reclaimed rocking chair or an armchair made from plastic bottles, recycled furniture is stylish, individual and kind to trees. For information on fairs and where to buy antiques visit **www.antiquesatlas.com**. A good place to sell and buy second-hand furniture is **www.ebay.co.uk**. For furniture made from cable reels visit **www.reelfurniture.co.uk**. Their furniture is fully seasoned and finished with eco-friendly lacquers. Visit **www.re-formfurniture.co.uk** for furniture made from polythene bottles. For information on recycled wood visit **www.smartwood.org**. SmartWood was set up by the Rainforest Alliance, to certify reused, reclaimed, recycled and salvaged wood products.

DON'T BUY FURNITURE TREATED WITH BROMINATED FLAME RETARDANTS Brominated flame retardants are a group of chemicals used in fabrics, computers and plastics to counteract the spread of fires. They contribute to indoor air pollution and build up in the environment because they don't biodegrade. Several of them are also proven to be hormone disrupters, interfering with the daily functioning of the body, and they can also disrupt the thyroid hormone and contaminate human breast milk. Some countries have banned them and some major furniture suppliers such as IKEA have stopped using them. Check the company's policy when you buy new furniture. See **www.greenpeace.org.uk/media/press-releases/swimming-in-dangerous-waters** to find out how bromine flame retardants are affecting our wildlife.

AVOID FURNITURE MADE WITH FORMALDEHYDE

Formaldehyde is a bonding agent used to glue wood and make insulating foam. It is also used in latex paints, fabrics, cheap furniture and MDF. It can take up to three years for all the fumes to be released – and inhalation can cause flu-like symptoms, rashes, cancer and neurological illnesses. Avoid buying furniture with formaldehyde, and if you're using MDF, make sure it's formaldehyde-free. See **www.oneecohome.co.uk**.

SYNTHETIC CARPETS VS NATURAL FLOORING Carpets hide a number of evils. The carpet, as well as its underlying pads and glues, can release formaldehyde into the air for months or even years. Carpets are also a haven for house dust mites that aggravate asthma. Most cleaning products for carpeting contain solvents and glycol ethers – chemicals that may cause irritation and coughing when inhaled. There's a range of alternatives – including carpets made from paper and plastic bottles! Find natural flooring at **www.flooringsupplies.co.uk/alternativeflooring.cfm**.

NEVER BUY WOODEN FURNITURE FROM OLD GROWTH FORESTS Over 78% of the world's original old-growth forests – also known as primary or ancient forests – have already been logged or degraded. If you do buy new furniture, ask the retailer where the wood comes from. Consumer pressure *does* work. In 1991, Friends of the Earth (**www.foe.co.uk**) launched a campaign against the stocking of 'unsustainably-sourced' tropical timber by the 'big six' DIY chains. The campaign became a consumer boycott and by June 1994, all six had agreed to stop selling mahogany. Mahogany imports fell 68% by 1996. Contact the Rainforest Action Network to find specific campaigns against companies that are destroying our rainforests and to find old-growth alternatives at **www.ran.org**.

Pest control

THE PESTICIDE PROBLEM **Most people associate pesticides with farming, yet 80% of our exposure to them comes from our homes and gardens. In 2001, 4,893 tonnes of pesticides were bought in the UK and that figure is rising by 38% per year. If you do use pesticides, keep yourself informed about their ingredients. Approximately one teaspoon of pesticide concentrate could affect 200,000 people a day. Many people are completely unaware of the harmful content of the products they use, as the packets don't always explain their contents. Pesticides are designed to kill – before you buy them, think about how your use of them will affect other people (particularly children), domestic pets and wildlife. Make a difference in your own pest control at home or in the garden. Contact Pesticide Action Network UK – an excellent source of information at** www.pan-uk.org **or call 020 7065 0905. There are invariably alternative environmentally friendly methods of pest prevention and control.**

DISPOSE OF CHEMICALS PROPERLY Of the 4,893 tonnes of pesticide active chemicals that we bought in 2001, only 5-10% were disposed of in special facilities. A massive 20-30% will have ended up down the drain where they pollute the water table and endanger wildlife. And the rest may still be sitting on the kitchen or shed shelf – where they can pose a threat to humans. Water companies use millions of litres of water to purify our drinking water and the cost of the energy used is added to *your* water bill. Make sure you dispose of chemicals and pesticides properly by taking them to a special facility. You can search for a local council pesticide disposal facility at **www.pan-uk.org/disposal**. Some councils also run a residential collection service.

TELL FLY SPRAYS TO BUZZ OFF! One squirt of a chemical fly spray, and the toxic gases emitted will stay in the air for up to 72 hours. Chemicals such as dichlorvos and pyrethrins that are found in fly sprays also kill bees and aquatic life when their residues enter water systems. Perversely, they can also cause fly populations to increase, by strengthening their resistance to pesticides and killing species that are natural predators. 'Integrated pest management' is the term given to controlling pests without resorting to chemicals, and involves altering the local environment to make it less attractive to pests. In the case of flies, this would involve cleaning out rubbish bins, disinfecting them and making sure there's no decaying food lying around. Natural fly deterrents include lemon, cloves, pine and cedar oils.

STRIKE A BALANCE Pests play a vital role in the lifecycle of nature, and some pests, no matter how hard you try to get rid of them, will always come crawling back into your garden to fulfil this role. So instead of trying to kill off the pest, try adapting the environment to minimise their impact. If a weed is taking over a shady area of your garden, prune back a tree to allow light through or plant something that flourishes in shady conditions to drive it out. With insects or pests, try eradicating their food supply and they will eventually move on. The RHS and Wildlife Trusts' *Wildlife Gardening for Everyone* has some great tips.

AVOID CHEMICAL HEAD LICE TREATMENTS FOR NITS
Chemicals used in conventional headlice treatments can disrupt the immune system, cause burning sensations, skin irritation, hyperactivity and dizziness. Instead, thoroughly wash the hair with normal shampoo and conditioner, wide-comb the hair to straighten it, then systematically fine-comb the hair from the roots to the tips to remove hatched lice. Or find Nice 'n' Clear Natural Headlice Lotion at **www.seeknatural.co.uk**.

GET RID OF ANY PRODUCTS THAT CONTAIN LINDANE
Lindane is an organochlorine pesticide that was banned from use in the UK in June 2002. It has been linked with breast cancer, and may

disrupt the endocrine system. In June 2002, an eight-year-old girl died after swallowing a tiny amount of ant powder that contained lindane. Because of its known dangers, it was banned for use throughout the EU. Check that you do not have any left in your cupboard and dispose of it properly if you do. Visit **www.pan-uk.org** for lindane factsheets and details of their successful Ban Lindane campaign.

TOP TIP – THE NATURAL COLLECTION

LADYBIRD LADYBIRD... Ladybirds eat greenfly. Encourage them to breed in your garden with a silver birch ladybird house, which provides a safe environment for 100 ladybirds to live and breed. Larvae are supplied with the house – simply place them on the plants with the greenfly infestation – they'll consume up to 8,000 greenfly a day. Hang the house up nearby – the ladybirds will take up residence as they grow! Visit Natural Collection **www.naturalcollection.com** or call 0845 367 7001 for more.

USE A FLY SWAT Houseflies are a nuisance and a health hazard. But resorting to chemical sprays won't solve the problem in the long run. Flies often come down the chimney in summer – so block your chimneys with cardboard, cover food and secure domestic waste. If you can't get rid of one annoying critter – use a fly swat.

USE NON-TOXIC METHODS OF SNAIL AND SLUG CONTROL Chemical slug treatments do not degrade, so their toxins remain in the environment indefinitely. And as slugs are the hedgehog's favourite food, you will be indirectly poisoning hedgehogs, too. There are several simple ways of deterring slugs from eating your beans or hostas. Interplant vulnerable species with lavender or rosemary – slugs don't like spiky aromatic plants – or spread ash, beer or eggshells on the earth. For patio pots put a strip of copper round the base of the pot – they won't go near it. Slugs' natural predators are frogs, so encourage frogs into your garden by providing a rock pile shelter for them to make a home. See **www.wildlifegardener.co.uk/naturalslugcontrol.html**.

INSTALL A BAT BOX Unlike many other insects, mosquitoes are very short-sighted and have to rely on their sense of smell. If you get bitten, you may not notice it straightaway as the mosquito injects an anaesthetic into the skin. Only when the anaesthetic has worn off will you start itching. If your garden is providing a home to mosquitoes, there are plenty of things you can do without reaching for chemicals. Make sure any stagnant water is covered and if you have a pond, stock it with mosquito predators – frogs, dragonflies and fish. Alternatively install a bat box. Bats will eat around 3,000 mosquitoes and gnats every night. Find out how to make a bat box at **www.bats.org.uk/helpline/documents/howtomakeabatbox.pdf**.

SUPPORT THE VICTIMS OF THE WORLD'S WORST CHEMICAL POISONING ON THE 'DAY OF NO PESTICIDES'
One night in 1984, in the Indian city of Bhopal, there was a leak of almost 40 tonnes of deadly gases into the atmosphere from Union Carbide – an American factory that produced pesticides. Parts of the city were surrounded by a chemical fog so thick that people could hardly see. It was the world's worst industrial pollution – to date over 20,000 people have died and more than 150,000 have become chronically ill. But the story is not over yet. There are still about 25 deaths every month, the contaminated factory site has never been cleaned, victims have not been properly compensated and Union Carbide and its new owner Dow Chemical continue to deny liability and refuse to pay for a clean-up. The anniversary of the Bhopal poisoning – 3 December – is marked as Day of No Pesticides. Support the Bhopal victims' campaign for justice or make a donation to help them with their medical costs. Visit **www.bhopal.org** for more information and **www.pan-uk.org** for details about Day of No Pesticides.

Clear water

ELIXIR OF LIFE Water is one of the most important resources on our planet – and with 60% of our body made of water it's vital for human survival. It transports blood and food around the body and helps remove waste. It also lubricates the joints, keeps our eyes in shape, is essential to the maintenance of our body temperature and to the development of foetuses. Yet we do not have an abundance of water. Of the total water supply on earth – 326 million cubic miles – only 0.3% can be consumed by humans. Use water thoughtfully – the average person in the UK now washes away a staggering 1,050 litres of water a week – and be conscious, even in rainy places, of what it takes to get that clean water piped to your home.

FILTER OUT THE CHEMICALS Much of the water we use has undergone quite a transformation since it first fell from the sky. Water is treated with chemicals, which find their way back into the environment when we use it a second time. Even ultra-violet light is now part of the used water treatment process. Some of these chemicals may be harmful – chlorine, for example, which is used to kill bacteria is a bleaching agent that destroys proteins in the hair and skin, it can dry hair out and make sensitive skin itchy. To filter out the chlorine in your household water, visit the Fresh Water Filter Company at www.freshwaterfilter.com.

IT TAKES ABOUT SIX LITRES OF WATER TO MAKE A PINT OF BEER... 10 litres to make a daily newspaper, 20 litres to make an aluminium can, 150 litres to make a cotton shirt and 20,000 litres to make the body of a steel car. There is a culture of wastefulness in some industries, despite the fact that companies can make great savings by auditing their water use. The UK government, for example, fitted controllers to urinals in their cabinet offices to stop them flushing continuously and saved 3,500 cubic metres of water and £2,600 a year.

Think about the things you use – the more processed they are the more water is likely to have been used. See **www.waterwise.org.uk** for details of the Waterwise Marque – designed to help denote water efficient products.

KIDS – HELP YOUR SCHOOL TO SAVE WATER On average, schools in the UK spend £2,500 a year on water (although a large secondary school could spend as much as £20,000). Schools that carefully manage their water consumption could, together with an effective education programme, reduce their water use by two thirds. A secondary school with 600 pupils could save as much as £5,000 a year – enough to buy eight new computers. To help your school save water visit **www.ecoschools.org.uk** or **www.ecsc.org.uk**.

USE SHORT BURSTS OF WATER FROM THE TAP WHEN YOU BRUSH YOUR TEETH You can waste up to six litres of water a minute by just leaving the tap on while brushing your teeth. Using short bursts of water to rinse your toothbrush can save 80% of the water that you would normally use.

ONLY USE A WASHING MACHINE WITH A FULL LOAD
A single washing machine cycle uses up to 100 litres of water, and the average family uses their washing machine five times a week. That's 26,000 litres a year. Find the most energy efficient washing machines at **www.waterwise.org.uk**.

WHY USE DRINKING WATER FOR FLUSHING THE TOILET, WASHING YOUR CLOTHES AND WATERING YOUR PLANTS? Use rainwater instead! Flushing the loo accounts for over a third of our water use, laundry for 12% and irrigation for 7%. To really make a difference, invest in a rainwater collection system that will enable you to use rainwater for all these activities. You can also arrange to have your bath water recycled through your cistern – it's a small matter of plumbing. But if that's a bit daunting, install a large water butt for your gardening and some washing needs. There's a huge range of shapes and sizes at **www.waterbuttsdirect.co.uk**.

TAKE SHOWERS INSTEAD OF BATHS The average bath uses about 80 litres of water, while the average shower uses something between 30-49 litres. Having a shower saves a significant amount of water, and time, too. Ideally, take a non-power shower for five minutes.

SAVE WATER IN THE GARDEN Sprinklers can use as much as 1,000 litres of water an hour – that's a minimum of 8,000 litres if left on for eight hours! Avoid sprinklers and use a watering can instead. Try to only water plants during the evening or early in the morning – not only does this save water, it prevents leaves from getting burnt in strong sunshine. Other water-saving garden tips include: installing a water butt to catch rainwater, building a soak-away (to distribute storm or surface water), leaving grass cuttings on the lawn, mulching around plants with organic compost and using drought-tolerant plants, such as lavender and thyme instead of bedding plants that are very heat sensitive and require more water. See **www.water-guide.org.uk/tips-garden.html**.

USE APPLIANCES CAREFULLY Use front-loading washing machines rather than top loaders. Energy-efficient washing machines now use less than 50 litres of water per wash (on average older machines use 100 litres). Energy-efficient dishwashers also use as little as 16 litres of water per cycle. When you buy new appliances check their water consumption on the energy-rating label to find out how much water they use. Visit **www.greenbuildingstore.co.uk** for more information on water-saving WCs and fittings, **www.waterwise.org.uk** for ranked dishwashers and washing machines and **www.environment-agency.gov.uk/savewater** for information on the energy-rating scheme.

CHECK YOUR SYSTEM FOR LEAKS The average family in the UK now uses around 5,000 litres of water a week, but out of this over 16% is lost due to leaks. That's a staggering 800 litres of lost water a week! Check your water meter just before you go to bed and then re-check in the morning. If it shows an increase, have your water system checked – it could save you money in the long run. For more information check **www.water.org.uk**. And while you're checking for your own leaks, make sure your local water company isn't wasting water either. In some areas of the UK more than one third of water is lost through leaking pipes. Find out about your local water company's record – if it's bad, write to them to protest that consumers should not have to pay rising costs if the company won't invest more of its profits managing its water storage. Find company details at **www.ofwat.gov.uk**.

KIT OUT YOUR HOUSE WITH WATER-SAVING DEVICES
For example, spray taps let out a smaller volume of water but achieve the same results as normal taps. Low-flow showerheads can be fitted to maximise water coverage and minimise the water used. And a dual flush toilet saves thousands of litres a year by discharging a small amount of water for liquid waste and a larger amount for solid waste. Contact the Centre for Alternative Energy at **www.cat.org.uk** or call 01654 705950.

HELP BRING CLEAN WATER TO THE BILLION PEOPLE WHO NEED IT We take water for granted. But the UN's Human Development Report in 2006 showed that 1.2 billion people in the world don't have safe water to drink and 2.6 billion don't have access to adequate sanitation. It estimates that 1.8 million children die every year as a result of diseases caused by unclean water and poor sanitation. That amounts to around 5,000 deaths a day. Water Aid is a charity that helps over 500,000 people from the poorest communities provide themselves with a better quality of life through water, sanitation and education. It also lobbies for more sustainable water policies on a global level. To become a supporter visit **www.wateraid.co.uk**.

Green fingers

THE ECO-GARDEN Your garden is an ecosystem teeming with life; and just as it contains its own micro-ecosystems, it is also part of the ecosystem of the surrounding area. Encourage biodiversity, by thinking about what species you plant and about the materials you use in your garden.

Where do they come from, how were they made and what knock-on effects do they have? For more information contact The Wildlife Trusts for a leaflet on wildlife gardening at www.wildlifetrusts.org, get a copy of *Wildlife Gardening for Everyone,* or visit www.wildaboutgardens.org. HDRA – the Henry Doubleday Research Association – is a mine of information on gardening methods. For more information, visit www.gardenorganic.org.uk or call 0247 630 3517.

TURN YOUR WINDOWSILL INTO A GARDEN You don't need a garden to grow things… think chillies in window boxes, tomatoes in grow bags and herbs on the kitchen windowsill. Read *The Window Box Allotment* by Penelope Bennett for ideas including wormeries and compost heaps in confined spaces, or *The Edible Container Garden: Fresh Food from Tiny Spaces* by Carol Klein, Michael Guerra and Patrick Whitefield.

DON'T USE A FUEL-POWERED LAWNMOWER One fuel lawnmower produces as much pollution in one hour as driving a car for 100 miles. Instead, use an electric mower – or better, a manual mower – instead. And bear in mind that grass is not always greener anyway. Grass needs a lot more water and treatment against weeds than other hardier ground covers, and the more ground area covered by grass, the less area available for other species. Devote a larger area of your garden to other types of habitat such as a rockery, flower beds, a wild area or a vegetable patch. See **www.applegategardens.co.uk/acatalog/lawn_ideas.html** for alternative lawn ideas.

DON'T POISON YOUR GARDEN Private gardens make up a significant proportion of green space in cities, and provide a refuge for urban wildlife. What you do with your garden can make a vital difference to the survival of wildlife species in your area. Don't resort to chemical warfare – learn more about the pests in your garden and search out other ways of dealing with them. See **www.safegardening.co.uk/poisonstoxinscategory.html**.

DON'T TREAT FENCING WITH CREOSOTE Breathing in creosote fumes irritates the windpipe, and if it gets into food or drinking water it can cause burning in the mouth, stomach pains, convulsions and kidney problems. Creosote dissolves in water and can then get through the soil to groundwater, where it takes years to break down. For alternative wood and timber preservatives see **www.greenbuildingstore.co.uk**. Why not create a hedge or tree border instead, or build a wall from old bricks with crevices that can become a home to plants, insects and beetles? Old brick walls are a haven for wildlife and can also support a variety of species or creeper. Get reclaimed bricks from **www.brickfind.co.uk**.

AVOID USING WATER-WORN LIMESTONE IN YOUR GARDEN The British Isles hold the world's most significant areas of limestone pavement – natural outcrops of limestone rock – of which only 3% has escaped damage by man. It has been sculpted by glaciers and weathered for over 10,000 years resulting in a unique splintered appearance, with fissures that are home to rare plants, snails and butterflies. Water-worn limestone, used in rockeries, is also known as Irish limestone, Cumbrian stone or weathered limestone. There are several alternatives – sandstone, granite deep-quarried limestone or York stone, as well as reconstituted and artificial substitutes made from fibreglass or cement. Find out more at **www.limestone-pavements.org.uk**.

SAVE OUR ALLOTMENTS! Allotments are a vital breathing space in city areas and give people who have no access to gardens a chance to develop green fingers. Over the past two decades there has been a 43% drop in the number of allotments in the UK. The National Society of Allotment and Leisure Gardens campaigns to protect allotments. See **www.nsalg.org.uk** or call 01536 266576. Use their site to find out how to source an allotment, what things you could grow and the most natural way to do it. Plus get more advice at **www.allotments-uk.com**.

DON'T USE PEAT COMPOST Over 90% of Britain's peat bogs have been damaged or destroyed – mostly in the last 50 years. Some are thousands of years old, and in their trapped remains, researchers and archaeologists have found seeds, plant remains, artefacts and even bodies – such as the 2,300-year-old man 'Pete Marsh'. These have helped us to understand our climate, environmental history and early civilisations. Gardeners account for 70% of all the peat used today in the UK. The area of lowland raised bog in the UK has diminished from an original 234,755 acres (95,000ha) to approximately 14,830 acres (6,000ha) today. Buy peat-free compost and make sure that the plants you buy are also in peat-free compost. To find out more visit the Royal Botanical Gardens, Kew site at **www.kew.org/ksheets/peat.html** or see **www.rspb.org.uk/advice/gardening/planting/peatfree.asp**. Find out more about our disappearing peat bogs and what you can do to help from Plant Life, an organisation that works to conserve Britain's wild plants. Visit **www.plantlife.org.uk/uk/plantlife-campaigning-change-plants-and-peat.html** or call 01722 342730.

URBAN FOXES AREN'T PESTS Foxes survive in a range of different environments – they can adapt easily to urban areas and eat many different types of food and it is now quite common to see them in cities. The Wildlife Trusts believes they have become an important part of the city's ecology and should be tolerated rather than persecuted. If a fox becomes a nuisance in your garden don't remove it by killing, trapping or transporting it – another fox will quickly take its place. Visit **www.wildlondon.org.uk** for humane and effective ways of controlling foxes in your garden.

FURNITURE IN THE GARDEN You don't have to make your garden hi-tech to enjoy it. Avoid energy-wasting gadgets such as patio heaters – put on a warm jumper! If you must install lights in the garden – go for solar powered. When you buy wooden garden furniture, avoid tropical hardwoods such as teak – which is fast disappearing. If you have to buy teak, make sure it's either reclaimed or from sustainable forests. Since the launch of Greenpeace's Garden Furniture Guide in 2004, many retailers have worked hard to improve their policies. Visit **www.greenpeace.org.uk/tags/garden-furniture** to see how you can support them in your choices.

TOP TIP – MALCOLM TAIT, WILDLIFE EDITOR

BE HEDGEHOG AWARE If you're planning a late autumn bonfire, carefully turn the contents over first. A hedgehog may have begun its hibernation inside. You can find out more about making your garden safe for wildlife by reading *Wildlife Gardening for Everyone* (ISBN 1-84525-016-8). Published in association with the RHS and The Wildlife Trusts, the book contains need-to-know answers to over 101 questions about cultivating wildlife in your garden. Visit **www.wildaboutgardens.org** for information.

Cool compost

BACK TO THE SOIL **Almost a third of our domestic waste could go straight onto the compost heap. Instead, 10 million tonnes of organic waste – food scraps and tea bags – go to landfill each year where, deprived of oxygen, they do not biodegrade. There is no reason why our organic waste should not be turned into compost, returning the nutrients and energy from your leftover food back to the soil where they can be reused. Composting reflects the world's cyclic patterns – recycling waste and reaping the benefits as you watch your garden grow, rather than the destructive resource-waste conveyor belt. Your plants love compost because...**

- **it slowly releases nutrients that benefit plants when they need them – unlike chemical fertilisers, which are released in a 'rush'**
- **it helps sandy soils to retain water (so you save on water, too!)**
- **it helps to suppress plant diseases and weeds without introducing chemicals into the ground**
- **it insulates soil and retains warmth in cold weather – so plants are better protected from frosts.**

SPREAD THE WORD

Compost Awareness Week is held every year around the world to encourage homes, businesses and schools to start composting. Show your support for composting by joining one of the planned activities – such as competitions to grow sunflowers, educational drives and roadshows. For more information, visit the Composting Association website **www.compost.org.uk** and **www.compostawarenessweek.org.uk**.

NOT JUST FOR THE GREEN FINGERED... Composting is easy. You throw your leftovers – uncooked food waste such as fruit and vegetables, tea bags and egg shells – together with your garden waste, such as mowings, old plants, flowers, weeds and leaves into a pile in the garden. With the help of worms and other creepy-crawlies, they'll decompose into five-star plant food. You'll save on plastic rubbish bags, buying nutrients for the soil and water, the Earth will be saved from yet more contaminating landfills and your plants will thrive. For information on how to create a compost heap visit the Composting Association **www.compost.org.uk**. Your local council should also be able to provide you with a food waste composting bin and collection service – more than 1.7 million bins have been provided so far, with 20 million more homes targeted in 2007. For enquiries and supplies call 0845 600 0323, visit **www.recyclenow.com/home_composting/index.html** or **www.wrap.org.uk/local_authorities/reducing_household.html**.

GET STARTED! Compost bins are easy to get hold of at garden centres but, even better, make your own from old tyres, scrap timber, bricks or wire mesh. By building your own bin you can recycle materials, which might otherwise find their way to the scrap heap.

KIDS – GO MAD WITH WORMS Set up a worm-composting bin, either inside your house or out. Worms eat kitchen waste and convert it into rich dark compost by passing it through their bodies. Each worm can recycle half its own bodyweight of waste every day – if you have a bin-full of worms, that's a lot of composting. You can buy worm-composting bins, but why not make your own? The best types of worms to use are tiger worms and red worms. Contact Wiggly Wigglers at **www.wigglywigglers.co.uk**, or call 01981 500391.

FEED YOUR COMPOST HEAP WITH FIBRE All your paper and card which cannot be recycled can be composted. That includes tissues, kitchen towels, the tubes from toilet rolls, cereal boxes and egg boxes. Like people, compost heaps need fibre to keep healthy (otherwise they go soggy!). Fibre keeps air spaces in the compost, so your heap will be bursting with beneficial creepy-crawlies. For more ideas of what types of waste you can add to your compost heap visit **www.gardenorganic.org.uk/organicgardening/compost_pf.php**.

GIVE YOUR FLOWERS COFFEE AND WATCH THEM GROW Did you know that coffee grounds are perfect compost material? Next time you're about to empty the coffee pot, tip it onto the flower beds instead of the bin. And if you use a paper filter – well that can go on the compost heap, too! If you've got a serious compost heap 'brewing' in the back garden, ask local coffee shops to donate their coffee-grounds – or take them to the nearest municipal compost heap.

NO GARDEN? NO EXCUSE! Find out where your nearest community composting project is. And if there isn't one in your area, set one up. The Community Composting Network provides composting sites around the UK that each serve about 100 households. The compost made from their organic waste is distributed around the community either for free or at a cheap price, and it's also used in local parks. Contact the Community Composting Network at **www.communitycompost.org**, or call 0114 258 0483.

GIVE YOUR COMPOSTING A TURBO BOOST Serious composters who want to cut down on landfill should look out for an Eco Food Waste digester. Unlike conventional composting bins, it can digest cooked food – including meat, fish, bones and dairy products – too. For more information visit Green Cone at **www.greencone.com**.

Happy families

There are so many ways – at all stages and in all areas of their lives – in which family members can collectively do their bit. Economies of scale are the key. Families consume more, waste more and spend more than individuals, so changing habits makes more of a difference. They also benefit from the ripple effect – if one family member starts recycling, volunteering or eating organic, others are likely to follow. Doing your bit doesn't have to cost more in terms of time and money, either. Sometimes it's just a matter of thinking before you act, or consciously deciding not to do something. Make the world one of your family's priorities, and there'll still be a world for your family's families to grow up in.

Love conquers all

GREEN RECIPES FOR LOVE AND ROMANCE Try to care about the world as you care about your valentine. After all, it's love that makes the world go round.

CANDLELIT ROMANCE Turn off the lights and eat by candlelight. It's more romantic and you'll save energy, too! Take care in your choice of candles, though – paraffin candles are made from petroleum residues so do neither your health nor the environment any good. Use natural beeswax, soy or other vegetable-based candles that biodegrade and are smoke-free. They last twice as long and burn brighter! Try **www.corfecandles.co.uk** for ideas.

CHOOSE A GREEN MATE Find a partner you can make a difference with by joining a 'green' dating agency – try Natural Friends at **www.natural-friends.com** (01284 728315) or Evergreen, **www.evergreenagency.co.uk** (0845 456 1274). For a more subtle approach, Friends of the Earth have groups across the country that meet to discuss green issues and campaign together. Visit **www.foe.org.uk** or call 020 7490 1555.

BE FAIR WITH FLOWERS Blossoming bouquets in florists' windows have usually been cultivated in mass plantations on the other side of the world, doused in pesticides, fed vast quantities of water in locations where it is scarce, and transported thousands of miles to reach you. Go for locally grown daffodils or tulips, or look out for Fairtrade flowers. You can find out more at **www.fairtrade.org.uk/products_roses**.

COOK UP A TREAT Don't give commercially made food or chocolates as presents. They're likely to be full of sugar and additives and wrapped in unnecessary packaging. Instead, make it personal and give your love something you've cooked up yourself. Home-baked biscuits or chocolates are delicious indulgences and fun to make. If you must buy chocolate, make it eco-friendly and Fairtrade with **www.fairtrade.org.uk/products_chocolate_buy**.

SAFER SEX You may be responsible when it comes to using condoms, but how good are you at disposing of them? Every year in the UK almost 150 million are flushed down the toilet, clogging water treatment filters and causing sewage overflows on rivers and beaches. Apart from being unwelcome guests when you're wading through rock pools, wrinkly rubbers are harmful to wildlife. Latex is a natural product made from rubber-tree sap and is biodegradable in landfill, so put latex condoms in the bin. For more information visit **www.bagandbin.org**. And if you're indulging in a bit of *alfresco* loving, don't leave the evidence behind.

STAY CLOSER TO HOME Heathcliff and Cathy's stormy love affair took place in the wild 'wuthering heights' of the Pennines, Henry VIII romanced Anne Boleyn at Hever Castle in Kent, and Tintern Abbey near the Forest of Dean inspired one of Wordsworth's greatest poems. Some of the world's most uplifting places are found in parts of Britain's remote and beautiful countryside, so you don't need to travel to far-flung places for romance. Turn to literature for inspiration, or visit **www.visitbritain.co.uk**.

PUPPY LOVE Kids can show they care too. Get them to take a small tray or used yoghurt pot and plant cress seeds on organic cotton wool in the shape of a friend's name. They should then tell the friend to water it regularly and wait. They'll be surprised when shoots start to spring up and spell their name. They can eat the delicious, healthy cress too.

GET TOGETHER AND COOL IT! All over the world, people have achieved change through linking their voices together, whether it's halting plans for the construction of an incinerator, or saving a species from extinction. One of the biggest threats to the future of our planet is global warming. CO_2, the main heat-trapping gas, is at the highest levels the planet has seen for 20 million years. Link up with people planet-wide to turn the heat down before it's too late. ClimateArk is a great campaigning tool against global warming – visit **www.climateark.org**.

Well matched!

WEDDINGS THAT DON'T COST THE EARTH The symbolism in traditional weddings implies that there are parallels between the union of two people and the union of those people with the Earth. But now a wedding is far more likely to cost the Earth, than bring us closer to it. Couples spend an average of £11,200 on a wedding. But you don't have to follow the crowd and run up the same bill. A green wedding saves not only your pocket but also the environment and is probably easier to arrange!

EARTH-FRIENDLY INVITATIONS This is so much more original than bleached-white heavily embossed traditional cards. Some paper comes ready-sprinkled with flower petals, or you can use plain paper and decorate each card individually with feathers, petals and leaves. Visit **www.recycled-paper.co.uk** for inspiration and stationery supplies, or call them on 01676 533832.

HAVE AN ETHICAL WEDDING LIST This is a great opportunity to introduce some of your friends to the benefits of green life. Ask for a wind-up radio or solar-powered garden lights. You can set up a wedding list at **www.greenfibres.com** or see **www.greenunion.co.uk** for ideas.

TREES FOR LIFE Rather than collecting more household goods, ask your guests to donate a tree to the MarryMe Wood. This scheme, run by the CarbonNeutral Company, will help protect the climate by absorbing greenhouse gas carbon dioxide. The trees are native species planted in natural woodlands protected from development for at least 40 years. Visit **www.carbonneutral.com/weddings** for more information. Alternatively, you could celebrate tying the knot by planting an apple or pear tree together in your garden.

ASK YOUR GUESTS TO MAKE A DONATION TO YOUR FAVOURITE CHARITY For advice on easy ways to set this up, without spending time collecting donations while busy organising your wedding, visit **www.firstgiving.com**.

MAKE A GREEN ENTRANCE Save the environment from the pollution of all those cars carrying just one or two people to your wedding. Include clear directions in the invitation for how people can reach the wedding by public transport and details of places for them to stay nearby. Try to persuade friends to share the drive together, and when you arrive at the church, do it without fuel but in the ultimate style – by horse or horse-drawn carriage.

ALL THAT GLISTERS IS NOT GOLD... Don't swap rings that have been made from materials excavated using cheap labour in exploitative conditions. Diamonds mined by insurgent groups in Sierra Leone and Angola cause misery to millions, while gold is mined with cyanide, which is highly toxic to both humans and the environment. The Kimberley Process, launched in January 2003, requires governments and the industry to implement import/export control to prevent conflict diamonds from fuelling war and human rights abuse. Visit **www.kimberleyprocess.com** for more information. *But*, there is currently no way of knowing whether a cut diamond is a conflict diamond or one that has been legally harvested. If you must have a ring, buy antique, or melt down and recast an old one. For an alternative to diamonds, **www.silverchilli.com** offers a range of silver jewellery bought at Fairtrade prices from Mexican craftsmen. Or try **www.credjewellery.com** for ethical jewellery, including wedding bands.

MAKE YOUR OWN WEDDING CAKE This way you can ensure that all the ingredients are organic and locally produced, and the eggs are from free-range chickens. Visit **www.ethicalweddings.com/diy-weddings/category/category/cakes** for ethical cake recipes.

BE A BEAUTIFUL BRIDE – NATURALLY
As a bride your natural beauty should shine through, but getting your make-up done can be half the fun. For natural cosmetics by ranges such as Earth's Beauty, Nvey and Miessence visit **www.theremustbeabetterway.co.uk**.

MAKE SURE YOUR CONFETTI DOESN'T HANG AROUND
If you throw plastic confetti at the happy couple on their wedding day it will still be around in a landfill site when they celebrate their silver

wedding anniversary. Choose a biodegradable alternative – recycled paper, rosebuds or dried bougainvillea petals. Visit **www.petalpot.co.uk** for biodegradable confetti. Better still, collect flower blossoms or petals yourself.

PICTURE PERFECT Taking photos digitally can save on harmful chemicals used to process conventional film. Plus, try to avoid the trend for giving out single-use cameras at your wedding – the resulting packaging is incredibly wasteful. Instead, ask guests to send in a copy of their digital images to complement your own. You can then print the best ones for you and post the rest to friends online.

MAKE YOUR HONEYMOON MATTER Explore the possibility of becoming eco-tourists on your honeymoon. Visit **www.exodus.co.uk**, **www.explore.co.uk** or **www.responsibletravel.com** for eco-friendly holidays, which include wilderness trails, hideaway hot springs in the forest and scuba diving in some of the world's most romantic destinations, but without damaging valuable ecosystems. In 20 years' time you'll be able to go back and find it's still there!

Birth right

GREEN TIPS FOR ECO-BABIES Excited parents-to-be and their families, encouraged by advertising, can spend huge sums with little consideration for the impact they are having on the environment, not to mention the money they waste on products they probably don't need or won't use for longer than a few months. It's easy to spend £2,000 on baby paraphernalia before and during the first year of a child's life... make those first 21 months calmer and easier by cutting down on clutter and making sure everything you buy is simple and natural. Think in terms of the essentials: clothing and nappies, a pram, a cot and feeding equipment.

VINTAGE BABY Good second-hand baby clothes are cheaper, as well as being well-worn and therefore often more comfy. And if you aren't keeping baby clothes for future children of your own, pass them on again to friends or take them into your local charity shop. You can also buy and sell unwanted baby items on the internet. Visit **www.baby-things.com** and the baby section on **www.preloved.co.uk** or get information on local nearly-new sales from The National Childbirth Trust at **www.nctpregnancyandbabycare.com** or call 0870 770 3236.

BREAST OVER BOTTLE? Breastfeeding can help protect your baby against infection because antibodies are passed from mother to baby through the breast milk. Research shows that on average breastfed babies have fewer infections in early life than babies who are bottle-fed, and it's thought that babies who are breastfed are also less likely to develop obesity, diabetes and heart disease. Breastfeeding is also good for mums – it reduces their chances of developing breast cancer and helps weight-loss after giving birth. It's also free! Formula milk is made with artificial additives and a huge amount of energy is needed to turn cow's milk into formula. If you do need to buy formula milk, there are organic varieties available – try **www.hipp.co.uk**. For breastfeeding advice contact La Leche League at **www.laleche.org.uk** or on 0845 456 1855. For general feeding information, visit the National Childbirth Trust at **www.nctpregnancyandbabycare.com**.

DON'T LET YOUR BABY BE A VICTIM OF HAND-ME-DOWN POISONS Mothers may unwittingly pass on chemicals or contaminants to their baby through being unknowingly polluted themselves. A WWF survey found that more than 350 man-made contaminants have been found in mothers' milk. These pollutants are thought to be linked to reduced intelligence and subtle behavioural effects in children. For more information visit **www.wwf.org.uk** or America's Natural Resources Defense Unit **www.nrdc.org/breastmilk/envpoll.asp**.

UNTREATED COTTON BEDDING Synthetic bedding can expose a baby to formaldehyde, solvents and other chemicals. Babies' bedding should be made from cotton, wool, hemp or silk – these natural fabrics breathe and feel more comfortable. Non-organic cotton is treated with pesticides and chemical fertilisers that remain in the material after they are applied. Contact **www.borndirect.com** or **www.gossypium.co.uk** (0870 850 9953) for organic bedding and baby clothes.

TAKE ACTION AGAINST INFANT DEATHS The World Health Organisation (WHO) estimates that 1.5 million infants die around the world every year because they are not breastfed. Instead they are given aggressively marketed milk substitutes mixed with unsafe water. Where water is unsafe a bottle-fed child is up to 25 times more likely to die as a result of diarrhoea than a breastfed child. In 1981, an international marketing code was set up to regulate the industry, but some companies continue to violate that code. Baby Milk Action is part of the International Baby Food Action Network and campaigns to expose these violations and make milk substitute companies take responsibility for their actions. Find out how you can help at **www.babymilkaction.org** or call 01223 464420.

CHOOSE ORGANIC FOOD FOR YOUR BABIES Organic baby food is already bought by 60% of mothers, and is available in most supermarkets and small retailers. Friends of the Earth have found high levels of pesticides in non-organic baby food. Pesticide residues have more impact on babies than adults, as the amount they eat in proportion to their body weight is higher. Visit Hipp at **www.hipp.co.uk** or find out about the Babynat range at **www.organico.co.uk** (0118 923 8767). Both specialise in producing organic baby food. If you want to make your own organic baby food get information from other mothers and exchange recipes at **www.babyorganix.co.uk**, **www.child.com** or **www.mumsnet.com**.

The bottom line

NAPPY FACTS Nappies are one of Britain's major waste problems. The average baby will get through a total of 5,480 during its early years. Each day eight million disposable nappies are thrown away in the UK, accounting for 4% of landfill waste, where they can take 500 years to decompose – and there is also the risk that viruses from human faeces can seep into groundwater supplies. As many as 100 viruses can survive in soiled nappies for up to two weeks, including the live polio virus excreted by recently vaccinated babies. It's not only babies' disposables that are harmful to the environment – older children and adult incontinence pads are, too. For information on eco-friendly incontinence pads and incontinence laundries, contact the Extra Large Nappy Company on 01386 700293.

READER TIP – TRACEY FARWELL

IS IT WORTH THE SACRIFICE?

It takes a cup of crude oil to produce the plastic for one disposable nappy. Use environmentally friendly nappies presoaked in an environmentally friendly nappy soak (**www.thebabycatalogue.com**) and then throw them in the washing machine using Eco-balls (**www.ecozone.co.uk**), not washing powder.

DISPOSABLES COST THE ENVIRONMENT – AND US – MORE With cotton nappies, you'll bear more of the environmental cost in terms of water and energy (if you wash them at home), but this is very little compared to nappy production costs and will make a substantial saving to the environment. The financial cost of disposable nappies per child per year has been estimated to be £1,200. But the cost of keeping one child in shaped cloth nappies has been estimated to be £300, and that includes washing. Think what you could do with an extra £900 a year! But it's not just the money. Nappies lined in plastic can interfere with a baby's cooling patterns, possibly decreasing fertility levels as an adult, and some nappies contain a super-absorber crystalline made of sodium polyacrylate, which turns into a gel on contact with urine. This chemical was linked to toxic shock syndrome in tampons and was removed from feminine products in 1985.

WHICH WOULD YOU PREFER TO WEAR? Cloth nappies have come a long way since the squares with safety pins. They can come in different shapes and sizes, colours and prints, with elastic or Velcro fastenings, breathable fleece or silk covers and biodegradable liners. If you had to wear them on your bottom, which would you choose – a sweaty plastic disposable or a breathable cotton fleece-lined one?

BUY ECO-DISPOSABLES If you're going on a long journey where changing and washing nappies is difficult, you could use eco-disposable nappies instead. Their manufacturing process does far less harm to the environment than normal disposables, not least because they don't contain bleaching agents. They are also free from perfumes and other chemicals which may harm your baby's skin, and are biodegradable. Visit **www.spiritofnature.co.uk** for more details.

GO VELCRO Pins too much hassle? Buy Velcro-fastening cotton nappies. Visit **www.thekidswindow.co.uk/nappies** (0800 542 50 93) for ranges of easy-to-use cotton nappies.

KEEP IT DRY Keep your baby's bottom as dry as possible – and don't use moist tissue wipes. Keeping dry reduces your baby's likelihood of contracting nappy rash, a reaction to chemicals in the urine and faeces. And if you thought that cotton nappies meant a higher chance of nappy rash – *wrong*! Research by the American Medical Association found that nappy rash occurs in 54% of babies using disposable nappies and only 18% of babies using cloth nappies. Most moist baby wipes are full of chemicals such as alcohol, preservatives, fragrances and moisturisers. If you have to use them, go for organic, unfragranced and biodegradable ones from Earth Friendly Baby at **www.earth-friendly-baby.co.uk**.

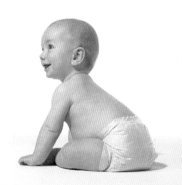

NEVER FLUSH A DISPOSABLE NAPPY DOWN THE TOILET The bleaching agent in nappies can pollute waterways and damage wildlife, fisheries and, ultimately, humans. The gel in disposable nappies absorbs water and the nappies swell so much that they block pipes. Any nappies that do get through the sewerage system will eventually end up on our beaches. Not a pleasant thought.

USE A NAPPY-WASHING SERVICE Nappy services use 32% less energy than home washing, and 41% less water. They also make life much easier for you. Contact the National Association of Nappy Services to find out about services in your area. Visit **www.changenappy.co.uk** or call 0121 693 4949.

MATERNITY WARDS SHOULD USE COTTON NAPPIES TOO Most women put their first nappy on their baby at hospital, so it makes sense for hospitals to encourage them to use cotton nappies to start with. Join the campaign for the NHS to use cotton nappies and lobby your local hospital to do so. Contact the Women's Environmental Network for more information at **www.wen.org.uk**.

READER TIP – GRACE EDWARDS

WEAR A NAPPY!

Support Real Nappy Week each April by wearing a nappy – a clean one, of course! Last year mums whose babies wear real cloth nappies supported Real Nappy Week by wearing scraps of terry nappy on their lapels – a great conversation point and a good way of spreading the news.

HELP MAKE THE CHANGE Real Nappy Week is a nationwide campaign to get people to switch from disposable to cotton. Get involved at **www.wen.org.uk/rnw**. You can also find out more by visiting The Nappy Lady at **www.thenappylady.co.uk**, and the Women's Environmental Network at **www.wen.org.uk**, which organises nappy activists' workshops as well as events for Real Nappy Week.

Kids' stuff

EARLY LEARNERS **Kids learn best by doing. One of the best things parents can do to make kids more aware of the environment is to lead by example. Show kids how to save water by turning taps off when they brush their teeth, and how to separate rubbish and recycling cans and plastic bottles at the bottle bank. Walk or cycle with them to school and local shops to save fuel, and point out interesting plants, animals and birds on the way. If you are aware of environmental issues, your children will become aware of them, too!**

DRAW UP A FUN ECO-CODE It's never too soon to get kids interested and involved in a lifestyle that's good for them and the environment. Drawing up an 'Eco-code' will give them a set of eco-friendly guidelines that they can stick to. Help them turn it into a fun, colourful poster and give them treats when they do a good turn. Include activities and tasks such as recycling, looking after animals and turning off lights to save energy. See **www.ecofriendlykids.co.uk/TheEcoCode.html.**

DOWN ON THE FARM If your kids are growing up in a city centre, take them to a green space – a park or a city farm – to learn more about how the countryside supports cities. There are over 60 city farms throughout the UK which breed livestock and grow crops – **www.farmgarden.org.uk** has all the details. You can find the location of your nearest park in the *Good Parks Guide*, a collection of over 500 of the best public, countryside, urban and historic parks in the UK. Find out more on **www.green-space.org.uk/goodparksguide**. If there aren't any green spaces near you, find out how you can create one. Visit the British Trust for Conservation Volunteers at **www.btcv.org** for information on community initiatives, a project that helps communities to develop or improve accessible 'green spaces' in urban and rural areas across England.

SADDLE UP Seeing the countryside on the back of a horse is a great way of getting back to nature. There are stables all over the country that offer riding lessons, and there are several organisations that arrange riding holidays. Details of these can be found at **www.horse-directory.co.uk**.

CHILDREN'S ENVIRONMENTAL HOLIDAYS If you want to send your kids on adventure holidays, choose a holiday that combines the excitement of activity with discovery of the natural world. The Field Studies Council runs eco-adventure holidays in England and Wales for children from eight years upwards; details are available at **www.field-studies-council.org**. Meanwhile, the Young People's Trust for the Environment runs Environmental Discovery Holidays for people aged 8-16, during the summer in the south of England. Visit **www.yptenc.org.uk/docs/residential_hols.html** for more information.

START VOLUNTEERING EARLY Young people are the decision-makers of the future, so encourage them to get involved and volunteer when they're young. The Young Person's Trust for the Environment provides courses, facts and ideas for kids aged 5-16 years and their teachers/parents. Search **www.yptenc.org.uk** for ideas and inspiration.

GET INTO THE WILD The best way to get children to care about the creatures and plants around us is to help them develop an active interest by visiting parks, environment centres or nature reserves. Visit **www.scampsandrascals.co.uk** for smaller wildlife sanctuaries and **www.safaripark.co.uk** for larger safari parks and zoos. Other museums well worth visiting are The Natural History Museum at **www.nhm.ac.uk** and the Eden Project in Cornwall at **www.edenproject.co.uk**. The IMAX cinema has informative films on the natural world. See **www.bfi.org.uk**.

KIDS – GO FLY A KITE Have you ever tried flying a kite off the side of a hill on a windy day? Kite surfing is an international sport and kites come in all shapes and sizes. For new and second-hand kites try **www.kiteshack.co.uk**. Alternatively, make your own kite out of a bin liner, some sticks, string and a bit of sticky tape! It's cheap and easy – **www.reeddesign.co.uk/kites.htm** will show you how.

KIDS – MAKE RECYCLED PAPER According to Recyclezone at **www.recyclezone.org.uk**, paper and card make up about a fifth of the contents of a typical household dustbin in the UK – that's about 6.3 million tonnes of paper a year. You can help reduce this by making sure all the paper – particularly newspaper – in your house is recycled. You can also make recycled paper out of old newspapers and water. To find out how easy and fun it can be visit **www.yptenc.org.uk/docs/actionsheets/recycling_paper.html**.

KIDS – HELP BIRDS TO NEST IN YOUR AREA... build them nestboxes! Some birds return to the same box each year, and as long as you don't disturb them, you can watch as they establish a home for their offspring, feed them and teach them to fly. To find out how to make a simple wooden nestbox for your garden or school visit **www.yptenc.org.uk/docs/actionsheets/nestboxes.html**, or get hold of a copy of *Birds in your Garden.*

KIDS – MAKE A FRIEZE OF ENDANGERED SPECIES

Thousands of animal species are threatened with extinction – from elephants that are killed for their ivory tusks to tiny insects in the Amazon who die out when their habitat is destroyed. Your own children may never be able to see them. Find out which animals are endangered and draw pictures of them – then stick them around your bedroom wall. Find out how you can protect an animal from extinction by reading *Going, Going, Gone? Animals and plants on the brink of extinction and how you can help.*

KIDS – PERSUADE YOUR PARENTS TO GET YOU A BICYCLE According to Sustrans at **www.sustrans.org.uk** nearly two thirds of car journeys in Britain are shorter than five miles. Don't let your family's car choke Britain with smoky fumes that contribute to climate change, polluted air and health problems. Persuade your parents to walk on local journeys or, better still, get bikes for everyone.

KIDS – LEARN MORE ABOUT THE ENVIRONMENT AND MAKE NEW FRIENDS A new website aimed at 12-16-year-olds has lots of information about air pollution, dealing with waste, conserving water and protecting endangered animals. There are also competitions, games and suggestions for group activities. Young people can join the Green Buddies Network through the site **www.europa.eu.int/comm/environment/youth/index_en.html**.

Play school

TOYS AND GAMES THAT MAKE A DIFFERENCE Toys can do so much damage. Often made on the other side of the world by children who receive next to nothing for their labour, they are transported from country to country, burning up fuel, and wrapped in packaging that contributes to global waste. And how often have you given a brand-new toy to a young child only to find them playing with the cardboard box it came in? Why not make a difference with the toys you give? It'll be fun for you as well as the children.

PLAY SAFE Are your children playing with toys that are safe? Look for the Lion Mark – a triangle with a lion inside it. This shows it has been made by a member of the British Toy and Hobby Association and meets government safety requirements. About 95% of toys sold in the UK have a Lion Mark so it's not difficult to avoid the few that aren't safe. For more information visit **www.btha.co.uk** or call 020 7701 7271.

Also, never buy a child a toy if it is aimed at an older kid – they can be especially dangerous for children under three. Check toys with loose or small parts that a young child could choke on, toys with sharp edges or finger traps, loose ribbons and small toys sold with food.

JOIN A TOY LIBRARY In 2006 the toy industry was worth £2.2 billion, with electronic gadgets as the fastest-growing area. However, you don't have to spend a fortune to keep up with the latest toy craze: join a toy library where – for a small fee – you can borrow toys, join play sessions and meet other families. There are over 1,000 toy libraries in the UK, run by the National Association of Toy and Leisure Libraries. Call them on 020 7255 4600 to find out your nearest library, or visit **www.natll.org.uk**.

BE PVC FREE Plastic toys, especially PVC or vinyl toys, can contain phthalates, harmful chemicals thought responsible for altering testes development as well as liver and kidney damage. Some toys made in Asia contain up to 55% phthalates by weight. Workers who produce these products have been found to suffer from a high level of liver and other cancers. Some researchers put the risk of liver cancer in vinyl plastics workers as high as 200 times greater than average. Don't let your child's toys be someone else's killer. Wooden toys are much kinder to the environment and last longer, too. Contact the British Toymakers Guild at **www.toymakersguild.co.uk** to find out where you can buy handmade wooden toys.

CHILDREN SHOULD PLAY WITH TOYS, NOT MAKE THEM
Before he stepped down in 2005, Michael Eisner, former CEO of Disney, paid himself US$133 million a year, or about US$63,000 an hour. It would take a worker in Bangladesh – some only children – sewing Disney garments for 12 cents an hour, 210 years to earn what Eisner earnt in an hour. When Bangladeshi workers went to America to highlight their situation, they said they had to work over 15 hours a day, seven days a week, were denied maternity benefits, beaten and paid just 15 cents for every US$17.99 Disney shirt they sewed.

Disney responded by cancelling its order, causing them to lose their jobs. Find out more and how to campaign for sweatshop workers, including children, around the world at **www.nosweat.org.uk**.

BRING FAIRNESS TO THE TOY INDUSTRY! BUY FAIRTRADE TOYS The International Labour Organisation estimates that over 200 million children are involved in child labour. Over 95% of these children are found in developing countries. Fairtrade shops sell toys made to strict ethical rules, and manufacturers get a fair price for making them. Find out more from Traidcraft at **www.traidcraft.co.uk** or the British Association for Fair Trade Shops at **www.bafts.org.uk**. The Natural Collection sells wooden animal jigsaws using non-toxic paints that are made by a craft enterprise in Sri Lanka, plus Fairtrade footballs and finger puppets. For details visit **www.naturalcollection.com**.

SAVE COMMUNITY PLAYING FIELDS Recreational space is a vital part of every community. Yet despite its importance, an average of one playing field every day comes under threat from building development, such as new houses and car parks. Once this land is built on, it's lost for ever. The National Playing Fields Association is responsible for acquiring, protecting and improving our fast-disappearing playing fields and playgrounds. Visit its website at **www.npfa.co.uk** to find out if any playing fields near you are under threat and to support its campaigns.

DON'T LET KILLING BECOME FUN In the twenty-first century, 'virtual killing' has become child's play in console games. But children under the age of eight are not always able to separate fact from fiction. MediaWise, an initiative of another US organisation (the National Institute on Media and the Family) runs KidScore, a rating system that evaluates videos and games from a family-friendly perspective – visit **www.mediafamily.org** for details. The UK is also looking into a rating system for video and computer games, similar to the one used for films. In the meantime it's up to parents to exercise some discipline in this area.

TOYS TO UNDERSTAND THE ENVIRONMENT An Australian study recently found that six out of 10 children who use computers at school and children as young as nine were being treated for chronic Repetitive Strain Injury (RSI) pain. Don't expose your children to 'Nintendo thumb' by buying them more computer games. For guidance on getting better habits when using computers, consoles and texting see RSI Action's Guide for Young People: *How to avoid RSI* at **www.rsiaction.org.uk/rsi-conditions-and-prevention**. You could also encourage your children to try games that get them outside. At **www.thekidsgarden.co.uk**, kids can find ideas on how to build a wormery, grow plants, make scarecrows, build a birdhouse and make a sensory garden. The Green Board Game Company makes board games that encourage knowledge of the natural world and are made of recycled products and wood from sustainable forests. Their All Around the World game is fun for all the family, while little ones will enjoy Where's My Home or Farmer's Market. Visit **www.greenboardgames.com** for details.

RECYCLE THEM If your child has grown out of a toy, it's not useless – another child will still get hours of fun from it. Following the news that 40 million toys were being thrown out each year in the UK, Toys to You set up a Toy Recycling in the Community initiative. Visit **www.toys-to-you.co.uk/acatalog/ToyRecycling.html** for ideas of how to recycle toys, including giving them to a charity shop, playgroup or hospital.

MAKE YOUR OWN Transform colourful old clothes into stuffed toys, beanbag toys or rag dolls. Some garments will have a whole new lease of life in a fancy-dress box. Look on the *Blue Peter* website **www.bbc.co.uk/cbbc/bluepeter/active/makes** for tips and ideas.

CHOOSE TOY BATTERIES CAREFULLY Most batteries contain toxic metals, such as cadmium, mercury and nickel, that leak into the environment when they are thrown away. When you do buy batteries, choose alkaline manganese ones, which are free from toxic heavy metals. And how about buying a solar-powered battery charger? You can find them at **www.getethical.com** and **www.sunshinesolar.co.uk**.

CELEBRATE MULTICULTURE Get your kids to learn about other countries and cultures from an early age so that they grow up with a healthy respect for diversity and each other. They can do this by playing with toys from around the world or by making their own. Get great global craft ideas at **www.dltk-kids.com/world/index.htm** or for multicultural, multilingual and inclusive games and toys see **www.kidslikeme.co.uk**.

Grass roots

BACK TO BASICS WITH ECO-EDUCATION Schools are the perfect place for environmental initiatives, bringing lots of people together from different age groups and backgrounds. Environmental projects can help create a sense of community and participation, while providing excellent teaching resources. And who knows – children may start bringing their good habits into the home and influencing their parents. Meanwhile we need to put the brakes on the increasing corporate takeover of our schools. In a school in America, for example, PepsiCo donated US$2 million to build a football stadium in exchange for exclusive rights to sell its soft drinks in all 140 of the district's schools and to advertise in school gymnasiums and on athletics fields. That deal is estimated to earn the company US$7.3 million over seven years. Education or exploitation?

TRAVEL TO SCHOOL ON FOOT OR BY PUBLIC TRANSPORT At 8.50am one in five cars on urban roads is taking children to school. One in four children travel to school by car – that's twice as many as 20 years ago. Contrary to popular belief, in slow-moving traffic, pollution levels are actually higher inside the car than out. Children who walk or cycle to school are usually fitter than those dropped at the gate, and arrive for lessons more alert. In the UK only 1% of kids cycle to school, while in Denmark, which has pioneered a cycle to school campaign, over 60% of kids do. Sustrans is a sustainable transport charity that encourages the use of environmentally friendly methods of travel. It facilitates Safe Routes to Schools in partnership with pupils, parents, teachers, the police and the local authority to provide safe routes to schools for children. Visit the website **www.sustrans.org.uk** or call 0117 915 0100 to find out more.

EDUCATION IS A BASIC HUMAN RIGHT... It's as fundamental as food and shelter. An education is the key to every child's development, bringing out their potential and helping them deal with the challenges of a changing world. It is also one of the most effective ways of breaking the poverty cycle. Around the world, 120 million children of primary-school age are not in school. In Nepal, only 44% of children complete primary school, and in Angola only 4% do. To find out more, and see what you can do to help, visit **www.unicef.org** or **www.savethechildren.org.uk**.

GET PLANTING! Growing food at school is a fun way of learning about the lifecycle of a plant and becoming more aware of where food comes from. And you don't even need a garden! Herbs can be grown on windowsills, while carrots, tomatoes and potatoes can be grown in buckets on a balcony. You can take this even further and encourage your school to make a conservation area, where you can all work together to make an exciting, growing garden. For ideas on how to start a garden in your school, visit the Campaign for School Gardening at **www.rhs.org.uk/schoolgardening**.

RUBBISH IN THE CLASSROOM Kids – ask your school to put recycling bins in the classrooms for white and coloured paper, and cans. See **www.wastewatch.org.uk** for information. Arrange for a 'robot recycler' to come to your school to teach everyone about recycling, and join the Schools Waste Action Club.

BRING THE OUTDOORS IN The countryside is a fantastic learning resource and studies have shown that children who spend time learning outdoors and in close contact with nature often develop better interaction and initiative skills, while children living in urban areas often miss out on its benefits. The Countryside Foundation is a charity that runs a scheme to bring the countryside into the classroom using excellent learning materials. Alternatively, the class can be taken to the countryside on an educational field trip or a simple nature walk. Find out more at **www.countrysidefoundation.org.uk** or call 01422 885566. Farming and Countryside Education (FACE) can also organise school visits to rural areas and sustainable farms at **www.face-online.org.uk**.

CUT COSTS AT SCHOOL UK schools account for 25% of public sector energy costs, spending nearly £400 million on energy and releasing eight million tonnes of CO_2 each year. One secondary school managed to save £10,000 of its annual fuel costs after an energy-saving project. Imagine what you could buy with that! Two thirds of a teacher, nearly 2,000 textbooks or 25,000 bars of (Fairtrade) chocolate! For advice on how to save energy and water see **www.sustainablelearning.info**.

CAMPAIGN AGAINST THE USE OF CHILD SOLDIERS An AK-47 is small, light and simple enough to be used by a child of 10. In some countries it can be bought for as little as US$20. More than 300,000 children are being used as child soldiers around the world and since 1990, it is estimated that two million children have been killed and six million have been seriously injured in wars. Support the campaign for an end to the use of children in warfare – visit the Coalition to Stop the Use of Child Soldiers at **www.child-soldiers.org** and support Amnesty International's child soldier letter-writing campaign at **www.amnesty.org**.

DON'T LET EDUCATION BECOME A COMMODITY; SAY NO TO GATS Students, teachers, campuses… normally we don't think of these as profit-making resources, or the institution of education as a market. But with the General Agreement on Trade in Services (GATS), all this may be up for grabs. GATS could start to replace the principles of learning with those of profit-making. Find out more about Education International at **www.ei-ie.org**, which wants to have education removed from the scope of GATS. If you are a student, campaign to turn your university into a no-GATS zone. Visit the students' campaigning group People and Planet at **www.peopleandplanet.org**, or call 01865 245678 for more information.

Fetch!

TURN YOUR PETS GREEN **Pets in the UK get it pretty easy compared to many in other countries. Hundreds of millions of pounds are spent annually on pet products by animal-loving Britain, which is not difficult considering pets are present in over half the UK's households. In 2007, the US petcare industry was estimated at around £40 billion a year, while around £3 billion is spent on petcare in the UK. An industry of such proportions won't leave the environment unscathed. Then there are the pets themselves. Could your treatment of them be greener? With a few small changes you could be kind to them and to the environment, too.**

RESCUE YOUR PET Keeping a family pet will help kids understand animals better. By taking responsibility for a pet they will learn about animal welfare first hand. If you're thinking about a cat or dog, get one from an animal shelter – there are thousands of mistreated or abandoned animals which need safe homes and caring owners. Contact Battersea Dogs Home (for cats as well as dogs) at **www.dogshome.org**, Cats Protection, which has branches all round the country, at **www.cats.org.uk**, or go through Rescuepet at **www.rescuepet.org.uk**. If you can't have a pet at home, encourage your kids to volunteer for the RSPCA, which welcomes young volunteers. See their website at **www.rspca.org.uk** for details.

PUT A BELL AROUND YOUR CAT'S NECK Domestic cats can plague local wildlife, killing birds, frogs, mice and voles, which can also litter people's lawns. Putting a bell round their neck could help to reduce that number significantly – a trial conducted by the RSPB found that cats equipped with a bell returned 41% fewer birds and 34% fewer mammals than those with a plain collar. Those equipped with an electronic sonic device returned 51% fewer birds and 38% fewer mammals, compared with cats wearing a plain collar.

DON'T FEED YOUR PETS PLASTIC Your pets are just as happy chewing and scratching on homemade toys as they are on resource-depleting, environment-damaging plastic. With a little care and attention, your pet can be your best friend – and the environment's, too. Screwing up a used sheet of paper into a cat's football can provide hours of fun, time and again. Visit **www.animalpure.co.uk** or call 01483 562669 for natural alternatives made from hemp and loofah.

HOMEOPATHY FOR PETS Applying arnica to bruises or giving aconite for a fever works just as well for pets that are poorly. And, as there's no difference between human and animal remedies, you don't have to buy them specially. Do get advice from the British Association of Homeopathic Veterinary Surgeons before you start, however. See **www.bahvs.com** or call them on 07768 322075.

SCOOP THAT POOP The 6.8 million members of the British canine population produce 900 tonnes of excrement a day. Dog excrement can contain the eggs of roundworm, which can live for up to two years in the soil. Once inside the human body, they can burrow through the gut, damaging the liver, lungs and eyes, and can lead to blindness. Children playing in parks are most at risk, so take a scoop with you, bag it and then bin it! Get biodegradable Poop Scoop bags from **www.envirobag.co.uk**.

DRY, NOT CANNED The UK spends £600 billion a year on canned pet food. Tins can be recycled, but their production and transportation requires energy and effort that's greatly reduced when you buy dry food in bulk. Find organic pet food for dogs and cats at **www.organipets.co.uk** or natural resources for all pets at **www.alotoforganics.co.uk**.

DON'T USE COMMERCIAL SPRAYS A female flea can lay around 25 eggs a day. If they all survive there could be 750 new fleas after just one month and 22,500 after two, wriggling about your pet and anything it comes into contact with. But many of the commercial sprays, which act by attacking a flea's nervous system, are associated with reproductive problems in pets. Use a non-toxic flea collar, try adding garlic pills or brewer's yeast (bought in pet shops) to your pets' food, or make a herbal flea collar. For less toxic options and alternatives, visit the Pesticide Action Network at **www.pan-uk.org/pestnews/homepest/Flea.htm**.

BIODEGRADABLE KITTY LITTER Instead of filling up the landfill with plastic bags of dirty cat litter, try using natural cat litter. Bio-Catolet natural cat litter is made from 100% paper and is biodegradable, and dust and odour free. See **www.veggiepets.com/acatalog/natural_cat_litters**. The cat litter can be composted, but cat faeces should be removed and disposed of in biodegradable bags.

LOOK AFTER THE ANIMAL YOU LOVE Pets can be treated for a wide range of illnesses now – ranging from a slipped disc to suspect lumps. But the treatment can be very expensive. You can insure your animals for as little as £6 a month for a cat and £9 a month for a dog. If you insure with the RSPCA you can receive a range of benefits, including the cost of up to £6,000 vets fees. Plus, 20% of your premium will be donated to the RSPCA to help animals less fortunate. Get an online quote at **www.rspca.org.uk**.

HAVE YOUR CAT NEUTERED One female un-neutered cat can be responsible for 50 million offspring and descendants in a lifetime if it has two litters each of six kittens. The surging cat population means that thousands are abandoned each year – in 2006, the RSPCA rehomed 32,221 cats, and had many more on waiting lists.

EXOTIC PETS? JUST SAY NO Exotic animals don't make pets. They grow faster, live longer and are unpredictable and dangerous if they escape, but few owners are fully informed. In 2007, the RSPCA carried out a survey of almost 300 pet shops in England and Wales. It revealed that only 20% of shops provided free care sheets to potential buyers; 20% of potential pet buyers were given no care advice whatsoever; 2% of pet shops sold crocodilians, such as caimans; and only 25% of cages displayed information about how big the animal inside would grow when fully adult. Visit **www.rspca.org.uk** or the Dangerous Wild Animal Rescue Facility at **www.dwarf.org.uk** for more details.

STAMP OUT PET CRUELTY Puppies bred intensively to be sold in UK pet shops are often kept in dark, cold and cramped conditions and are looked after by people more concerned with making money than the welfare of animals. Indiscriminate breeding increases the risk of genetic and behavioural problems and puppies are often separated from their mother at a very young age. Help Dogs Trust (formerly the National Canine Defence League) and its campaign against puppy farming at **www.dogstrust.org.uk** or call 020 7837 0006.

SUPPORT THE CAMPAIGN AGAINST TRAFFICKED ANIMALS A single shipload of green iguanas can contain 2,000-5,000 creatures, carrying them thousands of miles, often illegally, from their native habitat to an unnatural one in captivity and allowing their natural population to decline. Iguanas are the most commonly traded animals in the UK, but Britain imports a total of over one million live reptiles and amphibians a year, including boas, pythons, chameleons and geckos. It's not only reptiles, but also birds, fish and mammals that are swept up in this trade. Find out how you can help stop with Traffic International, the wildlife trade monitoring network, at **www.traffic.org** or call them on 01223 277427.

Christmas crackers

TOP TIPS FOR A GREEN CHRISTMAS At Christmas we go into an all-consuming, all-disposing frenzy. On the weekend before Christmas in 2002, British consumers spent a total of £630 million. In 2007 we spent a staggering £15.2 billion online between 1 October and 31 December. Our concerns for the environment often get thrown out of the window... but it doesn't have to be that way. Before you buy something, ask yourself: Do I really need it? How long would I use it for? Can I borrow it? Can I do without it? If the answer is still yes, then ask yourself: Is it recyclable? How will it be disposed of?

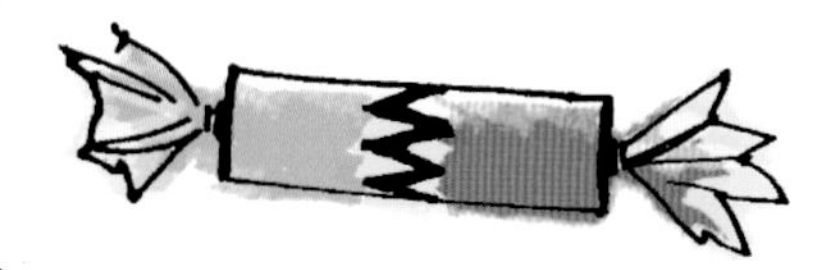

READER TIP – DAVID NILAND
A CHRISTMAS TREE FOR LIFE

For just £10 you can dedicate a tree from a choice of woods as a present. In return you'll receive a certificate stating the dedication and naming the tree's location. Trees are a lifelong gift and make an excellent present for weddings, anniversaries and christenings, too. See **www.woodland-trust.org.uk/plantatree** for details.

RECYCLE YOUR CARDS We have become so wound up in giving and receiving presents that the traditional spirit of Christmas is under threat. An estimated 1.7 billion Christmas cards were sent in 1997 in Britain – the equivalent of 200,000 trees. In Lapland the reindeer's habitat and the lifestyle of the indigenous Saami people is under threat because 95% of old forests have been lost in Finland and Sweden – where 40% of the UK's paper comes from. If more old forests aren't preserved, Rudolph may become a thing of the past. Help by taking old Christmas cards to a Woodland Trust recycling point at WHSmith, Tesco, M&S or TK Maxx in January. Visit **www.woodland-trust.org.uk/cards** for details.

BUY CHARITY CHRISTMAS CARDS Buy Christmas cards from charities and donate up to 20% to less fortunate people at the same time. Check on **www.christmas-cards.org.uk** or **www.charitycards.co.uk** for details. Charities such as The Blue Cross and the Royal National Lifeboat Institution make recycled cards. Or send an e-card – the British Library has some traditional designs at **www.bl.uk/ecards/indexxmas.html**.

JUST BUY NOTHING Instead of rushing to the shops to buy something, why don't you not buy something instead? Buy Nothing Day is organised to challenge the consumer culture and switch off from shopping and consumerism for a day. The day normally takes place at the end of November. For information and tips on what to do instead of shopping on that day visit **www.buynothingday.co.uk**.

CLOSING THE LOOP There's no point recycling rubbish if you don't buy recycled products – after all, the recycled products have to go somewhere! In 2002, we used 83 square kilometres of wrapping paper (enough to cover Guernsey) at Christmas. This year make sure your paper is recycled. You can buy recycled gift wrap and matching envelopes at Recycled Paper Supplies from **www.rps.gn.apc.org** and wrap your presents with string, ribbon and wool rather than sticky tape.

RECYCLE YOUR CHRISTMAS TREE In 2007 an estimated eight million Christmas trees were bought – enough to fill the Albert Hall four times over – most of which were thrown out after Christmas. Either buy a proper Christmas tree with roots and plant it in the garden afterwards or contact your local authority to see if they have a scheme which chips Christmas trees into garden mulch.

IF YOU'RE BUYING A TURKEY, MAKE IT ORGANIC Of the 10 million turkeys eaten at Christmas, most have been reared intensively in huge, windowless sheds holding up to 25,000 birds each. The birds have been genetically selected to grow as fast as possible, are fed antibiotics and are so overweight they cannot mate naturally. Visit Compassion in World Farming at **www.ciwf.org.uk/publications/reports/Christmas_guide.pdf**.

KIDS – MAKE YOUR OWN CHRISTMAS CARDS AND DECORATIONS Britain produced about three million tonnes of festive rubbish in 2007, with only around half of British adults recycling during this time. But house decorations can be made from recycled and scrap paper – old newspapers and magazines make great paper chains, and scrap materials can be used to make Christmas tree ornaments. This makes more sense than spending £20 on a sparkly angel that has been made by children in a far-eastern sweatshop to be thrown away after a few days on a Christmas tree. Usbourne's charming book *Christmas Decorations and Cards* is great for crafty ideas.

MAKE THE THOUGHT REALLY COUNT Avoid presents that rely on disposable parts, such as the paper filter on a coffee machine – look for a model with a permanent filter and choose solar-powered chargers rather than batteries. The best green presents are ones that will help their owners be kinder to the environment – a recycling paper kit, a worm bin compost kit, a sponsor an animal scheme, a subscription to the *Ecologist* or a copy of this book!

GIVE SOMEONE ELSE A HAPPY CHRISTMAS Christmas can be the worst time of year for people who have no one to share it with. Think about donating some money or time to a charity that works with the homeless, elderly people or those suffering from domestic violence. The Women's Royal Voluntary Service (WRVS) provides a range of outreach services to help people in need throughout England, Scotland and Wales, who might otherwise feel lonely and isolated. Find out how to 'be a star' this year by volunteering or donating to the organisation by visiting **www.wrvs.org.uk** or calling 0845 601 4670. For a register of all UK-based charities and their contact details go to **www.charity-commission.gov.uk** or call 0845 3000 218. Or Timebank can link you to a local volunteering project that works around the hours you have. Visit **www.timebank.org.uk** or call 0845 456 1668. Once you've chosen your charity, how about remaining loyal to it over the years with a regular direct debit donation?

READER TIP – LYN WEAL
KIDS – RECYCLE YOUR TOYS BY GIVING THEM AS GIFTS AT CHRISTMAS

Millions of kids around the world will receive nothing for Christmas because their parents can't afford presents. But you can recycle your unwanted toys and make a Christmas present for someone less fortunate. Samaritan's Purse International Relief runs Operation Christmas Child at **www.samaritanspurse.uk.com/occ/at**, where you can donate a shoebox of recycled toys, plus sweets and treats. These then go to needy children around the world. In 2007, they sent 1.24 million shoeboxes from the UK to children in hospitals, orphanages, Internally Displaced Persons camps, homeless shelters and impoverished neighbourhoods. You can also donate new toys, games, books, CDs, toiletries or accessories – maybe ones you haven't even used or opened – through the Salvation Army's Christmas Present Appeal. Find out how at **www.salvationarmy.org.uk**.

Present and correct

MAKE A DIFFERENCE WHEN YOU GIVE Sometimes it seems as if the year is one long gift-buying spree – with Christmas, Easter, Mother's Day, Father's Day, Valentines, leaving parties, not to mention birthdays! And what might the present be? Something made in China, transported to the US, then distributed to a UK warehouse before making its way to a local shop, burning up thousands of miles of transport fuel in the process. Then there's the wrapping paper, the gift tags and the ribbon bows which end up in the dustbin the following day. We spend so much money on the many presents we give, and use up so much of the world's resources in the process. With a little planning, we can find a way of giving presents, which are thoughtful, original and a real pleasure to receive and which make a positive difference to the environment as well.

GIVE A RECYCLED PRESENT Wastewatch is full of good ideas and details of where you can find original recycled gifts. Go to **www.wastewatch.org.uk** or phone 020 7549 0300. Charities such as Oxfam run year-round mail order services and are a good source of recycled present ideas. See **www.oxfam.org.uk**.

GIVE A GIFT OF TIME Your time is valuable, so give it as a gift! It will mean more than a hurriedly-bought present. Why not arrange for yourself and your friend to go on a trip to the theatre, a concert, the cinema or a sporting event? No wrapping involved, and the memory will last longer than chemical bath products or socks. Visit **www.seetickets.com** for ideas.

READER TIP – KATHERINE NORTH

BAG IT UP

Make your own gift bags from recycled paper or card and customise them to suit any individual. Better still, bought or handmade gift bags can be reused again and again, without the need for wrapping paper, sticky tape or string. Or buy recycled newspaper bags from **www.freesetbags.co.uk** – these donate towards and help raise awareness about social issues in India.

WATCH FOR BARBED FLOWERS The beautiful bunch of roses you buy in a florists or supermarket has probably been grown in a greenhouse the other side of the world at a huge environmental and social cost. Colombia provides 59% of flowers imported to the US, but two thirds of flower workers there suffer from illnesses caused by pesticide exposure. One fifth of the chemicals used there are carcinogens or toxins, the use of which is restricted in the US! Raise your awareness on the issue at **www.waronwant.org/cutflowers**. Then try to change your own flower-shopping habits. Ask your florist or market for locally grown cut flowers or choose an organically grown plant from your garden centre or **www.redhens.co.uk**, or grow your own with **www.gardenorganic.org.uk**.

GIVE A SQUIRREL! Well, not exactly. But through wildlife charities you can organise for a rare squirrel, seal, puffin or owl to be adopted as a present. The money you spend on the present (often as little as £15) goes towards the organisation's work to protect that endangered species. Two organisations that do this are The Wildlife Trusts – visit **www.wildlifetrusts.org** (01636 677711) – and the Barn Owl Trust – visit **www.barnowltrust.org.uk** (01364 653026).

A PRESENT TO RE-MEMBER Make a present of a year's membership of an environmental organisation. Most rely on their membership to be able to do the work they do. Hunt around for a small organisation that has a specific relevance for the person receiving the present. There are thousands, ranging from the British Beekeepers Association or the British Hedgehog Preservation Society to the British Cave Research Association. For an extensive list and website links go to **www.ethicaljunction.org**.

GIVE PRESENTS THAT MAKE US MORE AWARE For little thank yous and stocking fillers, buy Fairtrade presents – organic chocolate, handmade smellies, beeswax candles, recycled paper notebooks and pencils. And for someone who has everything, get them a wind-up phone charger. Three minutes of wind-up will provide eight minutes of conversation – it's a great way of learning about the cost of energy. Visit **www.greenshop.co.uk** for more ideas.

READER TIP – JUDI BRILL

GIVE A GIFT FOR CHANGE

Honour your loved ones with a gift that means the world for families and children in developing, poverty-stricken or war-torn countries. Mercy Corps has a range of Gifts for Change, including Child Health, Rainforest or School Supplies gifts. Use them to mark birthdays, weddings and anniversaries. They're also ideal for those lucky people who 'have everything'. Find out more at **www.mercycorps.org.uk/giftsforchange**.

MAKE A FAIRTRADE HAMPER Choose a basket from **www.onevillage.org** – made in cooperatives in Uganda, Bangladesh and the Philippines – then fill it with Fairtrade drinking chocolate, chutneys, preserves, biscuits and wine from **www.traidcraft.co.uk**.

Celebrations – green style

THROW A PARTY – SAVE THE WORLD! Parties are big business these days, especially for kids, and there's a whole industry devoted to making your celebrations go with a bang. Party poppers, paper hats, instant fancy-dress kits – it all adds up to a big pile of waste at the end of the evening. If you don't want to spend hours filling those bin liners with junk, plan a green party.

AVOID HELIUM BALLOONS Helium is the second most abundant element in the known universe. Here on Earth it is mined in conjunction with natural gas, mostly from around Amarillo in Texas. It's used for cooling MRI machines, deep scuba diving, cryogenic and superfluid research, the manufacture of optical fibres – and party balloons. Helium is formed from the radioactive decay of uranium and is a very slowly renewable resource – most of Earth's stocks eventually drift out into space. By 2012, it's estimated that there will be a severe shortage of helium (apart from the huge stockpile in Amarillo dating from World War II) and prices will rocket. Helium balloons are fun, but all things considered, staggeringly irresponsible. They use a valuable resource to drift around the world, depositing foil or treated latex that litter and can be swallowed by wildlife – turtles have been found beached with balloons hanging from their mouths. If you want balloons at your party, use your own puff and eco-friendly natural latex balloons from **www.littlecherry.co.uk** – they biodegrade at the same rate as an oak leaf – or get paper ones coated in PVA (which is soluble in water) from **www.tsumura.co.uk**.

FEEL BETTER THE MORNING AFTER It might not stave off your hangover but you can feel slightly better knowing that you've done your bit by taking some eco-action the night before. Make ready to recycle all your booze bottles plus leftover food and any paper waste. Then turn off all the lights and electrical switches before you go to bed. Switching off just one light can give you enough power to run a stereo for 24 hours – a great excuse for dancing in the dark!

SLAVE TO CHOCOLATE? Britons eat more chocolate per capita than any other country – over £1.20 per person per week. It's hard to believe that the type of chocolate we choose will determine whether a family can put food on the table, or a child goes to school. But the prices that most cocoa growers get for their crops make it difficult for them to survive at all. Don't let them be slaves to your sweet tooth: buy Fairtrade chocolate by Green and Black, Chocaid or Chocolala, plus more ranges at **www.fairtrade.org.uk/products_chocolate_buy.htm**.

COOK OUTSIDE WITH CARE Don't use disposable barbecues in the countryside, for example. In dry weather the heat can penetrate the ground, causing parched soil to burn below the surface and endanger plant, animal and human life. And don't add to the mountain of litter – take a bag and clear up any rubbish after you. For details of access – where you can walk, camp and gather – and how to act in accordance with the Countryside Code visit **www.countrysideaccess.gov.uk**.

HAVE A GREEN HALLOWEEN Traditionally, Halloween celebrated the change of seasons from autumn to winter, and was at one time considered to be the beginning of the year. Return this festival to its environmental beginnings. Avoid the glow-in-the-dark orange plastic and make your own Halloween figures and games, such as pumpkin lanterns, creepy string spiders, apple bobbing and floating beeswax candles. For fun free pumpkin-carving patterns visit **www.pumpkincarvingkit.co.uk**.

Down to Earth

MAKE A DIFFERENCE IN DEATH AS WELL AS LIFE

Death is part of the cycle of life – and just because we stop, it doesn't mean everything else does. While we may not be around to appreciate it ourselves, we can still make a difference when we're dead by signing up for a green funeral. This could mean being buried in woodland or a natural eco-coffin. The Natural Death Centre has lots

of advice on how to plan an environmentally friendly send-off in your area at www.naturaldeath.org.uk. You can also call their helpline on 0871 288 2098 or benefit from their regularly updated book *The Natural Death Handbook*.

GO FOR BURIAL INSTEAD OF CREMATION In the UK, 440,000 people – about 74% – are cremated, the largest proportion in Europe. Cremation releases toxins into the atmosphere, such as hydrogen chloride and formaldehyde. And crematoria discharge 1,300kg of mercury emissions in the UK every year. The mercury comes from amalgam fillings in teeth and its emissions will pollute the air, contaminate rivers and endanger the health of those you leave behind – it can attack the nervous system and cause brain damage.

HOW ABOUT A CARDBOARD COFFIN – OR EVEN MAKING YOUR OWN? Each year around 437,000 wooden coffins are burned in the UK. Do you really want to see those trees going up in smoke? Cardboard coffins are biodegradable and much cheaper than wooden coffins, costing as little as £53. See a range of natural designs made from cardboard, bamboo, banana leaf and water hyacinth, fixed with starch-based glue where required and lined with natural cotton at **www.naturalendings.co.uk/coffins.htm**, **www.ecopod.co.uk**, **www.ecocoffins.com** and **www.eco-coffin.co.uk**.

HAVE A TREE PLANTED IN YOUR MEMORY OR FIND A WOODLAND RESTING PLACE There are now over 200 woodland burial sites in the UK, and more are seeking planning permission. Woodland burial returns your body to nature – carbon is locked underground and land is saved from development. Many woodland burial sites are run by farmers and Wildlife Trusts. And what better headstone could you have than a living tree? The Association of Natural Burial Ground maintains a list of woodland burial sites at **www.anbg.co.uk/members.html**.

TAKING YOUR ORGANS WITH YOU? BE A LIFESAVER AND DONATE THEM INSTEAD! Over 8,000 people are currently waiting for a transplant, but only 3,000 transplants are currently carried out each year, with 1,000 people dying in 2007 while waiting for one. There are currently almost 15 million people – about 25% of the UK population – on the Organ Donor Register. The Human Tissue Act 2004 states that no organs and tissue for transplantation can be taken without the consent of the deceased or their relatives. If you would like to add your name ring 0845 60 60 400 or go to **www.uktransplant.org.uk**. For further enquiries call 0117 975 7518.

KEEP CAMPAIGNING AFTER YOU'VE GONE – WRITE AN ECO-WILL £1.6 billion was bequeathed to charities in legacies in 2007. Why don't you write an ethical will? Visit **www.ethicalwill.com** and preserve your legacy of values and hopes for future generations. Leave something to a charity or environmental organisation which means a lot to you. Will Aid works with nine charities including ActionAid, the British Red Cross, Help the Aged, the NSPCC and Save the Children at **www.willaid.org.uk**. Or find a charity that's close to home at **www.willtocharity.co.uk**. And on the subject of wills, if relatives are not going to need your old furniture, how about leaving it to a local community centre, school or old people's home? You can advertise goods on **www.reuze.co.uk**, **www.freecycle.org** or through the Furniture Re-use Network at **www.frn.org.uk**.

Power drills

In the next 20 years, global energy consumption is projected to rise nearly 60% due to population growth, urbanisation, and economic and industrial expansion, according to the Worldwatch Institute Report (WIS) *State of the World 2003*. The WIS report in 2006 showed that the rising demand for energy by 2.5 billion people in China and India is pushing figures even higher. Estimates of electricity consumption are even more dramatic, running at a staggering 70%. Much of this rise is in the developing world and the improvements this will bring to quality of life are immeasurable – but it's what it takes to generate the electricity that's worrying. Renewable energy targets have been set by the British government – by 2010 they intend for 10% of electricity to be generated by renewables such as wind, with the hope of reaching 20% by 2020. Power isn't just lighting, heating and cooking – everything you buy has a power history behind it – clothes, household items and even fresh fruit and vegetables. To make a difference, we need to use less energy. Get started now.

Energy saviours

CLEANER WAYS TO POWER YOUR HOME We're all responsible for global warming, each and every one of us – it's not just a problem for someone else to sort out. It's now one of the greatest threats to the global environment, so we need to take action now. Did you know that 25% of the UK's total CO_2 emissions come from our homes? So our actions can have important implications. An average house produces six tonnes of CO_2 every year – that's more than the average car. By reducing our household energy consumption, we can take responsibility for global warming. Find out more about how to save energy from the Energy Saving Trust at www.est.org.uk (0800 512 012) or from Action Energy at www.thecarbontrust.co.uk/energy (0800 085 2005).

SAVE ENERGY WHEN YOU BOIL WATER When you make a cup of tea, coffee or a hot drink, only boil the amount of water you need. If everybody did this for just one day, we could save enough energy to light every street lamp in the UK the following night.

TURN THE IRON OFF WHEN YOU ONLY HAVE ONE GARMENT LEFT TO DO Irons stay hot after they've been switched off, and so it will still be hot enough to iron the last item very well. Although this might seem a very small thing, it gets us into the habit of making small energy-saving actions that, collectively, can make a much bigger difference.

DON'T LEAVE YOUR TV ON STANDBY When you go to bed, switch off your TV, rather than leaving it on standby. If everyone in the UK did this over £50 million could be saved each year. That's the equivalent to 200 million cups of tea! And if you decide to upgrade your TV set, don't throw it away – take it to a second-hand shop so someone else can use it. Or recycle it safely with **www.restructa.co.uk**.

DON'T USE THE DRYER – HANG UP YOUR CLOTHES
Tumble dryers are the most energy-consuming appliances we use in the home and they can also affect the air quality around us. Instead, spin dry clothes first, then use an indoor airer from **www.ecowashinglines.co.uk**.

SHARE APPLIANCES WITH YOUR NEIGHBOURS How often do you really use that steam carpet cleaner? Or that garden shredder? Or that high-pressure washer? By sharing appliances, you can save energy and also form links within the local community. Local Exchange Trading Schemes (LETS) are a good way of organising tool pools. Find out more at **www.letslinkuk.org**, or call 020 7607 7852.

GO MAD WITH ALTERNATIVE ENERGY SOURCES You can install small-scale renewable energy systems in your home, and they needn't cost the Earth. Solar water heaters, solar panels and wind generators all help provide alternative sources of energy. For information about buying your own domestic wind turbine, and grants, contact the British Wind Energy Association at **www.bwea.com**, or call 020 7689 1960. For general information on renewable energy, contact the Centre for Alternative Energy at **www.cat.org.uk**, the National Energy Foundation at **www.nef.org.uk/greenenergy** and the Energy Centre for Sustainable Communities at **www.ecsc.org.uk**.

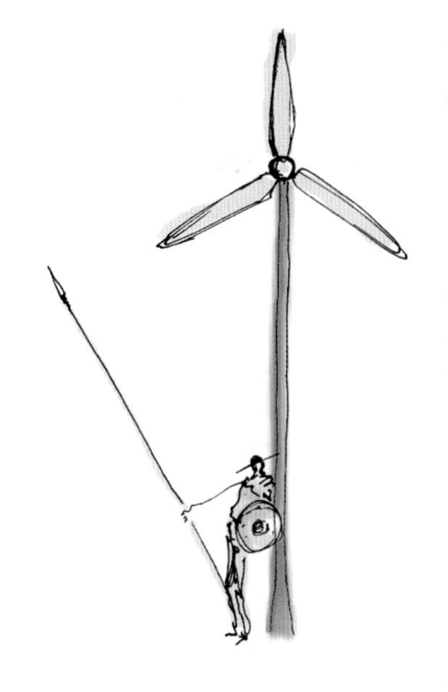

BUY GREEN ELECTRICITY Shop around to get the greenest electricity you can – and not always for a higher price. Friends of the Earth did produce a guide to green energy, but made the tough decision not to continue as they believe that the government should run this service. You can get free advice from the Energy Saving Trust at **www.energysavingtrust.org.uk** or by calling 0800 512 012. You can also compare deals and switch at **www.greenhelpline.com/green_energy**, **www.ukgreenpower.co.uk** and **www.greenelectricity.org**. Simplest of all, switch to Good Energy or Ecotricity, which invests money into building more renewable energy sources. Visit **www.good-energy.co.uk** or **www.ecotricity.co.uk**.

TOP TIP – GOOD ENERGY
GET HOME GENERATION

The government states that 40% of the UK's electricity could come from microgeneration by 2050. Good Energy currently operates in England and Wales, sourcing its energy from small-scale hydropower and wind farms across the UK. If you install a microgenerator, a wind turbine in your garden, a solar PV panel on your roof or a small hydro plant in a river, you can power your home and sell surplus units to Good Energy. To find out more see **www.good-energy.co.uk/gyo_home_gen**.

CURB YOUR GADGET ADDICTION By 2020, gadgets such as flat-screen TVs and digital radios will account for about 45% of the energy used in UK households. Ask yourself if you really need them.

TOP TIP – FRIENDS OF THE EARTH
PRESS FOR CHANGE

When an MP receives a hundred letters on a subject they have to take notice. When an energy company business director gets a thousand emails they have to take notice as well. It's not just the government or company bigwigs who get to make the decisions. You can help press for change and make things happen, too. Visit **www.foe.co.uk/campaigns/climate/press_for_change** to see what kinds of things you can do. This includes asking your MP to support renewables, asking the Minister for Energy for renewables support, asking your MP to support a strong Climate Change and Sustainable Energy Bill, supporting a local wind farm project, asking Ofgem to support renewables through green tariffs, and joining Friends of the Earth so that you can keep up with any relevant campaigns.

GRANTS FOR SOLAR ENERGY Get a government grant towards the installation of solar equipment in your home or business. Visit **www.energysavingtrust.org.uk/generate_your_own_energy/grants_for_renewables** or call 0800 512 012. You could save between 40% and 60% on total installation costs.

Hot tips for heating

GIVE YOUR HOUSE A HEATING MAKEOVER Every house is different, so tailor energy-saving devices to your home's requirements. There are currently around 50 Energy Efficiency Advice centres across the UK, offering free independent advice on how to make your home more efficient, especially through regulating your heating. To find your nearest one, visit the Energy Saving Trust at www.energysavingtrust.org.uk or call 0800 512 012. They are open 9am to 5pm Monday to Friday. You can request a call back by phone and speak to someone who can advise you about making the structure of your home more energy efficient and what grants are available, and put you in touch with qualified tradesmen in the area.

GET A HOME ENERGY CHECK Saving energy will reduce your household bills as well as improve the environment. Visit **www.energysavingtrust.org.uk/proxy/view/full/165/homeenergycheck**, spend a few minutes completing the questions and get a free Home Energy Check report that could save you £250 a year.

EXCLUDE DRAUGHTS Check for draughts and stop heat escaping from your house. Test your windows by holding a ribbon up to the window frame – if it flutters, air is coming in, and heat will be going out! Draught-proofing can make a big difference to heat leakage and could save you £20 a year (installation costs around a one-off £75 for a gas-heated semi). Plus, close doors when the heating is on to retain warmth.

ONE DEGREE OF SEPARATION In the summer, turn your thermostat down a few degrees and in the winter set your thermostat a few degrees higher. For each one-degree change, your family can save up to 10% on your home's heating bill and cut down on greenhouse gas emissions. And don't underestimate the power of warm clothing – pop on an extra layer if you feel chilly!

READER TIP – DAVID READ

INSTALL OR UPGRADE HEATING CONTROLS

You can save a lot of energy by only heating the rooms you need to use. Thermostatic radiator valves enable you to control every temperature separately. Installing these, together with heating time switches and thermostats, could save you up to £60 a year. Time switches automatically turn your heating and hot water on and off at pre-programmed times. Visit **www.inspiredheating.co.uk**.

READER TIP – SIMON FORT

GO SOLAR

You can obtain 70% of your household's hot water needs from solar thermal panels installed on your roof. Alternatively, covering your roof with PV (photo voltaic) panels can provide up to 50% of your electricity needs and save around 34 tonnes of greenhouse gases over their lifetime. Contact the National Energy Foundation's renewable energy website **www.nef.org.uk/greenenergy** (01908 665555), the Centre for Alternative Energy at **www.cat.org.uk** (01654 705950), or Future Heating at **www.future-heating.co.uk** (020 8351 9360).

CONDENSING BOILERS Condensing boilers are the most efficient type of boiler, converting 88% of fuel into heat, compared to only 72% for standard boilers. They also save an extra 12% on heating costs. When your current central heating system breaks down, replace it with a condensing boiler. They contain an extra heat exchanger, so when the boiler works at peak efficiency the water vapour produced in the combustion process condenses back into liquid, releasing extra heat. Find out more from **www.nef.org.uk/energysaving/boilers.htm**.

Keep cool

FRIDGE TIPS Fridges and freezers are probably the most expensive electrical appliances to run, costing an average £55-£65 each per year. But we can't get enough of them, and throw away 2.5 million per year as we replace them.

KEEP TEMPERATURE BETWEEN 3°C AND 5°C Fridges don't need to be kept cooler than 3°C. Below this temperature they are wasting energy and your money! Put a thermometer in your fridge so you can keep an eye on the temperature.

KEEP COILS FREE FROM DUST Get that feather duster out! When dust gathers on the condenser coils at the back of your fridge, energy consumption can increase by 30%.

BUY A FRIDGE-SAVER PLUG You can save 20% of your fridge's running costs by buying a saver plug to replace your existing fridge or freezer plug. When the appliance's motor is first switched on, full system power is needed, but not once it's running. The plug senses this, and cuts power to the motor in short bursts without changing the operation of the fridge. Every time the red light shows, savings are being made. Buy yours from **www.biggreenswitch.co.uk/around_the_home/fridge-saver-plug**.

FREE-STAND YOUR FRIDGE Your fridge works most efficiently if it's free-standing and in a cool environment. If possible, move it out of sunlight, away from the oven or boiler, and against an outside wall with a few inches around.

LET FOOD COOL FIRST Avoid putting hot or warm food straight into the fridge. The hotter the food is, the harder the fridge will have to work to try and keep it cool and this takes more energy. You can also defrost food in the fridge as this helps to keep it cool as it thaws.

NEVER DUMP, RECYCLE! The UK disposes of about 2.5 million consumer fridges and half a million larger commercial fridges each year. These contain an estimated 2,000 tonnes of CFCs and HCFCs, which are ozone-damaging chemicals. Since 1 January 2002, all fridges must have their insulation removed before they are recycled or scrapped, in order to prevent the release of ozone-depleting CFCs into the atmosphere. So when you are ready to get rid of your old fridge, make sure you take it to a recycling plant that can deal with it safely. Your local council is also obliged to pick it up, although they may charge a fee. Find a recycling plant with **www.wasteconnect.co.uk**.

NOW COOL IT! Not only can you recycle your old fridge safely, you can now buy 100% ozone-friendly fridges. 'Greenfreeze' fridges are widely available and work on a mixture of propane and butane. This means they don't contain any of the polluting CFCs, HFCs or HCFCs. According to the Energy Savings Trust, Energy Saving Recommended fridges and fridge freezers use over 60% less energy than a typical old one. If everyone upgraded their fridges and freezers, energy wastage would be cut by two thirds, saving nearly £900 million and the equivalent CO_2 emissions of 600,000 homes. Look for the Energy Saving Recommended logo before you purchase an appliance. You can also compare and buy products at **www.energysavingtrust.org.uk/compare_and_buy_products**. Also consider investing in an innovative new e-cube – this £25 black wax cube that fits onto your fridge or freezer's thermostat sensor could slash energy usage by 30%. See **www.ecubedistribution.com**.

Bright ideas

GREENER LIGHTING **The Energy Savings Trust wants the government to reduce VAT on energy-saving light bulbs to 5% – a step in the right direction. But what can you do to cut down on the energy-guzzling light you use?**

WIND IT UP Use your muscles to generate electric light with a clockwork torch. BayGen clockwork torches – created by British inventor Trevor Bayliss – use a winding handle to energise a constant force spring, and turning the crank provides enough energy to provide light for half an hour. The concept is catching on, and will help light the way for many people in developing countries, without resorting to expensive batteries. You can also buy other clockwork items, such as radios, computers, phone chargers and now MP3/video players. Visit **www.tangogroup.net** or **www.ecodigital.co.uk** to get yours and have constant light, music and energy while on the move.

IF EVERY HOUSEHOLD IN THE UK USED ONE ENERGY-EFFICIENT LIGHT BULB, WE COULD CLOSE A POWER STATION When your light bulb runs out replace it with an energy-efficient one – they last 12 times as long! Over their lifetime an 11-watt bulb saves £35 and a 20-watt bulb saves £57. If you have strip lights, don't send the fluorescent tubes to landfill – each tube contains enough mercury to pollute 30,000 litres of water beyond a safe level for drinking. Contact **www.reuze.co.uk/fluro_tubes.shtml** for recycling schemes.

FILL YOUR HOUSE WITH SUNLIGHT Tube skylights transform dark houses and mean you can keep the electric light off longer. These flexible tubes distribute light around the home by means of a reflector and prisms in a roof dome. Find out more from Solalighting Ltd at **www.solalighting.com** (0845 458 0101).

DON'T USE HALOGEN SECURITY LIGHTS Almost half of lighting complaints to local authorities are related to domestic security lights. These often use 150-watt halogen lights that are over-sensitive and are set off by roaming cats or blowing litter. Not only does this waste large amounts of electricity, it also means they're not an effective warning system, because neighbours become accustomed to the constant glare. Halogen lights are not that effective either, because the glare is so bright it darkens the shadows, providing more places for burglars to hide. Replace your wasteful halogen light with a low-power compact fluorescent light or get a handy solar-powered LED one from **www.greengizmo.co.uk/2008/02/15/duo-solar-security-light**. No need for wiring or a plug – the sun does all the work for you.

HELP PUT THE STARS BACK IN THE SKY Everyone should be able to see the stars. But over the past 40 years light pollution has increased so much that people in towns and cities now struggle to see them. The British Astronomical Society has set up a Campaign for Brighter Skies, aiming to improve light direction so the same area can be lit to the same brightness, but with less powerful bulbs to reduce the impact on the sky. Better lighting not only helps with viewing space, but it saves energy and is better for the atmosphere. You can help the campaign by looking out for floodlights on advertising hoardings that are left on all night, and for cloud spotlights above nightclubs. If you see them, report them to your local authority. Such schemes have met with considerable success, such as in Milton Keynes. After hundreds of complaints from the local community, the skybeam above the Milton Keynes Shopping Centre was extinguished. Visit **www.dark-skies.org** or **www.cpre.org.uk** for more information on how you can help.

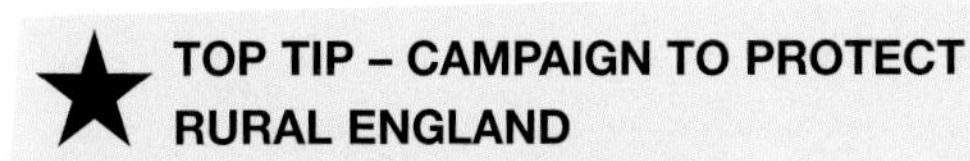

TOP TIP – CAMPAIGN TO PROTECT RURAL ENGLAND

DON'T WASTE LIGHT

Don't waste light outside your home. Angle outdoor lights downwards, fit hoods or shields to minimise light spill, use bulbs with minimal watts, and ensure lights are switched on only when needed. Approach any neighbours, including shops and businesses, with overly bright security lights and politely ask them to angle them downwards, shield them or fit a passive infrared sensor or a lower-wattage bulb. You can also contact local DIY stores and ask them to stock security lights that minimise light pollution. For more on CPRE's light pollution campaign see **www.cpre.org.uk/campaigns/landscape/light-pollution**.

CLOTHES THAT COST THE EARTH

Think before you buy!

Global warming, species extinction, animal testing, the arms trade and human rights abuses… all can seem way beyond our control. But as a consumer you *do* have control, because many of these problems are either caused or perpetuated by corporations funded by the money that you spend on their products. Every purchase you make has either a direct or indirect effect on the environment. When you exercise your power by choosing where and what to buy, and where and what *not* to buy, you help change the world for the better. The first step is to become a better shopper, and find out the stories behind the shelves. The *Ecologist*, **www.theecologist.org**, *Ethical Consumer*, **www.ethicalconsumer.org**, Ethical Junction, **www.ethical-junction.org** and Get Ethical, **www.getethical.com**, will keep you informed, and you can find the latest Ethical Consumerism Report at OneWorld's site: **www.oneworld.net.** The 2007 report shows that household ethical spending has almost doubled in five years, but is still a small proportion of total consumer spend.

Become an ethical consumer

SHOPPING TIPS In 2007, consumer pressure forced clothing retailer Gap Inc to fire an Indian company that made its clothes, after a video of children at work in a New Delhi sweatshop was posted on the internet. While investigating the story, *The Observer* spoke to children as young as 10, who said they had been working 16 hours a day for no pay. One 10-year-old boy told the paper he had been sold to the company by his parents. Clothes produced by the children were each retailing in the US market for US$40, but the company showed little interest in safety, wages or working conditions. The paper described the workplace as a 'derelict industrial unit' with hallways that were 'flowing with excrement from a flooded toilet'. Who is responsible? If the multinationals refuse to be, then it is us, the consumers, who buy products made in this way. Get informed, and think before you buy.

YOUR EMAIL CAN MAKE A DIFFERENCE When Polly Morgan noticed a 'Made in Myanmar' label on Kookai's clothes, she emailed the company to complain that they were supporting one of the world's most brutal military dictatorships by operating in Myanmar. The London buying director replied, saying: 'I agree with you that it is not ethical for us to produce our goods from Burma. I have stressed to Paris your concern and they have promised to eliminate production in Burma.' Find out more about her story on **www.ethicalconsumer.org/boycotts/boycottsarchive.htm** and write to retailers encouraging them to join the Ethical Trading Initiative (an umbrella group of companies aiming to improve workers' rights). Visit **www.ethicaltrade.org**, or call 020 7841 5180.

WREST THE POWER FROM THE MULTINATIONALS
Identify at least two multinational corporations (MNCs) with unethical environmental policies and boycott their products. You may

be surprised at how many different products they sell. Visit **www.boycottbush.net**. Boycotting is an effective way of registering your disapproval and dissatisfaction towards a company. Even a 5% boycott can significantly affect profit. Consumers collectively have the power to change the world for the better. Success is not just limited to isolated cases. Boycotting has helped make a difference to the Save the Children campaign and to the hugely successful awareness campaign in Europe against GM foods. Visit **www.ethicalconsumer.org** for more success stories or contact Corporate Watch at **www.corporatewatch.org.uk** or call 01865 791391.

AVOID SHOPPING IN SUPERMARKETS In the UK, 60-70% of the food we buy comes from one of the four largest supermarkets (Tesco, Sainsbury's, Morrisons and ASDA). This concentration of control forces farmers to accept lower prices for their products and means that food is often sourced from developing countries where supermarkets can profit from cheap labour and non-existent pollution laws. Transport pollution is probably one of the greatest threats to global warming – on average the item you buy in the supermarket has travelled 1,000 miles. Supermarkets act like giant vacuum cleaners, sucking money out of an area and putting it in the banks of distant shareholders, while hundreds of locals lose money as their jobs dry up. See supermarket websites for latest eco-pledges and **www.sustainablestuff.co.uk/supermarketspolicy.html**.

IF YOU CAN'T FIND IT LOCALLY AND HAVE TO HAVE IT, BUY FROM ETHICAL OR GREEN SHOPS ONLINE
Most ethical shops have online stores where you can find lots of gifts, clothes, food and products for the home that are either fairly traded, or made ethically, and without harm to the environment. Visit **www.naturalcollection.com**, **www.ethical-junction.org** or **www.getethical.com** for information and products. Buying online is now more popular than ever, and it is beneficial to the environment and your purse. The companies tend to deliver to your doorstep, so you don't have to travel there, cutting down on exhaust emissions, traffic pollution and the number of cars on the road.

TOP TIP – THE NATURAL COLLECTION

BAGS OF TROUBLE

New reports by Defra show that more than 13 billion plastic bags are given away in Britain every year – five billion more than previous estimates. And as plastics are difficult and costly to recycle, many of them end up in a landfill tip. When you go shopping, take a bag with you or reuse your shopping bags at home. Get an organic string bag for your vegetables or a fairly-traded shopping basket made of palm leaf from Malawi – you can get both from the Natural Collection, **www.naturalcollection.com** (0845 3677 001).

TOP TIP – BAGS OF CHANGE

SUPPORT LOCAL SHOPS AND SAY NO TO PLASTIC

Bags of Change is a new loyalty scheme for ethical shopping and winner of the Best Green Company at the 2007 Green England Awards (**www.green-england.co.uk/greenawards**). You can search for ethical shops across the UK at **www.bagsofchange.co.uk**, plus when you use one of their specially designed hemp-cotton bags you get a discount at participating stores. This means you can say no to plastic bags and have even more incentive to be an ethical consumer. To find out the latest government statistics, initiatives and suggestions on plastic bags see **www.defra.gov.uk/environment/localenv/litter/plasticbags/index.htm**. On 28 February 2007 they signed a voluntary agreement with UK retailers to reduce the overall environmental impact of carrier bags by 25% by the end of 2008. Bags of Change can help you do your bit.

BUY LOCALLY Just think of the resources wasted and the pollution created by shifting goods all over the world – and increasingly by air. Imported food and animal feed use 1.6 billion litres of fuel, and emit more than four million tonnes of CO_2 in the UK. Global transport costs can add as much as 16% to the price of food, while organic food that is locally grown is estimated to add as little as 3%. Other negative aspects of the global food industry are that it encourages farming monocultures to the detriment of local biodiversity, and it has caused the closure of independent grocers, bakers, butchers and fishmongers –

throughout the 1990s, around 1,000 independent local food shops closed each year. Investigate box schemes, farmers' markets, food co-ops and buy-local campaigns because we need to support and rebuild our local food systems! See **www.localfoodworks.org** and **www.farmersmarkets.net**.

BUY RECYCLED If there was no market for recycled goods, recycling wouldn't happen. And it's not as hard as you might think to find recycled products – the National Recycling Forum has all kinds of goods that started their lives as something else. See **www.recycledproducts.org.uk**. Look for the Mobius Loop symbol (the three arrows that make up a triangle), which means that a product has been recycled. And remember, reusing is a form of recycling. Charity shops and jumble sales are full of second-hand goods with years of use still in them.

BUY FROM CHARITY SHOPS Buying from charity shops is a really effective way of saving cash, donating money and picking up some unusual bargains. Some charities also sell a range of Fairtrade goods, many of which are available online. Visit the Association of Charity Shops at **www.charityshops.org.uk** to find charity shops, volunteer in one, donate goods and even set up one of your own. Do enquire before you donate, as many charities can only sell books in good condition, won't sell cosmetics unless new, and can't sell second-hand mains electric goods. Tatty clothes and worn shoes can be recycled, but sort and bag them to save the volunteers time.

SUPPORT BOYCOTTS AND SHAREHOLDER ACTIONS Support actions like the Nestlé boycott, which campaigns against all Nestlé brands and company subsidiaries to attempt to persuade the company to change its marketing of formula baby milk in the developing world. Boycotting products has a long history – in 1971, Britons boycotted Barclays Bank over its investment policy in South Africa. Visit **www.ethical-consumer.org/boycotts/boycotts_list.htm** for a list of current boycotts that you could support. You need to contact the registered company that is boycotting for advice and information.

Shareholder actions can also force a public company to change its policies to become more ethical or environmentally friendly. If you buy shares in a company (even one share) you will be entitled to go to their AGM and question directors on their policies, and even force a vote on the issue. Successful shareholder actions have forced companies to change their policies on their impact on the environment, human rights issues and executive pay. For more information, tips on preparing resolutions, and activism, visit Friends of the Earth on **www.foe.org/international/shareholder**.

SHOP FOR JUTE Jute – or hessian – is a plant related to European lime or linden, grown in Bangladesh and western India for its fibre. This semi-wild monsoon-watered crop takes little from the land compared to cotton crops, which need prodigious amounts of water, fertilisers and pesticides. Over 4.5 million people in one of the poorest parts of the world are supported by the jute industry, which turns the fibre into woven bags and sacks. Jute shopping bags are a worthwhile alternative to plastic bags – practical, inexpensive and good for the environment. For more information on jute, contact Canby at **www.canby.co.uk** or call 0845 277 0122.

Fashion victim

THE TRUTH ABOUT CLOTHES AND MAKEUP Clothes are a necessity for most of us, but we rarely question the processes they go through before we put them on. It may be a divine little black dress that clings to all your curves, but how much energy, water and lowly paid fingers went into its construction? Synthetic fabrics like polyester and nylon, made from non-renewable petrochemicals, use vast amounts of water and energy and take a very long time to

biodegrade. Some cotton, too, may not be as natural as it seems, as it's the world's most pesticide-sprayed crop. In 1995 in Alabama, up to 250,000 fish were killed after rain washed lethal concentrations of insecticides off the cotton fields into a nearby lake. The insecticides were used to deal with a budworm infestation, which is thought to have been caused when the crops were sprayed with the insecticide malathion – designed to kill the boll weevil, which also killed the budworm's natural predators. Look for ecological or naturally made clothing materials instead. See Ethical Consumer's buyer's guides and Ethiscore shopping guide at www.ethicalconsumer.org and www.ethiscore.org. Or visit the Personal Products section on www.greenconsumerguide.com. Look out for the Oeko-Tex label that guarantees the manufacture of clothes has met strict environmental standards.

WHO ARE THE REAL FASHION VICTIMS? Our clothes are mainly made in factories in developing countries where labour and production costs are cheaper, and governments are less likely to regulate. Sadly, only a few retailers respect their staff; many conglomerates believe workers' rights are less important than maximising their profits. In such sweatshops, staff may work up to 60 hours a week in conditions that are rarely safe, wages unreasonably low, children under 15 employed and unions almost always banned. In these countries a single pair of trainers sold in the UK can cost more than the monthly wage of the person who made it. Visit **www.sweatshopwatch.org** for a list of 'dirty' companies whose products you should avoid and a 'clean' directory of companies whose products are made ethically, avoiding sweatshop labour. Join No Sweat (**www.nosweat.org.uk**) where you can support the UK campaign to fight sweatshop bosses around the world.

DO YOU REALLY NEED ANOTHER T-SHIRT? Many of us have wardrobes bursting with clothes we've bought on a whim, but never worn. Before you shop for something new, look through your wardrobe

– you'll probably find something you love, but haven't worn for years, or a treasured item you put away for mending that hasn't been. By the time you've finished sorting, you'll have found something 'new' to wear, mended some old favourites, donated your rejects and saved money!

CARE WHAT YOU WEAR Cotton plays a vital role in the economy of several dozen countries, but its environmental impact is hugely damaging. Close to US$3 billion worth of pesticides are used annually in worldwide cotton production, and have resulted in cancer in humans, contamination of groundwater, erosion and degradation of soil, decline of animal populations and the overall depletion of biodiversity. You can buy cotton that doesn't harm the planet – Gossypium is an ethical eco-cotton store selling garments, yoga wear and bed linen made from fairly traded organic fibre. The company uses its profits to support the farming communities involved in clothing production, helping to steer them towards a dynamic rural lifestyle. Visit **www.gossypium.co.uk**.

AVOID OVER-PACKAGING Over 22% of the total product cost of perfumes and cosmetics comes from packaging costs. Many cosmetics are double-packed unnecessarily, for aesthetic purposes. If you buy a product in a plastic container and a box, leave the box at the checkout. And write to your favourite cosmetics company, asking them to set up a refill scheme. See the Industry Council for Packaging and the Environment at **www.incpen.org** for the latest research and member companies.

BOYCOTT ANIMAL-TESTED BEAUTY PRODUCTS One hundred million animals die in lab experiments around the world each year, and 'not tested on animals' labels are not always telling the truth: the finished product may not have been tested on animals, but this doesn't include individual ingredients. Look out for the Humane Cosmetics Standard (HCS) 'rabbit and stars' logo. It's an internationally recognised guarantee that the product has not been tested on animals at any stage. For cruelty-free products see the British Union for the Abolition of Vivisection at **www.buav.org** and **www.gocrueltyfree.org**.

TOP TIP – WWW.GREENCHOICES.ORG

CHOOSE GREEN SHOES

Vegetarian credentials do not guarantee green credentials! Leather substitutes can include problematic materials such as polyurethane, nylon and even PVC. Leather-free environmentally friendly shoes are available from Green Shoes **www.greenshoes.co.uk** and the Vegetarian Shoes Online Store **www.vegetarian-shoes.co.uk**.

OLD CLOTHES FOR NEW In early 2008 Marks & Spencer and Oxfam joined forces to create the biggest clothes recycling initiative in the UK. For every customer who drops off their old M&S clothing at an Oxfam shop, they will be given a £5 voucher towards their next clothing, homeware or beauty purchase at M&S, as long as goods retail over £35. This means that Oxfam gets more clothes and M&S helps to keep one part of their five-point Plan A policy – to send no waste to landfill. The store has also encouraged customers to reduce plastic bag use, construction waste and coathanger use. Plus they have drives in action for climate change, sustainable raw materials and animal welfare, Fairtrade partners and healthy food. It's great progress, but like all big stores, they're still encouraging consumers to buy more products. They therefore have a responsibility to keep to the guidelines of their Plan A and more. For further details see **http://plana.marksandspencer.com**. Find the locations of more than 700 Oxfam stores – including several specialist shops – at **www.oxfam.org.uk/shops**.

AS A LAST RESORT... If you really need to buy from one of the main UK chain stores, then there is a way of reducing the impact. UshopUgive is a new internet gateway to online retail outlets that donates a percentage of what you spend to a charity or school of your choice, without you paying an extra penny above standard retail prices. Visit **www.thegivingmachine.co.uk**. Charities include Scout groups across the UK, hospices and bigger organisations such as the Woodland Trust. You can find a list of affiliated stores online and these include Amazon, ActionAid Gifts in Action, Greenpeople, Greenfingers, WWF Adopt an Animal, Worldvision and eBay, as well as chain stores.

Waste not, want not

Nature has tremendously efficient ways of dealing with waste. Over time, everything – plant matter, human and animal remains, ancient building materials and even rock – breaks down and is recycled. Our modern waste problems stem from technological proficiency – the Earth just can't deal with the concentration of new chemical combinations in the quantities we're producing and dumping them. Defra's Waste Strategy Report for 2006/7 (**www.defra.gov.uk**) in England showed an increase of total municipal waste (29.1 million tonnes) of which 85% is from households, with an increase in recycling (12.2 million tonnes) and a decrease in the amount sent to landfill (16.9 million tonnes) – a mixed bag of results. Recycle Now, **www.recyclenow.com**, the national recycling campaign, is seeking to change this with better waste awareness. Over 60% of the contents of your weekly rubbish bin can be recycled, and if reduced by just 10% in a year, would be a saving equivalent to 8,687 times the height of Blackpool Tower. So make a difference and recycle what you can.

Not so rubbish solutions

ALL ABOUT RECYCLING **Here in the UK we're lazy about recycling waste, and only 18% of household rubbish is recycled. Yet the Zero Waste strategy in New Zealand (www.zerowaste.co.nz) has proved that by maximising recycling, incineration is unnecessary and the amount of rubbish going to landfill can be cut by 90%. Policy groups for Zero Waste strategies are slowly being introduced in Britain, such as by the Defenders of the Ouse Valley and Estuary (www.dove2000.org). Wherever you live in Britain, you can do your bit to help recycle. You may already be recycling bottles, cans and paper, but consider recycling your oil, stamps, glasses, office equipment and mobile phones. Visit www.recycle-more.co.uk to find out where your local recycling point is and how to recycle the waste you want. Friends of the Earth believes that it's possible for us to recycle at least 80% of our waste. For tips on how to do this, visit www.foe.org.uk. For information on how to recycle electronic and electrical waste, as well as hazardous household waste, visit the Waste from Electrical and Electronic Equipment Directive at www.weeeman.org.**

UGLY BUTTS A cigarette butt takes between one and 12 years to break down. So don't drop them. If you must smoke outdoors – and increasingly it's the only place you can smoke – carry a portable ashtray to store discarded filters in until you can dispose of them properly. Get one from **www.boodi.co.uk**.

MAKE MORE USE OF IT Make sure you only use a product if there's no reusable alternative available. Try to reuse everyday items like paper, envelopes and paper clips. If each of the UK's 10 million office workers used one fewer staple a day by reusing a paper clip, that could save a staggering 120 tonnes of steel each year.

GO BARE Nowadays almost everything we buy comes swathed in layers of excess packaging. Indeed, 90% of the material used in the production of, or contained within, consumer goods becomes waste within just six weeks of sale. Shop with a critical eye and avoid buying overpackaged goods. Also, reduce the amount of disposable products you buy and always look out for alternatives that will last. See **www.wasteonline.org.uk.**

FIND OUT MORE Get informed and find out about the recycling schemes run by your local authority at **www.recycle-more.co.uk**. Then campaign for them to be improved by writing to your local MP. Not only does recycling have environmental benefits, it also creates jobs. For every million tonnes of waste processed, landfill creates 40-60 jobs, incineration 100-290 jobs and recycling 400-590 jobs.

SAY NO TO INCINERATION Some people see incineration as an attractive alternative to landfill for waste disposal, and the government does have plans to increase the number of incinerators – largely because landfill space has run out. Although these are marketed as a renewable energy source, incineration plants still release a number of toxic pollutants into the environment, including dioxins, furans, acid gases and heavy metals. These pollutants can pose serious risks to human health, including hormonal defects, reduced immune system capacity and lung and kidney disease. Incinerators can also produce more greenhouse gases than gas-fired power stations. The millions spent on incineration plants would be much better spent on setting up recycling schemes. Visit Friends of the Earth at **www.foe.co.uk/campaigns/waste/issues/incineration_and_landfill** to find out the best way of sending letters to stop incineration in your area.

GIVE OLD CLOTHES TO A RECYCLING SCHEME In 2006, two million tonnes of clothes and textiles were thrown away in the UK, despite 75% of them being recyclable; and three billion gallons of oil is used to manufacture this amount. Textiles can be valuable to somebody, even if they appear worn out and useless to you. At present the consumer has the option of putting textiles in 'clothes banks', taking them to charity shops or having them picked up for a jumble sale.

The fibres from most clothes can be shredded and rewoven to make new clothes; as long as they are clean, they are usable! High-quality garments can be sold for reuse, whereas medium grade can be made into industrial rags, wiping cloths and low-grade filling and flocking for the furniture industry. Several charity shops run schemes that do this. Visit **www.oxfam.org.uk** (0845 3000 311) or British Red Cross shops **www.redcross.org.uk** (0844 412 2804) to find your nearest shop.

PICK UP ONE PIECE OF LITTER A DAY With the UK population standing at over 60.6 million, our streets would be a lot cleaner if everyone picked up one piece of rubbish a day.

TOP TIP – WWW.HIPPYSHOPPER.COM

HI-FASHION RECYCLING

Wearing clothes that are made from recycled fabrics, buttons and fastenings can be fashionable, too. Visit **www.ecobtq.com** for a range of sustainable fashion, accessories and beauty products that won't let you down in the style stakes – but don't let the world down at the same time. This online boutique chooses designers who work with recycled fabrics, vintage materials, azo-free dyes, Fairtrade components and manufacture in sweatshop-free factories. All their stationery and packaging is recycled, too, plus for every purchase over £5, £3.50 goes to Oxfam, WWF and Friends of the Earth. They also include a list of tips for greener living to help make sure you keep thinking about the waste that you could save.

Crystal clear

BOTTLES UP Recycling just one glass bottle saves enough energy to power a TV set for an hour and a half. In every tonne of glass recycled, 135 litres of oil and 1.2 tonnes of ash, sand and limestone are saved. For more information and the location of your local bottle bank go to www.recycle-more.co.uk.

GIVE MILK BOTTLES BACK TO THE MILKMAN Never put milk bottles in a glass-recycling bottle bank – always return them to the milkman. And you can recycle the aluminium bottle tops, too. In 2000, 35,000 tonnes of household aluminium foil (worth around £12 million) was used in the UK, of which only 11% was recycled. Most recycled aluminium foil is used to make cast components for the automotive industry, such as cylinder heads and engine blocks. Check if your local authority collects foil as part of its recycling scheme, or search for a local foil bank at **www.wasteconnect.co.uk**.

SORT BEFORE YOU BIN Successful glass recycling depends on you starting the process properly. Put different-coloured bottles in the correct bank, and remove all metal and plastic tops, corks and rings from bottles or jars. Importantly, light bulbs, cookware such as 'Pyrex' or 'Visionware', and flat glass (as used in windows), should not be put in bottle banks. Find out more and what to do with these other types of glass from Recycle More at **www.recycle-more.co.uk** (0845 068 2572) and WasteConnect at **www.wasteconnect.co.uk** (0905 535 0940).

RECYCLE YOUR SPECS AND SUNGLASSES Thousands of people in developing countries are hindered by poor eyesight, yet each year four million pairs of functioning glasses are discarded in the UK. By donating your old glasses you can transform people's lives for the better. Vision Aid Overseas has so far helped over 300,000 people with donations from the UK. Contact **www.vao.org.uk** or call 01293 535016 for more details. Many local opticians support the scheme – if yours doesn't, then let them know. Alternatively, hand your glasses in to any charity shop or high-street retailer that runs a recycling scheme.

TOP TIP – THE NATURAL COLLECTION

THE GREENEST GLASS

The Natural Collection sells frosted tumblers made out of old wine bottles. The transformation does not involve any melting, making them more energy-efficient than normal recycled glass. For details, visit their website **www.naturalcollection.com** or call 0845 3677 003.

Paper cuts

RECYCLING PAPER Recycling can start at home and in everyday practices. Use waste paper as notepaper. Reload your printer with paper printed on only one side – and don't print unless you need to. Reuse envelopes. Cut up old cards to make gift tags. Wrap gifts in old wrapping paper or old newspaper, even put down old shredded newspaper as animal bedding, or put it on the compost heap.

NO MORE JUNK MAIL Around one million tonnes of junk mail and magazines get binned every year! To stop the onslaught, you can register with the Mailing Preference Service. Visit **www.mpsonline.org.uk**, email mps@dma.org.uk, call 020 7291 3310 or write to: Mailing Preference Service, DMA House, 70 Margaret Street, London W1W 8SS. Simply include your details and state that you would like to stop receiving unsolicited direct mail.

READER TIP – AGNES SULLIVAN
FOREST-FRIENDLY TOILET ROLL
Start with the basics and use tree-friendly toilet roll. Lots of companies now produce this – you don't need to make your own! Greenpeace has a guide to forest-friendly toilet paper, kitchen towels and tissues made with recycled paper or Forest Stewardship Council approved at **www.greenpeace.org.uk/forests/tissue-guide**. Get yours from **www.traidcraftshop.co.uk** and then just try to use less, too!

KIDS – TAKE OLD WALLPAPER TO SCHOOL Old newspapers, magazines and even wallpaper can be easily recycled at school. They can be painted on, used to cover tables in craft lessons or used for making papier-mâché. So don't just throw it out, take it to school.

THINK HEMP Hemp produces up to four times more pulp per acre than timber, and produces higher-quality paper. It recycles more times than wood pulp and there are no environmentally damaging bleaching processes involved in its production. Unlike other fibre crops, it doesn't need the intensive use of herbicides and pesticides to grow, so it's the perfect ecological crop for the twenty-first century. Commercial hemp growth has occurred in Britain since 1993, but the UK government has been unwilling to support hemp farmers because of the connection with cannabis. For more information and products visit the Hemp Shop's website at **www.thehempshop.net** or call 0845 123 5869.

RECYCLE YELLOW PAGES The Yellow Pages telephone directory is delivered annually to households and companies. The dye in the pages means they can't be recycled with other paper and newspaper. To recycle them you could either place them on the compost heap, shred them for animal bedding, or have them specially recycled by your local authority. Nine out of 10 local authorities now recycle directories. Find out if you can at **www.recyclenow.com**.

BUY ADDRESS LABELS FROM CHARITIES Many charities, such as Trees for Life, sell labels you can stick over old addresses on envelopes – so you're saving paper and supporting a charity. See **www.treesforlife.org.uk/products/envelope_reuse_labels.html**. For more tips on reusing envelopes visit **www.conservatree.com**.

BIND IT Think before you staple. For less than five sheets of paper use a clamp that makes the paper thread through itself, making its own paper clip, so there's nothing to remove before recycling the paper. For up to 35 sheets, use a paper clip. For large amounts of paper, use a treasury tag.

TOP TIP – THE NATURAL COLLECTION

TURN IT BACK INTO LOGS

Transform old newspapers into pulp logs – one newspaper will usually make one log, which will burn for up to an hour. For log-making machines visit **www.naturalcollection.com**, or call 0845 3677 003.

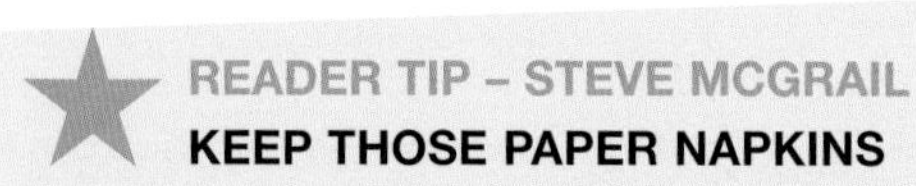

READER TIP – STEVE MCGRAIL

KEEP THOSE PAPER NAPKINS

If you eat out at a restaurant or café, retain the paper serviettes (furtively or triumphantly, depending on your temperament). Cut up, they're perfectly good for toilet paper… but not if they've first had to deal with curry spills!

PVC is not PC

RECYCLING PLASTIC **We only recycle 15% of our plastic packaging. Councils will only invest in better recycling facilities if you show just how much you, as voters, care about it! A pioneering unit called Reclaim was set up in Sheffield in 1989, providing employment for people with mental health illnesses, and now recycles 100 tonnes of plastic film a year and 350 tonnes of plastic bottles. The good news is that more local authorities now collect some types of plastic bottles door to door. If yours doesn't, write to your MP, or find out how to set up schemes in your area at** www.recoup.org **(01733 390021).**

A COOLER GLASS OF WATER Instead of using plastic cups, always use a glass when you take a drink from the water cooler. This will save on the wasteful use of disposable plastic cups, and will save your company money! Plus see **www.save-a-cup.co.uk** to find out about collection and recycling services for vending machines. Save A Cup has collected one billion cups so far!

SAY NO TO UNWANTED BAGS (SNUB) More than 13 billion plastic carrier bags are currently given out each year to shoppers in the UK. Support schemes to keep this number down, urge retailers to do more, and recycle any you do use. For example, Marks & Spencer has introduced a 5p fee on its plastic bags – in a trial of 50 stores this saw demand fall by 70%. It doesn't seem like we 'need' those bags after all!

READER TIP – LEANNE BELL
SEND PLASTIC BACK

If you like a product but are unhappy with the plastic packaging or components, do something about it and send it back to the manufacturer. This could include extra wrapping on food or plastic detergent scoopers where cardboard ones would work just as well – especially if the washing powder is ecological! If we all complain it might work.

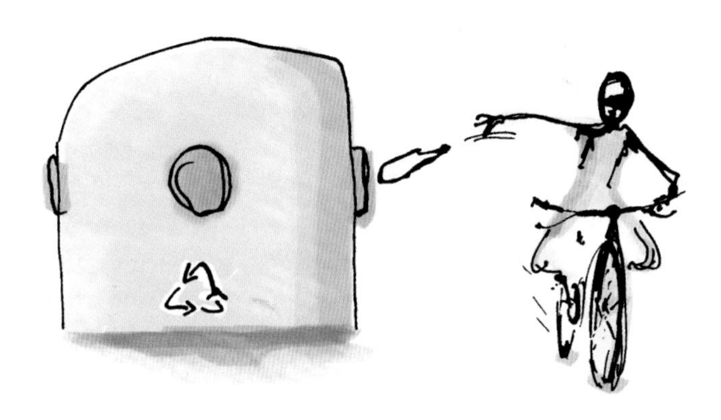

REUSE/RECYCLE PLASTIC DRINK BOTTLES If you buy a drink in a plastic bottle, don't just throw it away! In the UK, we use a colossal 3,300 million bottles a year, of which 25% are recycled. This is a huge step up from the 3% of bottles recycled in 2001, but we need to aim for zero waste to make a real difference. Recycling just one plastic bottle can save the energy needed to power a 60-watt light bulb for six hours. More than 60% of local authorities now offer kerbside recycling services for plastic bottles, which means that 13.9 million households get theirs picked up. There are also thousands of drop-off points. Now we need to campaign for local authorities to recycle other plastic products, too. See **www.wrap.org.uk/local_authorities/plastic_bottle_collection**.

DON'T BE LAZY WITH READY MEALS These often come with plastic trays in which to heat them up. Plus, you can cook a quick and easy meal with fresh ingredients in minutes – try cooking some tasty fast food with the help of a time-saving book such as *Nigella Express*.

AVOID PRODUCTS CONTAINING PVC PVC contains the softening agent phthalate, which leaks out during use. The most commonly used phthalate is DEHP, a possible carcinogen and a known cause of liver, kidney and reproductive damage. Wherever possible, avoid using products that contain PVC, such as Tupperware®, garden furniture and window frames. Find out more at **www.pvcinformation.org**.

Pack it in

WHAT TO DO WITH PACKAGING Recycle Now, the national recycling campaign, suggests you check through your rubbish to take a look at what you're throwing away. Next time you do your shopping, see if you can reduce your number of packaged purchases. If you can't avoid packaging, dispose of it carefully. Follow the tips below.

SQUASH YOUR RUBBISH Squashing rubbish and packaging before you throw it away means it takes up less space in the landfill sites and reduces the amount of land given over to these areas.

REUSE ALUMINIUM FOIL Every year 35,000 tonnes of aluminium foil is used in the UK, but just 11% of this is recycled! After using foil, where possible fold it and reuse it at a later date. Alternatively, use boxes with lids or cover food with bowls or plates instead of using foil, which can create unnecessary waste.

AVOID PAPER CARTONS The 'paper' cartons containing milk and juice are not paper alone. They are made up of 75% paper, 20%

polyethylene and 5% aluminium foil. Subsequently, they are a nightmare to recycle and all too often become incinerated or put into a landfill site. Find out where to recycle them, if needs be, from the Alliance for Beverage Cartons and the Environment at **www.ace-uk.co.uk**.

BUY REFILLABLES Reduce landfill waste. Cleaning products such as dishwasher soap, floor cleaners and washing-up liquid, or even personal toiletries such as soap, are now sold in refillable bottles. Bulk buy brands such as Ecover at **www.gonegreen.co.uk** and campaign for more great shops like Be Unpackaged where you can refill reusable containers with wholefoods, groceries and household goods. See **www.beunpackaged.com**.

HEAD DOWN THE MARKET Shopping at town or village markets, farmers' markets, and farm stores if you pass one, means you can choose goods without packaging – plus, the experience can be really fun, too. Your area has probably boasted a market for years and will offer great deals on an array of fresh ingredients including fruit, vegetables, fish and meat. Farmers' markets may be a bit more pricy but offer specialised and often locally produced goods that can really put the gourmet back into cooking. Find British Farmers' Markets at **www.farmersmarkets.net**.

READER TIP – DIANE BARNARD

SCRAPSTORE IT

Working in a playgroup, you can not only recycle your own packaging, but use that provided by local businesses via Scrapstore, which provides novel craft resources for schools and other groups working with young people. There are several warehouses countrywide, many with their own websites, which you can link onto from the general website **www.childrensscrapstore.co.uk**. Members may wheel supermarket trolleys down aisles containing shelves and barrels full of fabric, card and wood offcuts. If it's colourful and interesting, it'll be in the warehouse! Find out more by visiting the website or emailing enquiries@childrensscrapstore.co.uk.

REUSE CARDBOARD BOXES It might sound obvious, but don't throw away those cardboard boxes. Next time you buy a pair of shoes, or something else that comes in a box, keep it to reuse. It could be ideal for mailing gifts or moving house.

Good ore bad

RECYCLING METALS Scrap metal such as copper, brass and aluminium is worth money and has a long recycling history, though most households don't generate enough to interest dealers. Domestic waste – batteries, tin cans and cars, for example – can all be recycled, and aluminium cans could be recycled indefinitely. Find out more about metals recycling from Waste Online at www.wasteonline.org.uk.

CASH FOR CANS RECYCLING CENTRES Five billion drinks cans are sold in the UK every year, and throwing them away is incredibly wasteful. Your local authority should pick them up as part or your kerbside recycling scheme. Or you could take them to your nearest Cash for Cans recycling centre – if all the aluminium cans sold in the UK were recycled for cash it would raise £30 million! To find out where your nearest centre is, visit **www.thinkcans.net/cash-for-cans/where-can-i-recycle**.

KEEP HOUSEHOLD BATTERIES OUT OF LANDFILL SITES The average household uses 21 batteries a year, which adds up to around 650 million batteries throughout the UK. Of these, around 20,000-30,000 tonnes of batteries are landfilled annually – and only 1,000 tonnes of these are recycled. Batteries contain metals that can cause serious pollution problems, such as cadmium, which doesn't degrade and can't be destroyed. If it gets into the food chain it can damage the liver, kidneys and brain of humans and fish. Many local authorities now collect batteries as part of their kerbside recycling scheme – find details at **www.wrap.org.uk/local_authorities/batteries**. Or find a recycle point at **www.recyclenow.com**.

RECYCLE STEEL CANS Steel cans are recyclable, but not enough is being done. The steel plate recovered from cans each year in western Europe weighs the equivalent of 132 Eiffel Towers or 4,000 jumbo jets, but we could do better. For example, every year each Australian sends around 3.5kg of steel cans to refill – that's enough steel to make 40,000 fridges! So, make sure you're doing your bit. If your local authority doesn't pick your cans up, take them to one of the 2,000 Save-a-Can banks across Britain. For more information, visit the Steel Can Recycling Information Bureau at **www.scrib.org** or call 01554 712632.

The Tao of poo

SEWAGE AND STUFF Humans need to produce waste as part of our digestive system – but this waste also needs to go somewhere and be treated before it enters the UK's water network again. Every day in the UK about 347,000km of sewers collect over 11 billion litres of waste water. This is treated at about 9,000 sewage treatment works before the treated effluent is discharged to inland waters, estuaries and the sea. Without suitable treatment, the waste water we produce every day would damage the water environment and create public health problems. However, leaks and pollution do still occur. For more on how a group of environmental organisations are fighting back to ensure a sustainable water future visit www.blueprintforwater.org.uk. You can also help the campaigning group Surfers Against Sewage lobby for full treatment of sewage throughout the UK. Visit www.sas.org.uk or call 0845 458 3001.

THINK BEFORE YOU FLUSH Every time you flush the toilet, you use between 15 and 20 litres of water. You can help reduce your water consumption by placing a brick or hippo water saver in your toilet cistern. In just one year, you could save over 3,000 litres of water. Visit **www.hippo-the-watersaver.co.uk** or call 01989 766667 to order your water saver. Spare a thought for exactly what you flush away, too. We flush an enormous number of chemicals and loose items, with an estimated three quarters of blockages in water pipes being due to disposables such as sanitary towels, razor blades, syringes, even ladies tights and cotton buds. In 2005, over 75% of toilet debris on beaches was composed of the plastic sticks from cotton buds, and in the Marine Conservation Society's Beachwatch Survey 2006 these ranked second in a beach litter poll. Waste like this is not only unsightly, it's harmful to wildlife.

READER TIP – LAURA PEARCE

USE WATER CLEVERLY

When you're running the hot tap to do your washing up, you're wasting water while you're waiting for the water to turn hot. Rather than letting it run straight down the sink, save the water in another container. It can then be used around the house for watering plants or washing your car.

IF IT'S YELLOW LET IT MELLOW, WHEN IT'S BROWN, FLUSH IT DOWN If you can, avoid flushing the toilet every time you visit – particularly at night. And try not to use the toilet as the bathroom rubbish bin, as every flush will use 15-20 more litres of water.

REPORT INCIDENTS OF WATER POLLUTION In order to be removed, sewage needs to be identified. Don't assume that somebody else will report it! Even if they have, the pollution is clearly still there and has not been dealt with properly and the authorities still need notifying. If you see foamy scum or brown slick on the surface of rivers, lakes or sea, or smell sewage, get on the phone to the Environment Agency's hotline on 0800 80 70 60.

FILTER YOUR OWN WATER When you turn on the tap, the water you are about to drink has passed through an ageing infrastructure of water pipes and been through various cleaning processes which, when combined, can leave your water as more than just H_2O! It can contain chlorine, ammonia, bacteria, dissolved organic matter, suspended solids such as rust and dirt, and heavy materials such as aluminium, copper and lead. These can be removed using simple home water filtration methods. Find out how through the Fresh Water Filter Company (**www.freshwaterfilter.com**, 020 8558 7495) or the Pure H_2O Company (**www.pureh2o.co.uk**, 01784 221188).

TOP TIP – MALCOLM TAIT, WILDLIFE EDITOR

WATER TRAGEDY

The average household uses 355 litres of water a day, according to the Office of Water Services, all of which leads to depleted rivers and wetlands. In England, 26 sites that are designated Sites of Special Scientific Interest are being affected badly by water reduction, and nearly 200 more are in danger. Reduce your usage by turning the tap on and off when you brush your teeth, using a bowl for your washing up, and running the washing machine only when you have a full load.

Go wild

In the 3.5-billion-year history of life on Earth, there have been five major extinctions – events in which over 75% of all life disappeared. Today, experts from a whole range of fields – palaeontology, biology, climatology – in addition to statisticians are coming to the conclusion that we are on the brink of a sixth. 'Our activities have accelerated the rate of species extinction to hundreds – perhaps thousands – of times the normal background rate,' according to *New Scientist*, which reports Peter Raven, president of the International Botanical Congress, as predicting the extinction of about two thirds of all bird, mammal, butterfly and plant species by the end of the next century. This is not scaremongering. Since 1945, the UK alone has lost an estimated 95% of flower-rich meadows, 30% of ancient woodland and 80% of lowland grassland. Fauna has fared little better: nearly 10% of our butterfly species, for example, became extinct during the twentieth century, and 50% more are on downward spirals. Various agencies are looking for solutions, among them the Campaign to Protect Rural England (CPRE) **www.cpre.org.uk**; The Wildlife Trusts **www.wildlifetrusts.org**; and the Wildfowl and Wetlands Trust (WWT) **www.wwt.org.uk**. Get involved and you can help make a difference.

Close to home

WILDLIFE IN YOUR GARDEN There's an immense pleasure to be gained from preparing your garden for wildlife: as the birds move in to nest, the butterflies are attracted by nectar, the frogs make their home in your pond and bats swoop in the night sky above you, you realise that you have prepared a small oasis that nature now calls its own.

BUILD A WILDLIFE POND All wildlife needs water and countless species will benefit – you may find birds, badgers and dragonflies visiting your pond, and newts, frogs and toads making their home in it. If you're going to build a pond make sure it has shallow margins, deep areas and softly sloping sides so that small animals can get in and out easily. Placing rock piles nearby will give shelter to frogs, newts and even toads. It also needs to be deep enough for wildlife to survive in winter. For details of how to make your pond beautiful visit **www.beautifulbritain.co.uk/pond_pages**.

SAVE OUR HEDGEROWS The Department of the Environment estimates that between 1984 and 1990, 121,000km of hedgerows were lost. Hedgerows provide a rich and diverse natural habitat for plants, animals and birds, some of which are globally threatened. There is now less than 450,000km of hedgerow left in the UK (in 1947 there were 662,000km). CPRE – the Campaign to Protect Rural England at **www.cpre.org.uk** – can provide information on hedgerow management. You can also get advice from The National Hedge Laying Society at **www.hedgelaying.org.uk**, the British Trust for Conservation Volunteers (BTCV) at **www.btcv.org** and The Wildlife Trusts at **www.wildlifetrusts.org**.

TOP TIP – BUTTERFLY CONSERVATION

CHEMICAL WARFARE

More farmers are going organic and more of us want to buy organic food. It is, therefore, shocking that pesticide use in the garden increased by over 75% between 1998 and 2001. Pesticides do not specifically target greenfly and vine weevil (regardless of what it may say on the tin!) and such poisons kill countless beneficial or harmless butterflies, moths and other insects in gardens every day. They can also have nasty knock-on effects on garden birds, mammals and amphibians, which feed on insects in your garden. Cutting down your use of pesticides will be of great benefit to your garden wildlife, will save you money and effort and will give natural predators a chance to sort those pests out for you! For more tips and information about butterflies and moths contact Butterfly Conservation at **www.butterfly-conservation.org**, or call 01929 400209.

GIVE AN OWL A HOME Owls nest in hollow trees, old buildings or barns, and are often made homeless by modern developments. Encourage owls in your area by installing an owl box – it might just be the new des res an owl family is looking for. Contact the Hawk and Owl Trust for details at **www.hawkandowl.org**, or call 0870 990 3889. Alternatively, the Trust will tell you how to 'Adopt a Box' to provide homes for owl families. You won't be told where your box is (because the birds are protected), but you will get news of what's been going on in your box, a certificate, an illustrated guide to Britain's owls, a sticker and a regular newsletter.

TOP TIP – BUTTERFLY CONSERVATION
PUT YOUR FEET UP FOR MOTHS

You don't necessarily have to do extra things to attract wildlife to your garden – doing less can also help. Planting specific caterpillar foodplants can encourage butterflies to breed in your garden, but your patch is already home to many moths. An average garden will have scores of moth species breeding in it – a large wildlife-friendly garden in southern Britain might support 400 or more larger moth species alone. Some of these common moths are declining rapidly, yet all they need are the wilder, weedier parts of your garden or hedge. Not being too tidy in the garden and not using pesticides will help them to maintain their breeding colonies, which in turn provide vital food for hungry blue tits, house sparrow chicks and bats. Go out with a torch on a summer evening to see moths drinking nectar from flowers such as buddleia, honeysuckle, evening primrose and red campion. For more tips and information about butterflies and moths contact Butterfly Conservation at **www.butterfly-conservation.org**, or call 01929 400209.

GONE, BUT NOT FORGOTTEN They may be long dead, but they're still precious. Fossils are in constant danger from unscrupulous collectors who sell good specimens for a hefty profit – some have even been known to dynamite the rock in order to extract them. But even innocent collectors may inadvertently damage the resource, which in the proper hands can tell us much about the past – and therefore inform the present – life on Earth. There are codes of conduct for collectors – by the sea they recommend searching on the beach when the tide is going out, and in many places it's necessary to seek the landowner's permission. Certain fossils need registering, too. For more information visit the Discovering Fossils website at **www.discoveringfossils.co.uk**.

KIDS – COUNT CREATURES The Woodland Trust is recording nature's calendar, seeking the first signs of spring and autumn by counting the numbers of individuals of different species in their local area. The results are entered onto an online database, which will help us to understand the effects of climate change on wildlife. Recorders for the autumn 'count' should register in the summer for the following months and again in December/January for the spring 'flora and fauna census'. This includes recording trees, flowers and wildlife. Volunteer opportunities are listed on the website at **www.naturescalendar.org.uk**, or call 01476 584878.

SQUIRREL BANQUETS If you enjoy feeding squirrels remember they are actually hungriest in July, when their hidden stores are low and the new season's crop has yet to ripen. Try to provide food that approximates to their natural diet of tree seeds, tree flowers, tree shoots, mushrooms and fungi – they'll be grateful for peanuts, pine nuts, sunflower seeds, carrots and apples. Visit **www.overthegardengate.co.uk** for more wildlife tips.

TOP TIP – BUTTERFLY CONSERVATION
MAKING HAY WHILE THE SUN SHINES

Long grass and wildflower 'meadows' are great for attracting more wildlife into the garden. Common visitors such as the speckled wood, meadow brown and gatekeeper butterflies all lay their eggs on long grasses so it won't be long before they are breeding in your garden. The best way to look after such areas is to cut most of the long grass down in the autumn and take it off to the compost heap. If you cut in the summer, as soon as the grass turns brown (eg July/August), you'll be taking all the butterfly eggs and caterpillars away with the hay! Leaving the cut grass lying *in situ* is also detrimental, as it hinders the growth of wildflowers that provide vital nectar for butterflies. Leaving a few long tussocks over the winter will provide habitat for butterflies and other creatures during that time. For more tips and information about butterflies and moths contact Butterfly Conservation at **www.butterfly-conservation.org** (01929 400209).

LEAVE WOOD TO ROT Rotting wood is a common feature in the wild, and is an essential habitat for many species such as beetles. A log pile in even a city garden will attract a wide range of creatures and makes a good nature museum for kids.

BATMAN... Get a bat box to encourage bats to roost. Bats are an integral part of the ecosystem and – like many wild creatures – are suffering from the loss of their natural habitat. Of the 16 species left in Britain, six are endangered or rare and six others are vulnerable. Britain's commonest bat, the pipistrelle, is just 40mm long and weighs about 5g – less than a 2p coin. Despite its size it can eat up to 3,000 insects per night – so it's a real gardener's friend. You can find information on how to make or buy bat boxes at the Bat Conservation Trust at **www.bats.org.uk** (020 7627 2629). It also sells the Microbat, a tiny bat detector that enables you to identify bats in the field.

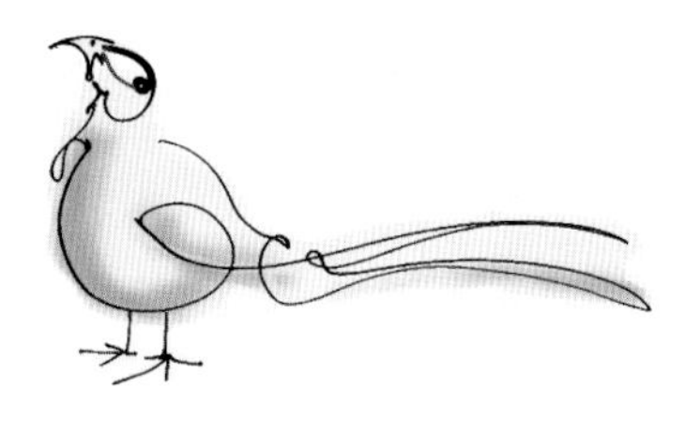

...AND ROBIN The RSPB recommends you feed birds year round – twice daily when the weather is severe – and don't leave uneaten food lying around. Feeding areas and utensils should be kept clean to avoid disease – salmonella can break out at unclean feeding stations. Black sunflower seeds, pinhead oatmeal, sultanas, raisins, currants, mild grated cheese, seed mixtures without loose peanuts, soft apples and pears cut up are all recommended. Avoid giving peanuts, fat and bread in the summer as they're not good for nestlings. And always leave clean water out, changed daily. For bird-feeding tips and more visit **www.rspb.org.uk**.

TOP TIP – WILDFOWL AND WETLANDS TRUST (WWT)
BUILD YOUR OWN WETLAND

Wetlands are the fastest disappearing habitat on the planet, with over 50% of the world's wetlands being lost over the past century, along with all their wildlife. Not good when you know that freshwater wetlands hold more than 40% of the world's known species and provide vital services to society: they store and clean water and protect us from floods and storms. So why not build your own mini wetland in your garden? Once you've made your pond, you can encourage wildlife such as frogs and newts to make their home there. Find out more at **www.wwt.org.uk**.

The loss of valuable wildlife habitats has been severe owing to changes in agricultural practice, new housing and industrial development. If you buy and plant native trees, shrubs, wildflowers and bulbs you will be helping to recreate some of these lost habitats and wildlife havens, and you'll also be safeguarding the future of a significant part of our cultural and landscape heritage. For a wide selection of native trees, plants and wildflowers, contact the British Trust for Conservation Volunteers (BTCV) on 01302 388 883 or visit **www.btcv.org.**

KIDS – KEEP SLOW WORMS IN THE GARDEN Slow worms are the only legless type of lizard in the UK. They grow up to 50cm long and can 'lose' their tail when frightened and grow it again later. You can tell a slow worm from a snake because unlike snakes they have eyelids. Slow worms feed on slugs, insects and spiders, hide in cool dark places during the day and come out at night to feed on their favourite meal, the slug. They are the perfect gardener's friend.

KIDS – HEDGEHOGS DON'T LIKE MILK (OR BREAD)
Nearly a quarter of the hedgehogs born into the world die before leaving their nest; probably half of the rest don't survive their first hibernation, according to the British Hedgehog Preservation Society. They're inquisitive creatures and will eat almost anything, but that doesn't mean that they should! They've been found with their heads stuck in tins, yoghurt pots and plastic cups, so keep your garden litter free of these items – especially if you live in a town. If you want to feed hedgehogs, give them tinned cat or dog food (not fish based), chicken leftovers, scrambled egg, chopped peanuts, grated cheese and breakfast cereal. Don't give hedgehogs milk – they can't digest it. Visit **www.britishhedgehogs.org.uk** to find out more.

READER TIP – LAURA PEARCE

DON'T THROW AWAY UNWANTED CDS

You can put the free CDs you receive in the post or with your Sunday paper to good use, even if they are not to your taste. Hang them from trees and bushes in your garden to prevent unwanted feline visitors – unwelcome predators will be frightened off once they catch sight of their own reflections in the CDs. You can also reuse the CDs in your home – they make perfect coasters, as the plastics they are made from are extremely heat resistant.

GARDENERS – HELP INCREASE THE BEE POPULATION

Since the 1960s, certain species of native bumblebee have declined by as much as 95%, owing in large part to the loss of wildflowers in the countryside. Some have declined so much they are rarely seen – the Cullem's bumblebee was last seen in 1941, the short-haired bumblebee in 1999. As the principal pollinators of soft fruit, they are essential to the ecosystem – their loss would render many gardens sterile. Natural England and the National Trust are calling for gardeners to spurn modern hybrids, such as petunias, and plant traditional cottage flowers – rich in nectar – in their garden. There are 15 million gardens in Britain. If all gardeners planted bee-friendly flowers, it could make a big difference. Visit Natural England on **www.naturalengland.org.uk** or call 0845 600 3078.

DEAD HELPFUL Graveyards, with their large expanses of open space, are perfect havens for wildlife. With the help of the Yorkshire Living Churchyards Project more than 1,300 graveyards in the York area are now thriving with native birds, mammals, insects and rare plants. Find out what your local churchyard is doing to manage itself in an environmentally sympathetic manner. It adds to the aesthetic appearance of the area and will also benefit wildlife. Visit **www.ecocongregation.org** to find useful links to organisations that help revamp or conserve church grounds.

A FAVOUR FOR FOXES If you leave your tin cans outside for collection, make sure you take the lids right off – don't leave them bent partially open for foraging foxes to cut their noses on. The National Fox Welfare Society at **www.nfws.org.uk** provides information on the UK's foxes.

KEEP YOUR POND FROST-FREE Throw a tennis ball or rubber duck into your pond – it will bob about creating gentle movement that stops the pond icing over in all but the severest of frosts, and save your fish and frogs from a chilly death.

DON'T REMOVE PEBBLES FROM THE BEACH Removing pebbles from British beaches is prohibited, and you could face a heavy fine if you're caught. Clearing beaches of pebbles can deprive coastal plants and animals of their natural habitats and shelters. In addition, removing shingle can interfere with the natural beach processes and sediment cycling. Pebbles can act as natural defences against cliff and beach erosion, so depletion could start to increase the rate of erosion. If you want to use pebbles for aquariums or gardens, make sure you buy them from stone merchants.

TOP TIP – MALCOLM TAIT, WILDLIFE EDITOR

BOXING CLEVER

If you have bird nestboxes in your garden, clean them out once the breeding season is over to reduce the likelihood of infection and parasites next year. Meanwhile, if you plan to tie a nestbox to a tree, try using an old rubber inner tube, as it expands as the tree grows, causing no damage. You can get more tips from *Birds in your Garden.*

SEEDS OF SUCCESS Although more woodlands are being protected than ever before, too many have already lost their carpets of wildflowers. Help repopulate them by simply helping to transfer seeds from established woodlands. To join a project like this near you, contact Landlife at **www.wildflower.co.uk** or call 0151 737 1819.

TOP TIP – WILDLIFE AND COUNTRYSIDE LINK
JOIN IN AND HELP

If you want to help wildlife in the UK or around the world, join one of the charities which work to protect nature. Almost seven million people are already members of wildlife and countryside organisations. A list of charities is available from us at **www.wcl.org.uk**. Don't know which one to join? Can't afford to join them all? Support a different one each year!

Wider world

DO YOUR BIT FOR THE WORLD'S WILDLIFE At present rates of extinction, 20% of the world's species of plants and animals could be gone within just three short decades. Habitat destruction is one of the key culprits, although climate change is not far behind. Faced with such daunting crises, can an individual really make much of a difference? You bet. Go wild.

SPONSOR A CHEETAH Your money could make a difference to some of the world's most endangered creatures. The Cheetah Conservation Fund (CCF) is working in Namibia to conserve

cheetahs in their natural habitat. They have launched an 'adopt a cheetah' campaign which, while not tied to a specific animal, will help protect and care for cheetahs worldwide. Visit **www.cheetah.org** for more information.

READER TIP – JUSTIN FRANCIS
VOLUNTEER FOR CONSERVATION RESEARCH

There are many great trips where you can help conduct valuable field research on lions, elephants, cheetahs, whales, dolphins, turtles and more. In addition to gathering vital data by staying with the conservationists some of the cost of your trip will support them and their work. Visit **www.responsibletravel.com** for conservation volunteering holidays.

PROTECT THE WHALES' SONG The song of a humpback whale is one of the most enigmatic and beautiful sounds of the natural world. These whales are extremely sensitive to noise and their ear drums can explode at 180 decibels. A new low-frequency submarine detection system being developed by the US and British navies together with NATO is blasting 240 decibels throughout the world's oceans. In areas where the system has been tested, huge numbers of whales have been beached with extreme auditory trauma. To find out more about the use of active sonar and add your voice to the growing protest, contact the Whale and Dolphin Conservation Society at **www.wdcs.org**.

STAMP OUT ILLEGAL WILDLIFE TRADE Traffic in wildlife is second only to the trade in narcotics in its size and value. The Environmental Investigation Agency (EIA) carries out undercover investigations into environmental crime, and exposes the horrific treatment we inflict on animals throughout the world. One of their current campaigns 'Species in Peril' focuses on species threatened with extinction because of the devastating impact of illegal trade in body parts. Bears in particular are highlighted, and the EIA is actively seeking to end the international trade in bear parts and derivatives. Visit **www.eia-international.org**, or call 020 7354 7960.

PROTEST AGAINST THE IVORY TRADE Despite the worldwide ivory ban which has saved large numbers of African elephants from widespread slaughter, the illegal trade in ivory continues. In 2002, six tonnes of ivory – the equivalent of 600 elephants – was seized in Singapore on its way from Africa to China and Japan, where ivory is still highly prized. And in 2001, seven tonnes was seized in India. Despite this, at the last meeting of the Convention on International Trade in Endangered Species (**www.cites.org**) delegates voted to allow three African countries to continue selling off ivory stockpiles even though evidence suggested this contributed to illegal poaching. China is becoming a major consumer of legally and illegally traded ivory. Support the Environmental Investigation Agency's campaign to ban the ivory trade. Lodge your protest with the Chinese ambassador – visit **www.eia-international.org** for details.

SAVE TIGERS' FORESTS In 2003, Friends of the Earth and the Environmental Investigation Agency discovered British cosmetic companies have been using talc illegally mined from a protected forest in India. These forests are home to endangered species, including tigers – only 5,000 are estimated to remain in the wild throughout the world. To find out more visit **www.eia-international.org**.

A LETHAL LUXURY A shatoosh shawl, made from the fine wool of the Tibetan antelope, became a 'must have' item among the rich and famous around the millennium, despite the fact that the antelope is in danger of extinction and only an estimated 75,000 animals remain in the world. Unlike pashmina wool, which is shaved, shatoosh is plucked from the antelope, so it must be killed first. Don't wear their pain. For more information contact **www.traffic.org**.

SUPPORT TURTLES Six of the seven types of marine turtles are listed as endangered. In the Pacific, the leatherback turtle is facing extinction and in the Mediterranean, numbers of green turtles are rapidly dwindling. Turtles take decades to mature, mate and produce offspring, but they have a battle to survive from the very moment eggs are laid – from humans who harvest turtle eggs to long fishing lines and pollution in seas. Visit the Caribbean Conservation Corporation at **www.cccturtle.org** to find out more.

TOP TIP – WHALE AND DOLPHIN CONSERVATION SOCIETY (WDCS)

DON'T BE A LITTER BUG

It is estimated that over 100,000 marine mammals and turtles die every year from entanglement, or ingestion of plastics. Often mistaken for food by marine animals, litter such as plastic bags can damage the animals' digestive tract and block the passage of food. This can lead to starvation and death, unless the blockage is removed. There are lots of things that you can do to help reduce marine litter: Take reusable bags to the shops instead of using plastic bags, choose items with less plastic packaging when shopping, dispose of waste responsibly, and never drop litter. For more about how to protect the UK's whales, dolphins and porpoises visit **www.wdcs.org.uk** or call us on 01249 449 500.

At your leisure

'When at leisure make preparations for a time of need' warns an ancient Chinese proverb. Well, we're rapidly heading for a global time of need, so what can you do? The joy of leisure is that it gives you time to think – and therefore act – a little more carefully. Recycling is not just for bottles, cans and plastic – all sorts of other things, like books, can be exchanged and recycled, too. You can go green when entertaining, and if you really want to make a difference, volunteer. A whole host of organisations, at home and abroad, need your help now. So have fun, but make a difference, too. As American philosopher and naturalist Henry David Thoreau wrote in 1852: 'Haste makes waste, no less in life than in housekeeping.' Take things slowly in your free time and you – and the world – will get more out of it.

In and out

BEING GREEN AT HOME AND ON THE TOWN To quote an old television programme: 'Why don't you just switch off your TV set and do something less boring instead?' Well, why don't you?

DETOX FROM YOUR TV On average, children in the UK aged 6-16 spend three hours a day watching TV. That's higher than the European average of only two hours a day. A survey by ChildWise also found that 80% of children aged 5-16 had a TV in their bedroom and most watched programmes on their own rather than with parents or other children. In contrast, only one quarter of the children read a book each day and just over half look at a book just once a week. Having a TV-free week would free up 21 hours of time to spend with friends, playing sport or reading a book.

TOP TIP – CAMPAIGN TO PROTECT RURAL ENGLAND (CPRE)

JOIN CPRE'S LETTER-WRITING TEAM

Letters really make a difference. CPRE's letter-writing team of members and supporters writes letters from time to time to key 'opinion formers' like local MPs, a government department or a member of the House of Lords. The letters – about important environmental issues and concerns – are straightforward, politically balanced and don't take long to write. CPRE supplies suggested text, highlighting key points, which you are free to amend. Volunteers also screen over 100,000 planning applications annually – raising the alarm when the countryside is threatened. Visit **www.cpre.org.uk** or call 020 7981 2800 for more information.

ADOPT A GREYHOUND Every year, tens of thousands of greyhounds are discarded by the ruthless racing industry. Of the estimated 60,000 greyhounds bred for racing each year, between 10,000 and 40,000 puppies are killed. The remaining dogs enter the racing industry. At least 10,000 are 'retired' before the age of four or five years.

You could boycott greyhound races, and encourage others to do the same. Alternatively, you could adopt an ex-racing greyhound. They make great pets and are surprisingly gentle. Find more details at **www.retiredgreyhounds.co.uk** or **www.adopt-a-greyhound.org**.

JOIN A GREEN GYM Green Gyms are conservation projects involving regular outdoor work, such as cutting down shrubs, clearing paths and repairing walls and fences. Not only does this work help the local environment, it also helps improve the participants' physical and mental wellbeing. For more information on Green Gyms, and how to join your local gym, go to the British Trust for Conservation Volunteers website **www.btcv.org/greengym**.

READER TIP – NICK HAY

JUST TURN IT OFF

Visit the International Campaign Against Television at **www.whitedot.org** for details on lessening the influence of TV.

BE ECO-ONLINE Led by search engine Google and processor heavyweight Intel, the computer industry recently made a pledge to reduce their energy usage by 2010. The scheme is expected to cut emissions by 54 million tonnes a year – equal to 11 million cars or 20 coal-fired power plants. Do your bit, too, by turning your computer off after use.

GET FESTIVE There has been a big growth in environmental initiatives at music and arts festivals in recent years. The green cause now also has a communal voice in the shape of A Greener Festival at **www.agreenerfestival.com**. It campaigns for events to take more responsibility for their environmental impact and to help promote causes to festival goers if it can. A recent survey it ran showed that music fans wanted greener festivals and were aware of the main issues, such as the negative impact of noise, waste and traffic. Find festivals that support A Greener Festival's manifesto in the site's links section, including Glastonbury, Bestival, Green Man Festival and **www.big-green-gathering.com**.

DON'T WAKE THE NEIGHBOURS Noise is as much of an environmental pollutant as carbon dioxide or nitrous oxide, so do your bit to reduce its impacts. From 28 February 2008, pubs and clubs exceeding the permitted level of noise could be subject to a fixed penalty of £500 or a fine of up to £5,000. For more information and reports on the effect of noise pollution, plus how to make a difference, check out **www.environmental-protection.org.uk/noise**.

TOP TIP – FRIENDS OF THE EARTH
QUESTION AND BADGER

Decision-makers like MPs and councillors are accountable to you. You have a right to know their position on an issue, and they want to hear from their constituents. They need your vote. Your troubles are their troubles. The same is true for businesses. Friends of the Earth helped to organise people's opposition to GM foods and all of the major UK supermarkets U-turned their position to give their customers what they want. Friends of the Earth could never have achieved successes such as doorstep recycling for all in England and Wales, and seeing the South Downs become a national park without people like you badgering decision-makers. Remember that trying to get a decent response is never pestering – it's lobbying! For ideas and advice on questioning and badgering visit the Friends of the Earth website at **www.foe.org.uk** or call the Friends of the Earth Information Service on Freephone 0800 581 051.

DON'T SEND THAT FILE Email is subject to pollution, too, so don't clog it! Be careful when sending large attachments, such as photographs. Large files can cause havoc when they become looped between two mail servers on the net. So, try to keep your photo files below 1MB, ask whether or not you really need to send that file, or put pics on a server such as **www.flickr.com** for friends to access at any time.

DON'T USE DISPOSABLES When you're giving a party, don't take the easy option and use disposable cutlery, plates and napkins. Just spare a thought for all those bags of rubbish you'd be producing.

TURN DOWN THE HEAT If you are having a lot of guests round, the chances are that their combined body heat will be enough to heat the house, so turn the heating off just before they arrive.

HAVE AN ECO-FRIENDLY EVENING Take advice from the Organic Food and Cooking chapters and make your party GM-free, organic and environmentally friendly! If you are having a lot of guests, try to limit the waste; buy a keg of beer instead of bottles, for example. If it's a dinner party, practice portion control to limit the food you waste.

Word power

ECO-READING **'To acquire the habit of reading is to construct for yourself a refuge from almost all of the miseries of life' wrote Somerset Maugham. Why not go one step further and use reading to construct a means of *tackling* those miseries?**

LET YOUR KNOWLEDGE FLOWER Green Books, publishers of *The Organic Directory*, supply a huge range of books on organic living, business, economy, renewable energy, ecological building, literature and poetry. Visit their website **www.greenbooks.co.uk** or call 01803 863260 for a catalogue. To order a copy of the Friends of the Earth publications catalogue, with books, briefings, reports and educational resources, visit **www.foe.co.uk** or call 020 7490 1555. For more on organic living, look at Green Guides. Published in nine regional editions, they contain listings of local shops, businesses, organisations and mail order services. Order a copy from **www.greenguide.co.uk**, call 01945 461452, or email subscriptions@greenguide.co.uk. The company also publishes *Pure Living*, a magazine for the ethical consumer.

ENSURE A GREENER READ The world's publishing industries remain vast consumers of paper. About 40% of the world's population use hardly any paper at all: most of Africa and much of Asia use less than 10kg a head. But per capita consumption of paper in the more prosperous countries is massive – the table-topping US uses 332kg while the UK and Germany are level in 13th place at 194kg. Responsible reading is one way of cutting down deforestation and ensuring the use of sustainable production methods in the paper industry. Always ensure that it's produced from recycled or sustainable paper sources, or better still check for a National Association of Paper Merchants (NAPM) Recycled Mark (**www.napm.org.uk/recycled_mark.htm**).

MEETING OF MINDS Get informed. Set up a book club where you meet friends to discuss major environmental issues, choosing a few relevant books beforehand. Try *Fast Food Nation* by Eric Schlosser, *Captive State* by George Monbiot, *Global Warming: The Last Chance for Change* by Paul Brown and *An Inconvenient Truth* by Al Gore. Publishers that specialise in environmental books include Green Books **www.greenbooks.co.uk** (01803 863260) and Earthscan **www.earthscan.co.uk** (020 7841 1930). Visit **www.oneworld.net**, which brings you news and views from a network of over 1,500 organisations working for human rights and sustainable development.

SHARE THE PLEASURE Once you've finished a book, pass it on to someone else. This is especially useful when travelling, as you can frequently exchange books with fellow travellers, making a single book purchase go a long way. Join Book Crossing (**www.bookcrossing.com**), the world's biggest free book club, to share with readers around the globe.

BECOME ECOLOGICALLY AWARE Staying informed is one of the best ways you can help make a difference. To find out more about the world's environmental and social problems, and what we can do to help, get onto the *Ecologist* website at **www.theecologist.org**. This monthly publication is the world's longest-running environmental magazine, and is read by people in over 150 different countries.

GREEN METROPOLIS Rather than letting piles of old reads gather dust in your home, turn them into cash and receive £3 for every book sold. The website **www.greenmetropolis.com** specialises in the 'recycling' of paperbacks, from the latest releases to golden oldies. All books cost just £3.75 (including free delivery) and by selling them on you save existing trees. Better still, 5p from every sale goes to the 'Plant a Tree' scheme run by the Woodland Trust.

Get involved

MAKE A DIFFERENCE – VOLUNTEER! Volunteering is easy, but to volunteer effectively requires a certain amount of commitment. Make sure that when you volunteer for something, you believe – or at least understand – the principles of the organisation you are working for. Not only will that encourage you to become more actively involved, it will also mean that you get more out of it. Visit TimeBank – a national volunteering campaign – at www.timebank.org.uk for details on how to get involved in your local community.

CHANGE PLACES You can help change the places around you by volunteering to work on local regeneration projects. Visit **www.changingplaces.org.uk** for details of schemes that transform derelict land into community gardens or playgrounds. You can also volunteer to work on sustainable development projects with Groundwork. This aims to build sustainable communities through joint environmental action between residents, businesses and other local organisations. At present 120,000 schoolchildren and 60,000 adults work on projects with Groundwork. Visit **www.groundwork.org.uk** for more information, or call 0121 236 8565.

JOIN THE WOODCRAFT FOLK The Woodcraft Folk is an educational organisation for children and young people aged 6-20, and provides an original alternative to Scouts, Cubs, Guides and Brownies. It doesn't just involve woodcraft! To find your local group, or to find out more information about the organisation, go to **www.woodcraft.org.uk**, or call 020 8672 6031.

TOP TIP – GREENPEACE

SAVE IT FOR THE FUTURE

Greenpeace is an independent non-profit global campaigning organisation that uses non-violent, creative confrontation to expose global environmental problems and their causes. We research the solutions and alternatives to help provide a path for a green and peaceful future. Our goal is to ensure the ability of the Earth to nurture life in all its diversity. Greenpeace organises public campaigns for the protection of oceans and ancient forest, for the phasing-out of fossil fuels and the promotion of renewable energies in order to stop climate change, for the elimination of toxic chemicals against the release of genetically modified organisms into nature and for nuclear disarmament and an end to nuclear contamination. To join Greenpeace call 020 7865 8100 or visit the website **www.greenpeace.org.uk**.

WIN A MEDAL The Duke of Edinburgh's Award scheme is run all over the UK and offers young people the chance to achieve things that they would not normally be able to. The Award scheme is open to boys and girls aged 14-17, and offers the opportunity to work towards bronze, silver and gold awards. In order to gain their Award, children must learn a skill, carry out a physical activity and volunteer to take part in community service. A great way of getting involved in the local community, visit **www.theaward.org** for more details.

BE A TREE WARDEN Get off your computer or away from the TV and get outside – there are plenty of fun things to do that will also help make your neighbourhood a better place. This includes planting and caring for trees. You can do this by becoming a Tree Warden for the Tree Council. Tree Wardens gather information about their local trees, get involved in local tree matters and encourage local practical projects to do with trees and woods. For example, trees that are growing need to be kept free of weeds and grass. Find out how to become a Tree Warden from the Tree Council at **www.treecouncil.org.uk** or from your local authority.

TOP TIP – MALCOLM TAIT, WILDLIFE EDITOR

LIFE'S A BEACH

Many of Britain's beaches are a mess, but you can help clear them up. Every year, the Marine Conservation Society (MCS) runs a September beach-cleaning weekend – although you can, of course, do your bit at any time of the year. For information about MCS Beachwatch visit **www.mcsuk.org** or call 01989 566017.

GET EXPERIENCE Everyone has skills or talent that could be used to help others, and Experience Corps believes that these skills only improve over time. This scheme is thus aimed at people aged over 50, helping them to put their skills to use in their local community. The Experience Corps now has over 423,000 imaginative and innovative voluntary work opportunities on its database. And this number is rising every week. Visit **www.experiencecorps.co.uk** to discover how your skills can be utilised.

GET ACTIVE! Anita Roddick founded the Body Shop in 1976 – and started a consumer revolution. In her years at the helm, she travelled all over the world, meeting an incredible range of inspirational people and campaigning relentlessly for change on a huge variety of environmental and humanitarian issues. Although, sadly, no longer with us, she still shares her knowledge on **www.anitaroddick.com**, a website devoted to global issues, with reports, updates and news of local action that people can participate in.

TOP TIP – THE SOIL ASSOCIATION

WANT A HOLIDAY WITH A DIFFERENCE?

The Organic Directory (**www.theorganicdirectory.co.uk**) lists places to stay from **www.organicholidays.co.uk**. Or visit Willing Workers on Organic Farms **www.wwoof.org** to find out about working on an organic farm in another country. You can find out more about the Soil Association on **www.soilassociation.org.**

EMAIL YOUR SUPPORT! Organisations such as Oxfam and Save the Children send their supporters email updates that profile key campaigns that need your help to influence decision-makers. To back the campaign, all you have to do is click on the link to send an email in support. It only takes a few minutes and it can also help keep you up to date with what's happening around the world. To sign up to receive the emails, visit **www.oxfam.org.uk** or **www.savethechildren.org.uk** and opt into the email update system. You can opt back out at any time.

Local heroes

WORKING FOR THE COMMUNITY There are many ways you can do your bit for your community. Join the local Women's Institute, Working Men's Club, or simply shop at your local newsagent, grocers or petrol station, which are fast becoming endangered species, even though they are often a cheaper and better-quality alternative. Lack of effort may mean the death of local shops. Visit www.impact-initiatives.org.uk to find out how you can do more.

TAKE OLD MAGAZINES TO YOUR DOCTOR Doctors' surgeries don't have large budgets to spend on magazines, but we could all do with something to read while we're waiting for our appointment. So, whether it's *Cosmopolitan* or the *Ecologist*, take your old copies down to your local surgery.

FAIR EXCHANGE Local Exchange Trading Schemes (LETS) are currently working to revitalise communities across Britain. They are local community-based networks, in which LETS members exchange goods and services with each other without the use for money. Using a special currency of LETS credits, people earn credits by providing a service, and can then spend the credits on whatever is offered by others in the scheme. For example, childcare may be exchanged for home repairs, or transport for the hire of tools and equipment. At least 30,000 people are involved in the UK's 300 LETS schemes at present, so visit **www.letslinkuk.org** to get involved yourself.

AIM TO SUSTAIN! Help your local area move towards a sustainable state. Local Agenda 21 was set up at the 1992 Rio Earth Summit, and is a comprehensive plan of action to help communities achieve sustainability through cooperation. Find out if your council is involved from the Improvement and Development Agency (IDeA).

Visit **www.idea.gov.uk**. You can get more involved by joining up to organisations such as the Bio Regional Development Group. Bio Regional is founded on the green ideal of local production for local needs. Local production helps create employment and wealth in the local area, reduce waste and limit our ecological footprint so we can live within the planet's resources. Visit **www.bioregional.com**, or call 020 8404 4880.

JOIN A CAMPAIGNING ORGANISATION Join a campaigning organisation and get involved. Just as you encourage your employer to do green things (recycle, compost waste, turn off unnecessary lights, etc) get your church/youth club/social club to do the same.

Play on...

MUSIC It has been proven to make people happier, healthier and smarter. Children who received music education in school have improved critical thinking and spatial-temporal reasoning, which resulted in better reading, language and maths skills, as well as higher self-esteem. Statistics have also shown that kids involved with music are less likely to abuse drugs and alcohol, and are more likely to stay in school. Music for Youth at www.mfy.org.uk and www.vh1.com/partners/save_the_music provide more information on music and its many benefits.

BUY USED CDS Sell your old music and buy second-hand CDs online at **www.amazon.co.uk**. Or switch to MP3s and donate your CDs to charity. Not only can you save yourself money, you're also limiting the wasteful use of resources.

REJECT CD PACKAGING CD packaging can be extremely wasteful. CDs sometimes come in long boxes, cardboard packaging that is twice the size of the actual CD jewel case. This excess packaging was designed to stop shoplifting. Do your bit by refusing to buy CDs at stores that use the long box.

GO TO CHARITY CONCERTS Many artists donate proceeds from their concerts to a local or national charity, so you can give back to your community while enjoying a night out. The Forestry Commission runs a series of concerts through summer, with proceeds helping to conserve valuable woodland – see **www.forestry.gov.uk** for listings. Plus, Live 8 (**www.live8live.com**) and worldwide Live Earth (**www.liveearth.org**) events in 2005 and 2007 have paved the way for future environmental benefit concerts.

RECYCLE CDS CDs are made from polycarbonate; a non-renewable, non-biodegradable petroleum-based product that usually ends up in landfills. Now there's a company – Polymer Reprocessors – that takes these CDs and turns them into items such as burglar alarm boxes, street lighting and lenses. Visit **www.polymer-reprocessors.co.uk** or call 0151 707 3684.

The great outdoors

It might look OK on the surface, but our outdoors is in crisis. Infinitely varied sources of pollution, the effects of intensive agriculture, urban and industrial encroachment and exploitation means the actual picture is pretty bleak. But all this has brought the outdoors sharply into focus. Never before has there been more study, understanding and awareness of the state of the countryside and the effects of our actions. We are rediscovering the ecological and practical benefits of forgotten techniques of land management, developing greener methods of agricultural and industrial production, and finding more sustainable and less damaging ways of doing things. This goes right down to the nuts and bolts of what – and what not – to do when out and about. US President Theodore Roosevelt (1901-1909) said: 'The nation behaves well if it treats the natural resources as assets which it must turn over to the next generation increased, and not impaired, in value.' Behave well as individuals and we can affect the behaviour of nations and the outcome of our great outdoors.

Play fair

GREEN SPORTS It's not whether you win or lose, but how you play the game that counts.

THINK WHERE YOU DRIVE Off-road vehicles and motorbikes can do untold damage in the countryside if not driven with a bit of consideration. Deep ruts caused by tyres can scar green lanes – non-metalled routeways bounded by hedges – making walking and horse-riding difficult. A survey undertaken in 2001 by JW Dover at the University of Stafford found that there are no accurate estimates for the UK stock of green lanes, which makes policy and conservation difficult, and that neglect is as much of a problem in certain cases as overuse. Green Lanes Environmental Action Movement (GLEAM) campaigns to prevent damage caused by recreational motor vehicles. Contact 01635 200764 or see **www.gleam-uk.org** for details. The Countryside Agency is compiling a national register of Greenways and Quiet Lanes – to help, visit **www.greenways.gov.uk**.

VOLUNTEER FOR SPORT Be a sport and get involved in your local community. Without volunteers, there would be no sport and leisure activities as we know them in this country. As well as keeping us fit, sport can play an important role in tackling social exclusion and giving young people a good start in life. To volunteer, visit TimeBank, the national volunteering campaign at **www.timebank.org.uk**. The 2012 Olympics will also need 70,000 volunteers – see **www.london-2012.co.uk**.

THE SLOPES ARE CHANGING If you're considering a skiing holiday, choose your ski resort on the basis of what it's doing for the environment. Global warming will have severe impacts on winter sports and recreation, so it's vital that resorts move towards the use of renewable energy resources. In February 2003, a new campaign was launched by the US National Ski Areas Association to 'Keep Winter Cool'. This involves the promotion of simple, innovative efforts to reduce carbon dioxide and other heat-trapping emissions using wind-powered ski lifts and car-pooling for guests and employees. Visit **www.nsaa.org**.

HITTING GREENS The Wildlife Trusts has long recognised that golf courses can make a significant contribution to wildlife conservation. For example, the Fynn Valley golf club in Suffolk has planted many native trees, such as the oak, and provides valuable habitats for dragonflies, barn owls and skylarks. Friends of Conservation has set up a new campaign to stimulate golf courses to introduce wildlife-friendly practices, such as restricting herbicide use, setting up birdwatching platforms, and training caddies to give wildlife talks. Visit **www.foc-uk.com** for details of how your local course can get involved. Also, see **www.english-nature.org.uk** for 10 top tips on how to make your golf course wildlife-friendly.

RAISE THE STANDARD OF YOUR LOCAL PARK The Pesticide Action Network UK (PAN UK) at **www.pan-uk.org** is helping to raise the quality of local parks, making them cleaner, safer, more environmentally friendly and better for the whole community. In 1997, it helped to set up the Green Flag Park Awards, rewarding parks that are well maintained, sustainable and do not use harmful chemicals and pesticides. Hundreds of parks across Britain expressed interest in the award and are endeavouring to improve the quality of their environment. See **www.greenflagaward.org.uk** for participating parks, or find a great park near you with the help of the *Good Parks Guide*.

CLEANER SWIMMING There are approximately 100,000 swimming pools in the UK, and while swimming may be healthy, the stuff we put into the pools isn't. Pools can be heated by the sun (see **www.energysavingtrust.org.uk/generate_your_own_energy/types_of_renewables/solar_water_heating** for details). They can also be made completely green by being chlorine-free. You can get a 100% chlorine-free purification system installed with e-clear at **www.eclearuk.com** or with Pristine Blue at **www.pristineblue.co.uk**. This is less harmful to you, the environment and your pets.

TOP TIP – WWW.GREENMATTERS.COM
HAPPY CAMPING

According to VisitBritain, domestic camping trips between 2003 and 2005 totalled around 4.9 million and are becoming more popular every year. If you go camping anywhere, leave no trace that you have been there. Carry all trash out with you; don't burn or bury garbage, without exception. Check your campsite carefully so as not to leave anything behind. If you are camping with a vehicle this is easy. If you are backpacking, plan wisely and take only minimally packaged items to reduce the garbage you generate and to make packing it out easier. Visit **www.greenmatters.com.**

Wood works

FORESTS OF THE FUTURE Urgent measures are needed to save the remaining 2% of Britain's ancient woodlands, which are fast being gobbled up by urbanisation. Broadleaf forests are home to 50% of the UK's threatened species, so it's vital that we stop their destruction before it's too late. To find out if woodland near you is under threat, or to make a report, visit the Woodland Trust's site at www.woodland-trust.org.uk or its dedicated site with the Tree Forum at www.woodsunderthreat.info. You can also help axe illegal logging in the European Union and save global forests by writing to the UK minister for Europe. Visit Friends of the Earth's website www.foe.org.uk for a sample letter.

BUY RECLAIMED WOOD Ancient forests are being lost at a rate of one football pitch every two seconds, and every year the wood trade throws away thousands of tonnes of wood as waste. You can help by only buying wood that's produced sustainably, and by purchasing reclaimed wood. For more advice on how to buy second-hand furniture, and furniture manufactured from reclaimed wood, order the *Good Wood Guide* from **www.foe.co.uk/campaigns/biodiversity/resource/good_wood_guide**, or call 020 7490 1555.

BIOREGIONAL CHARCOAL Every year, Britain imports 60,000 tonnes of charcoal. This is despite the fact that our own woodlands could meet this demand many times over. About 90% of imported charcoal comes from the developing world, which leaves British woodlands uncoppiced and derelict. BioRegional is working to encourage British charcoal production, thus restoring our forests. At present, 68 woodlands covering 4,000 hectares of land are certified by BioRegional Charcoal and the FSC (**www.fsc.org**). See **www.bioregional.com**. Not only do these provide local employment, but the coppiced forests also provide habitats for endangered butterfly species, such as the pearl-bordered fritillary. For more information visit **www.butterfly-conservation.org**.

RECYCLE WOOD AS COMPOST The next time you have a pile of waste garden wood, don't take it to the local dump. You can recycle fallen branches, garden canes or any other type of wood in your compost heap. The larger the pieces, the slower they'll break down and the harder the pile will be to turn, so make sure you break them up into small pieces first. For more ideas on composting, and help on recycling projects, visit **www.diynet.com**.

SAVE WOOD BY CUTTING UP MONEY Did you ever wonder what happens to old money? It's recycled! You can now buy recycled pencils made out of denim, paper and even money, instead of wood. By using a pencil made out of recycled money, you save a tree and create a new use for an old product. Learn about recycled products at **www.amazingrecycled.com**.

BRING TREES BACK INTO YOUR LOCAL AREA Trees can have enormous benefits for your local area. One hectare of woodland grown to maturity will absorb the carbon emissions of 100 family cars for a year. And a single large beech tree can provide enough oxygen for the daily requirement of 10 people. As well as these benefits, trees can make an enormous difference to the appearance of urban communities. You can help out by volunteering for a community tree-planting scheme, or by

joining the Million Trees campaign and sponsoring a tree for yourself or a friend. Contact Trees for London (**www.treesforlondon.org.uk**, 020 7587 1320) or the Woodland Trust (**www.woodland-trust.org.uk**, Dedicate a Tree/Woodland Creation Scheme 0800 026965).

GREENPEACE SAVE OR DELETE CAMPAIGN Ancient forests play a key role in the lives of people, are home to millions of plant and animal species and also help regulate the world's climate. This is why Greenpeace wants everyone to get involved in their Save or Delete campaign, which aims to protect the world's forests from total destruction. Visit **www.saveordelete.com** to join the campaign. The site contains useful information on how to send letters to put pressure on the government to ban illegally logged timber imports to Britain.

Out and about

WALKING, HIKING AND CAMPING There are 12 simple guidelines to remember when out and about:

- **Enjoy the countryside and respect its life and work**
- **Guard against all risk of fire**
- **Fasten all gates**
- **Keep your dogs under close control**
- **Keep to public paths across farmland**
- **Use gates and stiles to cross fences, hedges and walls**
- **Leave livestock, crops and machinery alone**
- **Take your litter home**
- **Help to keep all water clean**

- **Protect wildlife, plants and trees**
- **Take special care on country roads**
- **Make no unnecessary noise**

For more information and to see the Countryside Code, visit www.countrysideaccess.gov.uk.

TOP TIP – THE TREE COUNCIL
SUPPORT SEED GATHERING SEASON

The Tree Council runs a Seed Gathering Season every year between September and October, starting on the autumn equinox. Its aim is to inspire everyone, particularly children and families, to gather seeds, fruits and nuts and grow the trees of the future. Growing trees from local seed can have great benefits in restocking areas with trees of local provenance that are likely to flourish. See **www.treecouncil.org.uk**.

COUNTRY LOVERS UNITE! Check out **www.countrylovers.co.uk**, which has details of various conservation organisations, as well as advice and information about several issues concerning the countryside across the UK. All of this is very relevant to hikers and campers, who pass through the countryside on their travels.

HIKING ETHICS The Hiking Website **www.hikingwebsite.com** has a whole section devoted to 'Hiking Ethics' and how to behave out in the wild. Recommendations include not building another fire ring if one already exists, not digging trenches or building walls, and not cutting down plants or killing animals unless your survival depends on it. Visit the site for more details. Also, try **www.camping.uk-directory.com** for information about camping across the UK.

BLOCKED PATHS If you come across a blocked path or other difficulty, such as a broken stile or field path that has been ploughed over, contact your local highway authority (usually the local county council or unitary authority) or the local Ramblers' Association footpath officer. Call 020 7339 8500 to find out how to get in touch. Visit **www.ramblers.org.uk**.

HIGH PERFORMANCE, HIGH IMPACT High-performance trekking and walking wear makes a real difference to our life in the outdoors – but how does it affect the environment itself? Manufacturing and production practices need to be improved in a lot of companies, but certain brands are making an effort to reduce the environmental and humanitarian impact during manufacture. Patagonia (**www.patagonia.com**) is one of the most environmentally friendly for waterproof jackets and rucksacks, and Ethical Wares (**www.ethicalwares.com**) rates highly for boots. To find out more visit **www.ethicalconsumer.org**, or call 0161 226 2929.

TOP TIP – THE RAMBLERS' ASSOCIATION
USE PUBLIC TRANSPORT TO GET TO THE START OF YOUR WALK

As well as being better for the planet, not being reliant on a car enables you to do linear walks and these can be a lot more fun than the circular ones you have to do in order to get back to where you parked your car. For example, you can take a bus to somewhere, do your walk and come back on a different bus or train. You can do a far greater variety of walks this way. Visit **www.ramblers.org.uk**.

GET INVOLVED IN FOOTPATHS WEEK Statistics from the Audit Commission on England's footpaths 2006 show that on average 25.4% of paths are difficult or impossible to use. This is a rise of over 5% from 2002. If you want to make a difference to the accessibility of England's footpaths, take part in Use Your Paths Week every June. Visit **www.ramblers.org.uk** or call 020 7339 8500.

A healthy attitude

'A wise man should consider that health is the greatest of human blessings', according to the Greek physician Hippocrates, but how can you be healthy if your environment isn't? As a species we have been spectacularly successful, colonising the far reaches of the globe, but successful doesn't necessarily mean beneficial. For the individual, healthy living is mostly down to common sense and attitude, so think healthy, but think global. It's the health of our soils, rivers, forests and the very air we breathe that matters. Just one small action will make a difference.

Good vibrations

HEALTHIER LIVING Humans are outdoor creatures, just like any other species. But we now spend at least 80% of our time indoors. The Environmental Protection Agency has found that outdoor air is often five times better and can be up to 100 times fresher than the stale air indoors. If you do spend a lot of time indoors, keep fresh air circulating. Studies have linked ill health – even cancers – to the quality of the air we breathe. So open the window and banish the musty air caused by a mix of fungi, bacteria, furnishings that give off carcinogenic chemicals and gas heaters and stoves that release carbon monoxide.

EAT FRUIT AND VEGETABLES EVERY DAY Eating five pieces of organic fruit or vegetables a day protects against coronary heart disease and some cancers, but people in the UK eat far less fruit and veg than other countries in Europe, and one in five kids in England eats less than one piece of fruit a week. Fruit and veg also provide essential minerals and vitamins that are not available in other foods. Find out about the '5 a day' scheme from **www.5aday.nhs.uk**. It has lots of tips and advice, including why we should eat five pieces of fruit and veg a day, what counts as a portion and what to do if your kids are fussy eaters or you don't have much time to prepare meals.

GO BAREFOOT Your feet have a tough time of it. With each step you take, they absorb three times your body weight, so it's no wonder your feet like the chance to breathe. Going barefoot gives you a gentle foot massage, and because your feet contain thousands of nerve endings connected to different parts of your body, it keeps the rest of your body happy, too.

DRINK 2.5 LITRES OF WATER A DAY Our blood is 92% water, so if you're not drinking enough your complexion will look tired and dry: drink just a litre of water a day and you'll be glowing from top to toe. But when you're exercising don't overdo it. Medical experts are increasingly concerned about the amount of water we consume during exercise – drinking too much can cause water intoxication, diluting the body's salts, making people feel dizzy and, if serious, causing them to collapse. Drink a quarter of a pint of water for every hour of exercise you do.

Keep it clean

GREENER HYGIENE Aggressive marketing shouts at us everywhere we look, promoting a supposedly cleaner lifestyle. However, the products we use to create this illusion of purity do so by damaging the environment we live in. This takes place at every stage of their lifecycle – the manufacturing process pollutes, their usage gives off harmful chemicals into the atmosphere and when they are disposed of they are rarely recycled. And getting dirty can be good for you! Scientists in Germany have recently discovered that children who grow up on farms are 50% less likely to suffer from hay fever, asthma and other allergies than kids who grow up in sanitised environments. This is said to be because children who come into contact with dirt build up stronger immune systems, protecting them from illness later in life.

BUY RECYCLED TOILET PAPER The average Briton uses 110 rolls of toilet paper per year. The amount of Andrex alone sold in a year is enough to wind round the M25 80,000 times. In Britain, less than 10% of toilet paper is recycled – and while the paper may come from sustainably managed forests in Scandinavia, these forests are replacing ancient woodland that is home to thousands of endangered species. Save the forests and use recycled toilet paper instead. It comes from office paper and wood pulp that has already been used at least once. It's nice and gentle, too! Buy yours from **www.traidcraftshop.co.uk**.

TAKE YOUR SHOES OFF! Even the cleanest-looking carpets can harbour a cocktail of toxic chemicals and pesticide concentrations brought in from outside off the soles of your shoes. When you whip round with a vacuum cleaner, most of these residues cling on tight to the carpet, building up over the years. Do yourself, your family and your pets a favour and leave your shoes at the front door.

SAY NO TO AEROSOLS CFCs are no longer allowed to damage our environment, but hydrocarbon propellants such as isobutane still do. Used in aerosols, they contribute to air pollution and are thought to be responsible for respiratory diseases. Say no to aerosols and use pump dispensers or roll-on alternatives instead.

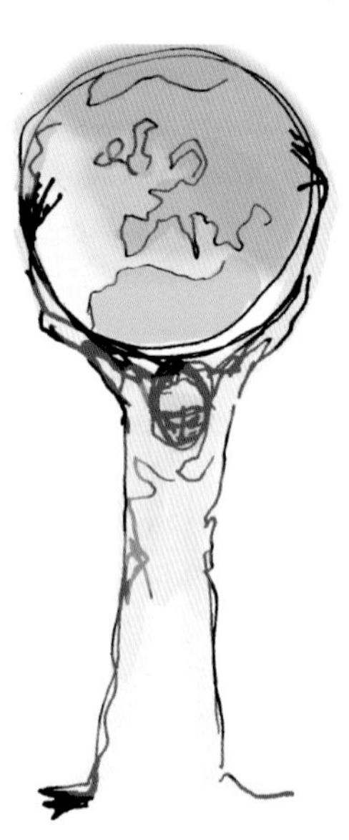

AVOID DEODORANTS CONTAINING ALUMINIUM If you use a commercial deodorant, the chances are it has got aluminium in it. Daily exposure to aluminium can be harmful. When absorbed through the skin it can pass into the liver, kidneys, brain, cartilage and bone marrow, increasing the risk of blood poisoning. Aluminium-containing antiperspirants can also block our pores and prevent us from sweating. A 'Deodorant Stone' is a healthier alternative, based on natural mineral salts and free from aluminium chlorohydrate. Find out more from **www.deodorant-stone.co.uk**, or call 01559 384856. The makers of Deodorant Stone have also now harnessed their stone magic in a convenient roll-on and spray format.

READER TIP – LOUISE SHEAR AND PENNY WETHERILL

USE A MOONCUP

Biodegradable sanitary products are kinder to the environment – they don't get flushed into the water system or pile up in landfills. Or you could try a reusable Mooncup Menstrual Cup. It's a 5cm cup that is inserted like a tampon but collects fluid rather than absorbs it. Mooncups last for years, save on waste and save money, too. See **www.mooncup.co.uk** or get them from **www.ecotopia.co.uk**.

SWITCH TO NON-BLEACHED SANITARY PRODUCTS... a big step when we're used to easy-to-use sanitary products. Women have been convinced that bleached disposable pads and tampons are the only option and few consider the risks to their health. A woman can use up to 11,000 tampons in her lifetime, increasing exposure to dioxin, a chemical by-product of bleaching, linked to cancers and immune system depression. Tampons also have additives to increase absorbency such as surfactants, which may also pose health risks. Ask your doctor about the risks of toxic shock syndrome, which can be caused by tampons, and opt for unbleached organic cotton pads and tampons, which are healthier for you and less damaging to the environment. Get Natracare products from **www.ecotopia.co.uk** or contact Spirit of Nature at **www.spiritofnature.co.uk** (0870 725 9885).

READER TIP – TERESA POWELL

CARE FOR NAILS NATURALLY

Nail varnish and remover can contain toxic substances, such as toluene, acetates, formaldehyde, phthalates and acetone. Alternatives such as Suncoat use natural ingredients, mineral pigments, soya oil and corn fermentation to colour and care for nails. See **www.naturalcollection.com**.

CHOOSE SAFE TOOTHPASTE Many commercial toothpastes contain polishing agents and whitening chemicals, which can be directly absorbed into the body through the teeth, the tongue and the gums. Sodium lauryl sulphate can irritate the skin and cause ulcers, while triclosan, a synthetic antibacterial agent, has been linked to cancer, decreased fertility and immune suppression. Toms of Maine has a selection of natural toothpaste for sensitive teeth and gum disease, with strawberry flavour for kids (**www.tomsofmaine.com**). Kingfisher sells natural toothpaste in lemon, mint and aloe vera flavour, as well as toothpaste without fluoride (**www.kingfishertoothpaste.com**). Or find a range of natural toothpastes at **www.buyorganics.co.uk**.

CAMPAIGN FOR WATER COOLERS IN SCHOOLS
Dehydration affects health, wellbeing, performance and learning. Long-term risks include constipation, continence problems, kidney and urinary tract problems, and some cancers. A child should have four to five glasses of water a day at school, but access to drinking water in some schools is insufficient. Visit **www.wateriscoolinschool.org** to find out if your school has joined the campaign to ensure drinking water in school.

USE REAL HANDKERCHIEFS Every person in the UK uses an average 215kg of paper or card a year. That's equivalent to 426 cornflake boxes, or over eight boxes per person per week. Help reduce the amount of paper you use by switching from paper tissues to real handkerchiefs. Paper tissues come in a bewildering array of types, colours, textures, thicknesses and shapes, so using handkerchiefs will also reduce the energy and expense involved in their production and packaging.

A spoonful of sugar

MEDICINE THAT'S GOOD FOR THE PLANET The average Briton spends £137 on medicine per year. Much of it is necessary and life-enhancing, but all too often we seek short-term answers from our pills, which can cause long-term problems. We need to make sure that our drive to make ourselves feel better not only does the job, but looks after the health of the planet, too.

SUPPORT YOUR LOCAL PHARMACY Supermarket pharmacy counters have threatened the future of 12,000 local pharmacies, which are essential to the wellbeing of a local community. Groups that will be particularly affected by their loss are elderly and disabled people and young mothers, who rely heavily on the free advice and range of services offered by local pharmacies. When the pharmacies go, you will have no choice but to go to the supermarket for medicines. Find your local pharmacy, plus doctors, opticians and hospitals, at **www.nhsdirect.nhs.uk**.

ALTERNATIVE MEDICINES If you're stressed, can't sleep or are simply feeling under the weather, try an alternative treatment before reaching for the pills or ringing the doctor. Homeopathy works by stimulating a person's immune system and resolving problems from within. People have turned to homeopathy for almost 200 years as a natural alternative and a specialised treatment. To find your local homeopathy practitioner visit the Society of Homeopaths website at **www.homeopathy-soh.org**.

READER TIP – MELANIE DANIELS

MAKE YOUR OWN EVERYDAY MEDICINES

Be your own doctor when it comes to the simple needs of your body. Home-made natural remedies can often reduce or prevent symptoms. Tea tree oil is excellent to gargle with when you have a sore throat, or to massage on sunburnt skin and insect bites; a few drops of lavender oil on your pillow will help you sleep; and eucalyptus oil dabbed on a tissue will help clear out stuffy noses. Make sure your ingredients make suitable medicines, and before experimenting consult a good book for expert advice. Check Herbal Safety News at the Medicines and Healthcare Regulatory Authority website **www.mca.gov.uk** if you are unsure of any ingredients. If you want to consult a professional, the National Institute of Medical Herbalists can provide you with a list of herbal medicine practitioners in your area – visit **www.nimh.org.uk**.

CHUCK OUT OLD MEDICINES Open your bathroom cabinet and chances are, you'll find some old medicine – an out-of-date painkiller or a nasal spray. Don't leave them lying around – medicines can be dangerous if they find their way into little hands. And don't flush them down the loo where they'll poison the water supply. Take them to your local pharmacy, where they can be disposed of safely, without harm to others or the environment.

Skin deep

REAL BEAUTY TIPS Women (and men!) can absorb up to 2kg of chemicals through toiletries and cosmetics each year. If you can reduce the amount of creams, moisturisers and make-up you use, or switch to natural and organic products, the benefits will be more than just skin-deep. Clear out your make-up bag, throw away the old products you haven't used and choose ones that are kind to your body as well as the environment. Get natural beauty products from www.theorganicpharmacy.com.

WHEN NATURAL IS NOT NATURAL A product that claims to be 'natural' may be far from it: the ingredients might have been natural at first, but by the time they reach your skin they may have been processed. In fact, for a commercial product to be called 'natural', it only has to consist of 1% of that natural product. Anita Roddick of the Body Shop said that the marketing blurb on cosmetic labels often amounted to 'a scandalous lie'. Protect yourself from the hidden dangers of cosmetics and support the campaign to end the cosmetics cover-up. Find out more from the Chemical Safe Skincare Campaign at **www.chemicalsafeskincare.co.uk**. Or get more information from the Women's Environmental Network at **www.wen.org.uk**.

BUY PURE SOAP We all need soap, but we don't have to poison our world in the process! Commercial soaps often come bearing overpowering artificial scents and many layers of wrapping. Various brands of pure, organic soap are sold in health-food shops and chemists, without additives and without wasteful packaging. Or find a pretty range of natural soaps at **www.woodspirits.com** or **www.naturalsoap.co.uk**.

MAKE UP YOUR OWN MAKE-UP Many cosmetics are made in science laboratories from chemicals, which can cause harmful side effects, such as skin irritation and allergic reactions. But women have been making their own cosmetics for thousands of years – in ancient Greece women used harmless berries and seeds to create beautiful blushers. Check out **www.makeyourcosmetics.com** for recipes and information on ingredients that are kind to your skin. For tips on natural face masks go to **www.wittyliving.com/recipes/facial-mask-recipes.html** and for more general natural beauty products information visit **www.natural-skincare-4u.co.uk**. For a more extensive selection of natural cosmetics tips and recipes check out *Natural Beauty at Home: More than 200 easy-to-use recipes for body, bath, and hair* by Janice Cox, and *Neal's Yard Remedies: Recipes for natural beauty* by Romy Fraser, both available from **www.amazon.co.uk**.

USE NATURAL FRAGRANCES

An extravagant bottle of perfume could contain a mixture of 600 synthetic chemicals. Over 95% of chemicals are made from petroleum and many are designated hazardous. As an alternative use essential oils, plant extracts or aromatherapy oils, which can be applied to the skin. Find out more from Culpeper at **www.culpeper.co.uk**, Cariad at **www.cariad.co.uk** or Neal's Yard at **www.nealsyardremedies.com**.

CHOOSE YOUR HAIR DYE CAREFULLY You may be dying to colour your hair, but have you thought how the chemicals in the dye may harm you? Hair dye uses harsh chemicals – ammonia, peroxide, p-Phenylenediamine (PPD) or diaminobenzene, and repeatedly dyeing hair, especially dark brown or black, can increase the chances of developing some cancers, such as non-Hodgkin's lymphoma, multiple myeloma and cancer of the bladder. Henna, made from the leaves of the desert shrub lawsonia, is a safer alternative. It can also be customised using natural ingredients: coffee to darken, tea to lighten and apple cider vinegar to cover grey hairs. Your salon may also use natural alternatives. Find a natural dye home kit or a salon that uses natural hair dyes and care products through **www.herbatint.co.uk** and **www.colourherbe.co.uk**.

BUY PHTHALATE-FREE PRODUCTS Make sure you are not buying any products containing dibutyl phthalate (DBP) or any ingredients ending with phthalates. Used in some makes of hairspray, perfume, body lotion, deodorant and nail varnish, animal studies have linked this chemical to damage to the lungs, liver, kidneys and the testes of unborn offspring. Manufacturers aren't required by law to list this product on their labels. To find out if the products you are using are safe visit **www.wen.org.uk** or see the Campaign for Safe Cosmetics at **www.safecosmetics.org**. Recent studies have shown that women aged 20-40 are especially at risk of multiple exposure from beauty products, so be on your guard to persuasive advertising, too.

IF A FRAGRANCE SAYS 'MUSK' ON THE BOTTLE, DON'T TOUCH IT! Artificial musks are 'bioaccumulative': they build up in body fat, blood and breast milk, and in the environment. Other side effects can be headaches, dizziness, rashes and respiratory problems. Some are also hormone disrupters, interfering with the hormones, which regulate our daily bodily functions. They are found mainly in perfumes and cosmetics, but also in laundry detergents. Find out more from **www.foe.org.uk**. Musk deer populations in Mongolia and Russia are also at risk for real musk products, so avoid them, too. See **www.wwf.org.uk**.

BOYCOTT ANIMAL-TESTED BEAUTY PRODUCTS A label that says 'not tested on animals' is not always telling the whole truth. Just because the finished product hasn't been tested on animals, it doesn't mean that the individual ingredients haven't been. Look out for the Humane Cosmetics Standard (HCS) 'rabbit and stars' logo. It is an internationally recognised guarantee that the product has not been tested on animals at any stage. A full list of HCS-approved products is available free from the British Union for the Abolition of Vivisection. Visit **www.buav.org** or call 020 7700 4888. Beauty Without Cruelty can also send you a list of companies that produce cosmetics without causing harm to animals. See **www.beautywithoutcruelty.com** or **www.animalaidshop.org.uk/cosmetics.htm**.

CHOOSE ELECTRIC RAZORS Our obsession with smooth skin is having devastating effects on the environment. Every day, Bic sells 10 million disposable razors, which end up in landfill. Once there, they don't biodegrade, and can even release toxic chemicals into the ground, contaminating soil and water. Avoid disposables and buy electric or traditional razors instead. And when you are shaving, avoid foams, gels and depilatory creams that contain alkylphenols and potassium thioglycolate. The former is a hormone disrupter, while the latter is a derivative of thioglycolic acid, which is listed in the US as a highly toxic material.

PROTECT
THE
HUMAN
Amnesty International
JOIN
AMNESTY
PROTECT
THE
HUMAN
Amnesty International has successfully
campaigned to protect human rights for over
40 years. We work to protect individuals wherever
justice, fairness, freedom and truth are denied.
To join Amnesty International today visit
www.amnesty.org.uk/join or text the word
Join1 to 64118.

Food for thought

The pursuit of cheaper, readily available 'food for all' that began after World War II has been astonishingly successful and has led to us getting whatever we want, whenever we want – for which we ought to be truly grateful. It's what lies beneath that is a little less palatable: unsavoury and cruel methods of production; the damage caused to the environment by the constant trafficking of food around the world; and a farming industry being squeezed by the need to constantly cut costs. And that's not all. Overprocessing and lack of sensible eating is causing a frightening range of health problems, including obesity and heart disease. Measures taken to counteract our slide into crisis are at best ineffectual: the words 'healthy food' are shamefully overused by the food industry. But it's not all bad. The response has been a flowering of organic and buy local movements. According to the Soil Association 80% of British households now shop organic. And now there are 500 thriving farmers' markets in the UK, selling all kinds of produce from cheese to flowers – in 1997 there were none. As consumers, we are in a position to make food a pleasure, both to eat and to produce. Exercise your choice and the whole world will be a healthier place!

Green groceries

THE WORLD OF FOOD The average item of food in a supermarket travels over 1,000 miles. Assisted by free trade, with no tax on aviation fuel, supermarkets transport food all around the world – a report in 2000 showed that seven of the UK's biggest supermarkets travelled more than 408 million miles a year to deliver their goods! Are the costs in transport emissions and packaging worth it? One kilo of New Zealand apples accounts for its own weight in CO_2 transmissions by the time it arrives in the UK, while 10 litres of orange juice need 1 litre of fuel (for processing and transport) as well as 220 litres of water for irrigation and cleaning. The food in a typical Sunday lunch could have been transported 49,000 miles – that's equivalent to twice around the world – releasing 37kg of CO_2. Buying locally is one of the most important things you can do to improve the environment. You can get tips on how to reduce food miles and find local suppliers at www.foodloversbritain.com, www.soilassociation.org.uk and Cultivating Communities at www.cuco.org.uk.

PROTECT CHILDREN FROM JUNK-FOOD MARKETING
The last National Diet and Nutrition Survey in 2000 found that 20% of boys and 27% of girls (aged 2-19) were overweight in England, with numbers growing by up to 3% since 1995. Type 2 diabetes, closely associated with obesity and previously only found in adults, is also making an appearance in children. But despite these alarming figures, UK children face the heaviest onslaught from TV ads that market junk food directly to them. In 'TV Dinners', a report published in 2001, Sustain (The Alliance for Better Food and Farming) found that 95-99% of food advertising aimed at children was for fatty, sugary and salty food. Since then, the government has made moves to restrict these ads. Now help campaign for a total ban – see **www.sustainweb.org/childrensfoodcampaign**.

GROW YOUR OWN Don't buy it from a supermarket – grow your own! Home-grown food contributes to the reduction of CO_2 emissions caused by transporting food around the world, minimises packaging that ends up in landfill, composts green waste effectively, and enables you to try out a whole range of non-commercial organic varieties, which challenges the supermarket monoculture. Tending a garden also relieves stress, and reduces environmental pollution and can be a great educational tool for children. Better still, it's cheap and the feeling you'll get when you see your first tomatoes on the vine or apples on the tree will surpass any sugar high! Get advice on what's seasonal, how to get the best crops and which varieties to choose at **www.growfruitandveg.co.uk.**

A SLIM CHANCE According to The Alliance for Better Food and Farming, 88% of slimming advertisements make claims that are in breach of the British Code of Advertising and Sales Promotion put out by the Advertising Standards Authority (ASA). Watch the diet products you buy. Are their claims realistic or just hype? If in doubt, get the ASA to investigate. You can file a report at **www.asa.org.uk.**

SAY NO TO GM CROPS The global use of GM crops increased by 12% in 2008, to reach 114 hectares across 23 countries. Biotech companies insist on the benefits, claiming that they will significantly increase food production in areas of scarcity, such as Africa. GM crops are developed either to tolerate herbicides, enabling farmers to use a

broad spectrum herbicide that kills off every other plant in the field, or imprinted with a toxin that kills off pests that feed on the crop. But concerns about contamination of non-GM crops are mounting, as experience shows GM crops contaminate far more widely than the 50-100 metres the biotech companies claim. In 2000, British farmers were sold rape seed that had been contaminated by GM crops over two and a half miles away. We can only speculate what could happen to disturb our ecosystem if wild plants or weeds were contaminated, as not enough research has been carried out. But if GM continues to contaminate, it will threaten organic farming and reduce consumer choice. Moreover, it will concentrate the world's food supply in the hands of five biotech companies, with one – Monsanto – owning 90% of the business. To find out more visit Friends of the Earth at **www.foe.org.uk** and see their Real Food campaign. They will tell you if your local council has declared itself a GM-free zone. Many councils already have – if yours hasn't, write to ask why.

A FISHY BUSINESS In 2003, the world's fish farmers and fishing fleets harvested 135.2 million tonnes of seafood for us to eat and more than 200 million people depend on fishing for their livelihood. But our seas are being over-fished – roughly two thirds of the world's major stocks have been fished at or beyond their capacity and another 10% have been harvested so heavily that fish populations will take years to recover. You can help address the problem by eating lower on the seafood chain – clams and squid rather than salmon – and looking out for Marine Stewardship Council (MSC) labelled produce that ensures it has been caught or farmed sustainably. Find more tips and advice at **www.msc.org**.

SUPPORT FARMERS In 1991, the farm gate price for a kilo of potatoes was nine pence and the retail price 30 pence – a mark-up of 233%. In 2000, the farm gate price was still nine pence a kilo, but the retail price was 47 pence – an increase in the mark-up to 425%. Farmers can do little against the global profiteering of supermarkets – if they don't like the terms the supermarkets offer, the multinationals will simply source elsewhere. Farmers are forced to accept crippling farm gate prices or go out of business, and they are also frequently made to supply supermarkets without the security of contracts, to pay for food wasted in-store, packaging, in-store promotions and buyers' expenses. As a result, agriculture in the UK is in crisis. We are losing 11 farmers every day, largely because on average farmers earn £11,000 a year – compare that with Tesco's chief executive who was paid £4.6 million in 2007. Agricultural charities are paying out record amounts to farmers to help them make ends meet. To arrest this decline, support rural farmers and buy from farmers' markets, independent shops and market stalls. You'll be doing yourself a favour, too – according to Sustain, fruit and vegetables are 30% cheaper bought this way. Farmers' markets provide good-quality, locally grown produce, and by cutting out the middle man, prices can be reduced by up to 40%. In just five years, farmers' markets have multiplied – there are over 500 in the UK today. Find a farmers' market or farm shop at **www.farmersmarket.net** or **www.farmshop.uk.com**. You can also find out more about local foods from **www.cpre.org.uk**.

CAMPAIGN FOR MORE RESPONSIBLE SUPERMARKETS

It's been estimated that the opening of a supermarket will result in the loss of 276 jobs in the area and the closure of all village shops within a seven-mile radius. Friends of the Earth is campaigning to hold supermarkets to account for their negative environmental and social impacts. You can also see **www.tescopoly.org** to see what one alliance of organisations is doing to halt the negative impact of supermarkets.

EAT SEASONAL PRODUCE All fruits and vegetables have seasonal lifecycles – vast amounts of land on the other side of the world have been deprived of growing the crops their people need, so that they can produce mangetout for our Sunday roasts and satsumas for our summers. Having given up their land to produce export crops, the farmers are then forced to spend the money they earn growing crops they don't eat, just to buy back the crops they once grew for free. Seasonal fruit and vegetables haven't been hanging around for a few months, they taste fresher, and they save on food miles and pollution. See **www.eattheseasons.co.uk**.

PRESERVE BIODIVERSITY Of all the 7,000 species of plant that are edible, only about 100 are considered essential to feed the global population! And 50% of the world's dietary energy comes from just four crops: rice, maize, wheat and potatoes. We don't help our environment by eating in this limited way. Agricultural biodiversity sustains diverse ecosystems, maintains food security and promotes genetic diversity. But this is all threatened by industrialised agriculture production. Annual seed fairs across Africa help to keep diversity alive, but more can be done to encourage diversity. Buy food that is specific to an area or country. Try to eat a wide variety and if you are growing food, plant a wide variety of seeds, too. Also look out for rare types of food, such as purple carrots, and buy produce local to you. See Practical Action at **www.itdg.org/html/advocacy/web_of_life.htm** for more details. Or the Henry Doubleday Research Association runs a scheme to 'Adopt a vegetable' to help sustain its Heritage Seed Library – find out more at **www.gardenorganic.org.uk.**

AVOID CHOCOLATES WITH LINDANE RESIDUES Lindane is a dangerous pesticide that was banned for use in the UK in 2002. In the same year, an eight-year-old girl died after swallowing a tiny amount of lindane in ant powder. Lindane is extremely hazardous to those who use it as well as those who are exposed to it – both in the environment and food. But it is still used in Africa, especially in the cocoa industry, and there may be remnants of it in your chocolate bar. Join the Ban Lindane Campaign at **www.pan-uk.org/pestnews/actives/Lindane.htm**.

BEASTLY GENES In a few years' time, we could be eating salmon that has been genetically altered to grow at twice the rate it does normally, or sheep that have had medicine added to their genes. Is this safe? Environmentalists, concerned about whether genetically modified animals may produce poisonous proteins, or the impact on wild animals if GM herds escape, are battling against biotech companies who claim their products are safe, even though there is insufficient research to prove it. Equally concerning are the efforts to clone animals – such as Genesis the cow, cloned from the Dairy champion Zita in the USA.

There are well over 1,000 cloned farm animals in the US and the agri-cloning lobby is eager to sell genetic material from them, which may mean we will be drinking cloned milk in the future. Cloned animals appear to be more susceptible to obesity and diabetes, but a report by the US Food and Drink Administration thinks food matter from them is safe for human consumption. To find out more visit **www.organicconsumers.org/patent/clonedmilk720.cfm**. At a 2007 public consultation by the European Group on Ethics in Science and New Technologies, the Farm Animal Welfare Council spoke on behalf of the majority of British and European public opinion to oppose the use of cloned farm animals and their produce here. We do not currently use cloned farm animals in the UK, but must carry on campaigning to keep it that way. Find out more from **www.fawc.org.uk**.

AVOID PESTICIDES IN FOOD A government study found that one in three pieces of fruit or vegetables contained pesticides. More than 300 different chemicals have been found in our bodies, but since there has been little research on the effects of such chemicals, we don't know how they will affect us in the long term. Some chemicals known as hormone disrupters can interfere with hormones, while others accumulate within our bodies. In many cases, washing or peeling the fruit or veg won't make a difference. To find out more, including links to a Safer Shopping website, visit **www.wwf.org.uk/chemicals/feature.asp**.

BUY FAIRTRADE CHOCOLATE We spend £700 million extra on chocolate at Christmas. In the last 10 years, the price of cocoa beans has halved, while the price of a bar of chocolate in the UK has increased by two thirds – so it's definitely not the farmers who are making the extra money. The Day Chocolate Company, which makes Divine and Dubble chocolate bars, ensures that cocoa farmers are paid a fair price. In fact, the cocoa bean farmers from Ghana own a one third share of the company. See **www.divinechocolate.com** and **www.dubble.co.uk**.

BUY FAIRTRADE FOOD Next time you shop, look out for the Fairtrade logo. Fairtrade ensures producers in developing countries get fair prices for their goods. In early 2008, Fairtrade Labelling Organisations were working in almost 80 countries, with 632 producer partners from 58 countries and across 21 Fairtrade markets in Europe, North America, Australia, New Zealand, Mexico and Japan. And seven million people – farmers, workers and their families – were benefiting from the system. By buying Fairtrade products you can help more farmers to survive, and not put more dollars in middlemen's pockets. The UK now has the most dynamic Fairtrade market in the world – here you can find the widest range of products, the most diverse range of companies involved and the most active grassroots campaigning network. Find out more at **www.fairtrade.org.uk** or call them on 020 7405 5942.

BUY BETTER BANANAS The banana industry is dominated by five international companies whose operations are so huge they dwarf the export revenues of all the banana-producing countries combined. But few benefits are passed on to the plantation workers. On the contrary, the social and environmental cost of producing bananas is huge, and has brought misery to thousands. Indigenous people have been driven out of their lands to make way for new uncontaminated plantations, workers earn as little as US$1 a day in some countries, unions are banned and unionised labour blacklisted. Worse, thousands of tonnes of toxic pesticides have been poured on the plantations – often sprayed from planes overhead, drenching workers still in the fields. You can read more about it and find Fairtrade bananas at **www.bananalink.org.uk**.

GO WITHOUT MEAT FOR A WEEK Meat production consumes vast amounts of resources – 10,000 litres of water are needed just to produce 1kg of beef, compared with only 500 litres of water needed to produce 1kg of potatoes. The less meat we as a population eat, the better the conditions under which the animals are reared will become. Go without meat for a week and see how many other options there are. To make sure everything you eat is meat-free, look for the Vegetarian Society logo, which guarantees food is free of animal products and genetically modified organisms – visit **www.vegsoc.org**. Or look out for Vegan Society logo products – see **www.vegansociety.com**.

ACHIEVE REAL CHANGE FOR ANIMALS Did you know that a battery hen often has no more space to stand on than the size of an A4 sheet of paper? Or that a broiler chicken's muscles grow faster than its skeleton, making it difficult to walk? Or that dairy cows are normally forced to give birth every year to keep them producing milk? Or that pigs are kept in such crowded conditions they often can't turn around? Support Compassion in World Farming. Visit **www.ciwf.org.uk** to find out more. And look for the Freedom Food scheme, set up by the RSPCA to ensure welfare standards are followed – see **www.rspca.org.uk**.

'BEGGARS CAN'T BE CHOOSERS...' – according to one US official approached over the policy of linking GM food aid with assistance for famine and HIV-inflicted countries in Africa. Many feel that food aid is being used as a marketing tool to force the African continent to accept GM food so that US agribusiness giants can capture new markets. In 2002 Zambia succeeded in rejecting all GM crops, but is still under pressure to take it or starve. In 2007, famine-stricken Darfur was forced to accept GM sorghum grain as food aid, even though Sudan had a bumper harvest that year and GM-free grain could come from them. Get to the root of issues at **www.i-sis.org.uk/GM-freefoodaid.php** and find out about the United Nations World Food Programme at **www.wfp.org**.

Nature's way

ORGANIC FOOD We often read that organic is better, but we often find that it's costlier, too. Is it worth the hassle? The answer is a definite yes. In order to be registered organic, a farmer is allowed to use only seven natural pesticides on a restricted basis. Conventional farms, however, can use as many as 450 registered pesticides, as well as fertilisers. The full health implications of this vast range of chemicals lingering around our food are still being studied, but it is now accepted that neurological disorders, a lowered sperm count and certain cancers are caused by

exposure to pesticides. The World Health Organisation estimates that 20,000 deaths are caused worldwide each year by pesticide exposure. In addition, pesticides damage soil structure and destroy organisms living naturally within. They also disrupt the food chain. Pesticide contamination of drinking water supplies in the UK costs £120 million annually. For more information on pesticides visit www.pan-uk.org. And for details on how organically grown food benefits the environment and you, visit www.gardenorganic.org.uk and www.organicfood.co.uk. Organic producers can observe guidelines at www.soilassociation.org and www.organicfarmers.uk.com.

CHOOSE ONE ORGANIC PRODUCT TO BUY REGULARLY

The more people demand organic products, the more farmers will decide to produce organic food and the cheaper they will become. Choose to buy one organic product, such as milk, bread, eggs or chicken, regularly. It's a good way of getting into the organic shopping routine.

LOOK AT THE LABELS Although many shops, stores and supermarkets have organic sections for fruit and veg, other products, such as organic baked beans, may not be so easy to find. Look for the UK Register of Organic Food Standards (UKROFS) UK1 certification, which sets the basic standards to which the various organic bodies and producers have to adhere. The Soil Association Certification (SA Cert) code UK5 means the product has met the more exacting standards of the Soil Association, which certifies 70% of UK organic food. For information on the many types of food labelling see **www.soilassociation.org.uk** or **www.aboutorganics.co.uk/organic_information/organic_labelling.htm**. Check products' origins, too – if the item you want has been transported from the other side of the world and local alternatives exist, put it back and buy local. You can pinpoint suppliers near you at **www.bigbarn.co.uk**.

DON'T JUST EAT ORGANIC, DRINK ORGANIC! The alcoholic drinks industry uses as many pesticides as the food industry. Hops, for example, are sprayed 12-14 times a year with an average of 15 different pesticides. The sprays are intended to minimise weed growth in hop fields, but they also kill off the wildlife living within them. Vinceremos Wines and Spirits (**www.vinceremos.co.uk**, 0800 107 3086) delivers organic drinks countrywide, including beer, cider and soft drinks, as do several online organic food companies.

JOIN A BOX SCHEME Box schemes and organic delivery companies save you the effort of searching out organic products – they deliver fresh local vegetables straight to your door. Box schemes source most of their produce from local farmers and consequently invest more into the local economy than supermarkets. There are over 550 box schemes in the UK, with organic produce sales from them doubling to 440,000 in 2008. To join one, visit **www.freerangereview.com** and type in your postcode. You can then choose to find various local food suppliers, including veg box, veg and meat box, and meat box schemes.

TOP TIP – THE SOIL ASSOCIATION

REDUCE THE TRIP OF YOUR SUNDAY LUNCH

The food in a typical Sunday lunch could have been transported 49,000 miles – equivalent to twice around the world – releasing 37kg of carbon dioxide. You can reduce food miles by buying local produce. To find out about your nearest box scheme, farmers' market, local farm shop or independent shop, visit the Organic Directory online at their website **www.whyorganic.org/involved_organicDirectory.asp** or order the book. Find out more at **www.soilassociation.org** (0117 314 5000).

SAY NO TO FOWL DINNERS Top chef Jamie Oliver launched a campaign in 2008 to raise awareness about the 95% of meat chickens and 63% of egg-laying hens that are still intensively farmed in this country. His show *Jamie's Fowl Dinners* highlighted the welfare implications for the birds as a result of our persistent demand for cheap food. The programme pulled in a massive 3.8 million viewers, illustrating that people are interested in making a difference. Jamie's top tips to help pull the poultry and egg industry into line include: try to buy the best welfare bird you can afford – preferably British-farmed and organic; look out for the RSPCA's Freedom Food logo; buy a whole bird and make several meals; choose free range and organic eggs. See **www.jamieoliver.com/jamiesfowldinners** for more tips.

SAVE SEEDS WITH GREENPEACE Proposed amendments to the EU's Seed Directives would allow GM contamination of seeds by thresholds of 0.3-0.7% without labelling them as genetically modified. But Greenpeace and other organisations feel that any detectable GM contamination is unacceptable, and are arguing for 'zero tolerance'. Support this campaign by logging on to **www.saveourseeds.org** and signing the online petition.

READER TIP – STEVE MCGRAIL

FOOD FROM THE WILD

Create the world's shortest food chain by eating what grows in hedgerows, on trees or in the ground. Consult the excellent books *Wild Food* by Roger Phillips, *Food for Free* by Richard Mabey or *Wild Food for Free* by Jonathan Hilton, all from **www.amazon.co.uk**. Remember to follow their advice on safety carefully, to avoid eating anything not good for you.

Hints for the hob

GREENER COOKING **Life used to revolve around the kitchen. Now we often rush in, pop a pre-prepared meal in the microwave, wolf it down and then hurry off to the rest of the day's activities. Taking the time out to cook not only creates a peaceful and relaxing interlude in the day, which you can share with other people, but it also means you can eat better, too. It enables you to select ingredients, which are locally produced where possible, and which you know haven't been processed.**

READER TIP – LAURA PEARCE

GET SOME EXERCISE

Use manual implements in the kitchen instead of electric – the majority don't save time as they are usually so awkward to clean and require ridiculous amounts of cleaning materials. You'll also get a free workout and save on electricity, too!

PLAN YOUR MEALS AND SAVE When you cook, plan ahead so everything is in the oven at the same time. Where possible, cook things in the oven rather than over the hob; oven cooking is more efficient because the heat stays in the oven. And if you can, avoid opening the door to take a sneaky peek. Every time you do, the blast of cold air from the kitchen can cause the temperature in the oven to drop by as much as 24°C. Then the cooker needs to use more energy to bring the oven back to its original temperature. Instead, be satisfied and look through the door.

BUY A PRESSURE COOKER OR A SLOW COOKER Improve energy efficiency by investing in a pressure cooker. They're not just easier to use, they can decrease cooking times by a third. Pressure cookers can be used for meats, beans, fruits and vegetables, and they have greater vitamin preservation than ordinary cooking, which makes them a great choice for today's healthier lifestyle. A slow cooker uses little more electricity than a light bulb – and makes delicious slow-cooked energy-efficient meals. Get one from **www.tefal.co.uk**.

READER TIP – GAVIN BUTTERWORTH

CONSERVE WATER WHEN YOU COOK

When cooking vegetables or pasta on the hob, don't overfill the pan with water and always use a pan with a lid. This way, the water doesn't vapourise into steam and it cooks more efficiently, heating the whole pan rather than just the bottom – so you use less energy. If you're boiling meat or vegetables, don't throw the water out – use it to flavour soups, gravies and jus. Alternatively, steam vegetables – you'll use less water, and conserve vitamins. Find recipes on **www.vegbox-recipes.co.uk**.

TAKE YOUR TIME! The SlowFood campaign started in Italy and spread all over the world, and now has 80,000 members in 90 different countries. SlowFood is a movement that tries to bring the pleasure back to eating by taking your time. That doesn't just include the time involved in cooking and eating the food, but also in growing and preparing it – giving the control over what we eat back to us! And with slowness comes diversity. Mass production means we have less choice. For instance, in Italy in 1900, there were 200 species of artichoke, but now there are only a dozen. For more information on global SlowFood initiatives visit **www.slowfood.com**. There's also a UK-based group at **www.slowfood.org.uk**.

READER TIPS – ANDREW FISHER

RELEASE THE HEAT

When you've finished using the oven in the wintertime and turned it off, leave the oven door open to allow the remaining warmth into the room. This saves having to switch on the central heating for some time, as the extra heat keeps the room nice and warm.

STEAM AND SAVE

If you're boiling pasta or rice, and you want to steam some veg, remove the saucepan lid, place your vegetables in a colander on top of the saucepan, and put the saucepan lid back over the vegetables. This works just like a steamer, but saves plugging in an extra electric gadget.

PEEL BEFORE YOU COOK Friends of the Earth estimates that half of all UK fruit and vegetables sold contain pesticide residues, some of which can accumulate in our bodies and harm our hormone systems. Recent studies have revealed that pesticides found in unpeeled potatoes can exceed the safety level for toddlers by a staggering 21 times! So when you're preparing fruit and vegetables for children, make sure you peel them first.

ORGANIC ADVICE To encourage your kids to eat organic food, **www.organics.org** has recipes and a Kids' Club. If you're searching for gluten-free products and recipes, visit **www.dovesfarm.co.uk**. Alternatively, to learn more about organic food in general, visit **www.greencuisine.org** where you'll find details of organic cooking courses on the Welsh borders.

Fine dining

EATING OUT There's little more frustrating than having to compromise your organic standards when you eat out. You can search for organic restaurants and pubs in your area by visiting www.alotoforganics.co.uk or www.aboutorganics.co.uk (01789 491610). The Organic Directory also has details of organic restaurants throughout the country; visit the Organic Directory page at www.whyorganic.org/involved_organicDirectory.asp.

CHOOSE COD AND TUNA CAREFULLY Since 1972, there has been a seven-fold increase in tuna catches in the South Pacific and, since the price of tuna is so high, a dramatic increase in the incidence of illegal fishing. Bluefin tuna is now listed on the WWF Endangered Seas Campaigns needing immediate action to avoid extinction. Cut down on your tuna consumption, especially in Japanese sushi bars, where raw bluefin is a speciality. And it's not just tuna that's under threat. Cod and chips could be off the menu, too, unless cod consumption is restricted. Scientists and conservationists say that for cod populations to recover, juvenile cod must be allowed to survive long enough to reproduce, and mature fish given the chance to spawn. The International Council for the Exploration of the Sea (ICES) is therefore calling for cod fishing in Kattegat, the Irish Sea and the west of Scotland to be reduced to zero as stocks are at dangerously low levels. Cod levels in the North Sea are showing signs of recovery, but limits must be enforced to ensure it continues. Choose your fish carefully. When you're eating out, ask where the fish is sourced from. If buying fish to cook at home, consult your local fishmonger or see consumer guidelines from MSC at **www.msc.org**.

DOES YOUR RESTAURANT RECYCLE? Britain's pubs, restaurants and hotels use about 350,000 tonnes of glass each year, and 80% of this goes to landfill. Ask if your local café or restaurant recycles its glass and, if not, find out why. If it's because the local collection schemes are inadequate, suggest they lobby the council with other restaurants to set up a better scheme. Visit **www.wasteconnect.co.uk** to find out about the schemes that are currently available.

SUPPORT RESTAURANTS WITH SMALL MENUS The larger the menu, the more likely it is that more food will go to waste each day. This is because the restaurant has to have a greater number of foodstuffs ready for consumption. If choosing between eateries, go for the one with the smaller menu. While you're choosing restaurants, try, too, to eat in an independent restaurant or café. You'll help preserve the individual nature of your community, and support local people. Restaurants such as the celebrated St John Bread and Wine in London cook food that make a delicious virtue of every part of the animals they cook, served up with seasonal and locally sourced vegetables and home-made bread and pastries. Cook up your own similar feast with founder Fergus Henderson's book *Nose to Tail Eating*.

VISIT MCSPOTLIGHT 2003 was a bad year for McDonald's, with dwindling profits and outlets closing, but there have been other setbacks, too. First, scientists declared food high in fat and sugar to be as dangerously addictive as tobacco – paving the way for more obesity lawsuits against the company; then a policeman was hospitalised after glass was found in his burger; a restaurant was shut in Buenos Aires after bacteria was found in food samples – the second time that year; an outlet in Greece was set on fire by anti-capitalist marchers; a man in America claimed he found chewing gum in his salad; and residents have successfully campaigned against having new McDonald's outlets in the UK, the US and Australia. Then to top it all off came the eye-opening fast-food exposé *Supersize Me* in 2004. McDonald's is never far from the battering ram when the subject of healthy eating comes up. You can keep abreast of what's going on at **www.mcspotlight.org**.

Cheers!

BETTER WAYS TO DRINK **While water used to be the only drink available – and still is in most parts of the world – many of us are now substituting it with fizz: flavoured, coloured and in fancy packaging. They may keep our taste buds happy, but not our bodies, the environment or local economies. Two companies control 77% of the soft drinks market: Coca-Cola® and PepsiCo. They have swept their way through the developing world, flooding the market of locally produced drinks and replacing healthier drinks in children's diets. Coke's active ingredient is phosphoric acid, which can dissolve a T-bone steak in two days, or a nail in four. Back in 1969, 54% of babies who were hospitalised for malnourishment in Ndola in Zambia had the diagnosis 'Fantababy' written at the foot of their beds. Their parents had fed them Coke and Fanta believing it to be the best drink for their children – a problem reflected all across the developing world. The chairman of Coca-Cola® is on record as saying: 'The only business we don't want, is the business that does not exist.' Do you want to drink to his health?**

TAP IS TOP! Bottled water isn't better and it costs us and the environment more, too. In 1997, the Food and Agricultural Organisation said that bottled water was not any cleaner or more nutritious than ordinary tap water. Bottled water costs twice as much as petrol, three times as much as milk and 10,000 times as much as tap water. Add to that the 1.5 million tonnes of plastic used every year to make water bottles – each of which could take untold years to biodegrade. And when you think that water companies pay nothing to extract water, while 1.1 billion people are living without adequate water supplies… doesn't it make you want to turn on the tap again? See the Drinking Water Inspectorate website for more information on tap water quality at **www.dwi.gov.uk/pubs/tap/index.htm**.

NOT WORTH A BEAN In 1992, the global coffee economy was worth US$30 billion – US$8 billion of which went to producers. In 2006, their profits totalled US$80 billion and less than three cents from a $3 cup of coffee goes to the 25 million coffee growers in the world. In fact, the farm gate prices of tea, coffee and cocoa have not risen in real terms for 40 years. Moreover, the international prices of these products are so low that frequently they fall below the cost of producing them, forcing farmers into a spiral of debt and destitution. At the same time, coffee companies make huge profits – in 2006 Starbucks made profits of US$117.3 million. Buying Fairtrade coffee, tea and cocoa will ensure that the producers are paid a living wage. In 2006, Fairtrade schemes accounted for about 4% of the instant coffee market and 18% of the roast and ground coffee market, although there are now more than 300 brands on the high street. For more information, visit the Fairtrade Foundation **www.fairtrade.org.uk** or **www.cafedirect.co.uk**. Cafédirect works with 39 grower organisations across 13 developing countries, encompassing 264,666 farmers and directly improving the lives of more than 1.4 million people.

MAKE YOUR OWN Squeeze your own fruit juices and invent flavours never experienced before. Make your own lemonade, for example. By using locally grown, organic fruits you can make a drink that's cheaper, healthier and much, much tastier than any you can buy.

RIP UP THE PLASTIC RING HOLDERS FROM BEER CANS
If these rings get into the sea or other ecosystems they pose a real danger to wildlife. Animals can get their heads caught in the near-invisible rings, and they either choke or starve to death. Small birds can get their wings trapped, and larger aquatic birds can catch the rings around their bills when they dive for food. So, get ripping and do your bit for wildlife.

CHOOSE WINES WITH NATURAL CORKS Between 5% and 8% of wine becomes corked when sealed with a traditional cork stopper and the wine industry has increasingly turned towards plastic corks in an effort to improve quality. But the move away from traditional corks is having devastating effects on the unique habitat of the oak cork woodlands in Spain and Portugal. Falling demand has meant forest owners are increasingly turning to more profitable, but less environmentally friendly methods of agriculture, and the wildlife is suffering. The forests are home to the critically endangered Iberian lynx – in 2004 an estimated 100 remained in the wild, of which only 30 were breeding females. Visit **www.soslynx.org**. For centuries, cork stoppers have been an effective, environmentally friendly method of corking wine – why change to plastic with its associated health and disposal problems?

SUPPORT LOCAL BREWERIES AND PUBS In the UK we consume an average 95 litres of beer per person per year, but 83% of it comes from just four multinational brewing companies. The ingredients in a locally produced beer might travel a total distance of 600 miles during production, but beer from a large brewery can be transported as many as 24,000 miles, belching out CO_2 all along the way. In addition, small breweries suffer from having to pay the same level of duty on alcohol as large ones, so their production costs are higher, making it harder for them to survive. In Germany, a Progressive Beer Duty system to help smaller breweries has been operating for a number of years, and in the UK the Society of Independent Brewers is trying to impose a similar duty. For more information see **www.siba.co.uk**. The Campaign for Real Ale also has details on supporting small breweries in order to stimulate local economies. Visit **www.camra.org.uk** or call 01727 867201 for more information.

TOP TIP – ADNAMS

BUY BEER FROM AN ENERGY-EFFICIENT BREWERY

Breweries don't need to waste so much energy producing beer. Some breweries, like Adnams, are installing energy-efficient equipment to recycle waste steam to heat the next brew and building energy-saving distribution centres with grass roofs, lime, chalk and hemp building blocks and solar panels. For more information, visit **www.beerfromthecoast.co.uk** or call 01502 727200.

borneo-travel.com
Giant Tapang Trees,
Metre wide Rafflesia,
wild orchids and carnivorous pitcher plants.
Primary jungle, hideaway islands,
world class diving and surfing.
Elephants and Orangutans.
Locally owned, sustainable tourism from our
offices in Borneo and Sumatra
01492 650 225
ATOL T7156

Volunteers needed on
conservation expeditions
All training provided, including dive
or language training where necessary.
Tanzania
Ecuador
Call 020 7470 8888
for a brochure or email info@greenforce.org
Borneo
Fiji
Bahamas
www.greenforce.org
GREENFORCE
GLOBAL CONSERVATION EXPEDITIONS

exodus

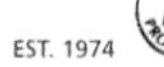

ATOL
PROTECTED

Responsible travel

Tourism represents about 6% of the world economy and 35% of the world's exports of services, rising to over 70% in Least Developed Countries. In 2006, almost 846 million people travelled worldwide, and according to the World Tourism Organisation (UNWTO) this is expected to reach nearly 1.6 billion by the year 2020. With CO_2 emissions, airport expansion issues, archaeological damage and threats to world ecology in the news, critics might argue that the only green traveller is the one that stays at home. However, the industry provides income, jobs and foreign exchange to countries and communities that badly need them, and can make a difference in other areas, too. Many developing countries, for example, can't afford the luxury of conservation funding. Without tourists – and the money they bring – many national parks would probably cease to exist. So get out there and travel – but travel thoughtfully. Think about where you go, and what you do when you get there. Plenty of organisations can offer you help and advice – **www.responsibletravel.com** provides holidays that give the world a break; and the charities Tourism Concern (**www.tourismconcern.org.uk**, 020 7133 3330) and Tearfund (**www.tearfund.org**) give up-to-date information.

Do not disturb

HOTELS THAT DON'T HARM THE PLANET It is estimated that five million people worldwide opt for all-inclusive holidays each year. In some destinations, such as the Bahamas, all-inclusive holidays account for up to 80% of UK bookings, and the sector is growing at a rate of 22% per year. But tourists in these resorts spend very little money outside the resorts, making them exclusive, rather than inclusive, for the local economy. Such resorts also swallow up large areas of land, often in the most beautiful parts of the country, restricting access for local people. So think before you book – your holiday should benefit you, but it's best if it benefits local people and the environment at the same time.

ALWAYS THINK LOCAL Of each US$100 spent on a holiday in a developing country by a tourist, only around US$5 actually stays in the country's economy. This 'leakage' may be as high as 80% in the Caribbean, with money spent by tourists leaving the countries via tour operators, airlines, hotels and imported food and drink. Always use local tour operators, stay in locally run hotels and only buy locally produced goods. The *Special Places to Stay* series by Alastair Sawdays provides local travel choices across Britain and Europe at **www.sawdays.co.uk** (01275 395430). Also see VisitBritain at **www.visitbritain.co.uk** for destination ideas, events and accommodation. For holidays further afield visit Conservation Corporation Africa at **www.ccafrica.com**.

NO CHANGE Most hotel guests are willing to use their sheets and towels for more than one day. The largest chunk of a hotel's energy use – 42% – is for heating water, and much of this goes on laundry. If each room had a sign for guests to leave out for the chambermaid requesting that they don't change sheets or towels, it's estimated hotels would reduce their energy use by at least 5%. If the hotel you're staying in doesn't have a 'no change' policy, try writing your own no change note.

DON'T USE THE FREEBIE MINIS Mini they might be, but the impact on the environment is far from small. The production of mini bottles and containers causes significant waste of resources and energy. Hotels could save on thousands of bags of waste each year by using refillable dispensers for shampoo and skincare lotions, and by recycling soaps – consider suggesting this to hotels you stay in.

LOOK OUT FOR THE GREEN GLOBE SIGN The Green Globe Programme is the travel and tourism industry's only global environmental programme. Initiated by the World Travel and Tourism Council, it is based on Agenda 21 and principles for sustainable development agreed at the Rio Earth Summit in 1992. It now offers four standards of accreditation. The programme gives certification to hotels, airlines and travel agents that meet standards for the responsible and sustainable development of world tourism. For more on Green Globe and members in over 100 countries, see **www.ec3global.com**.

TOP TIP – WWW.RESPONSIBLETRAVEL.COM

CHOOSE YOUR TOUR COMPANY CAREFULLY

Ask your tour company or hotel for their written policies with regard to the environment and local people. If they don't have one, ask them why not. For some of the world's best responsible and eco-tourism holidays from tour companies and hotels with responsible travel policies, visit **www.responsibletravel.com**.

TAKE AN ORGANIC HOLIDAY Both in the UK and abroad, there are an increasing number of organic hotels, guesthouses and B&Bs, which provide organic venues for catered and self-catered holidays or short breaks. With their organic lifestyle standards, not only would you be eating healthier, but you would also be supporting the local areas' businesses and economy. For more ideas, and a list of organic holiday destinations in Britain and worldwide, visit **www.organicholidays.co.uk** or call 01943 871468. For information on holidays and accommodation in the UK, Italy, France, Spain and Bulgaria try About Organics at **www.aboutorganics.co.uk/organic_holidays/organic_holidays.htm**.

HOSTEL IT! Hostelling has moved on – it's no longer just about dormitories and Boy Scouts. Today, many hostels are not unlike budget hotels, where the only significant difference is the price. For the biggest hostel database on the internet, visit **www.hostels.com**. As well as offering online booking, the site gives in-depth advice on what makes a good hostel. Also see **www.carbonneutraltourism.co.uk/category/hostel**.

SAVE WATER Conserve water when you're in areas with limited supply. When abroad, the average tourist can use over 800 litres of water in 24 hours. That's more than a villager in the Developing World would use in 100 days. Encourage hotels to become water efficient by harvesting rainwater, fixing leaks and switching to low-flow showerheads, sink aerators and toilets. Installing inexpensive tank-fill diverters in older toilets can save four litres of water on each flush. British tour operators, take note!

Broaden the mind

TIPS FOR THE ECO-TRAVELLER 'Tourism' is derived from the Hebrew word *Tora*, meaning 'to study'. Travelling shouldn't just take us to see new horizons, but should also expand them. Do a bit of background reading on the places you plan to visit, and always remember that your holiday destination – no matter how remote – is someone else's home.

USE SMALL, LOCATION-SPECIFIC TOUR OPERATORS Around 80% of British package holidays are booked through the big tour operators. With a tendency to undercut prices and use mass-purchased, imported goods, they may destroy the livelihood of local hotel owners and tour operators. Instead, use small, location-specific travel operators that either serve a specific market or cater to a specific interest group or activity. Visit **www.responsibletravel.com** for a comprehensive list of eco-aware operators.

OFFSET YOUR CARBON Each year, aviation produces nearly as much CO_2 as is produced by all human activities in Africa. One long-haul return flight can produce more CO_2 per passenger than the average UK motorist produces in a year. As a result, scientists have predicted that, by 2015, over half the annual destruction of the ozone layer will be caused by air travel. Now you have the choice to pay a voluntary tax at airports and with airlines you book through in the UK. This helps fund tree-planting programmes and other offsetting schemes that soak up carbon emissions pumped out from planes. For more details on how to become carbon neutral, visit **www.carbonneutral.com**. Or offset emissions and get great travel ideas from *Wanderlust* magazine at **www.wanderlust.co.uk**.

READER TIP – LOUISA RADICE

TAKE THE TRAIN

Over distances of less than 500km, air travel generates around three times more CO_2 per passenger than rail. For alternatives to air travel, check out **www.seat61.com** for information on how to travel to destinations in Europe, Africa, Asia and America by train and boat. It's also now even easier to travel by train with the expanded Eurostar (**www.eurostar.com**).

CALCULATE THE REAL COST For more information on aircraft emissions, and to work out the greenhouse warming effect of any flight, visit **www.carbonneutral.com/cncalculators/flightcalculator.asp**.

WALK, BIKE OR TAKE THE BUS When you travel, try to use public transport whenever possible – or, better still, walk or hire a bike. You'll see your destination in a completely different light.

LEAVE NATURE WHERE IT IS Natural souvenirs made of wood, coral, shell or ivory can be tarnished with environmental damage. Plant and tree life is also under threat from the souvenir trade. Between 2006 and 2007 customs confiscated more than 163,000 illegal wildlife trade items – many made from highly endangered species of animal or plant. So buy your souvenirs with a critical eye! Get details from WWF at **www.wwf.org.uk/news/n_0000004243.asp**.

DIVE RESPONSIBLY Coral reefs are the foundation of marine life and possess extremely high levels of biodiversity. For example, the Great Barrier Reef in Australia is home to more than 400 species of coral, 1,500 species of fish, 4,000 types of mollusc and 200 species of birdlife. Yet all over the world reefs are dead or dying. Already, 10% have been lost, and it is estimated that 70% of all corals will disappear by 2040 unless they are properly protected. When you go on diving holidays, you can reduce the tourist pressures on reefs by following a diving code of practice. This includes not touching the corals or sea life, not removing anything you didn't bring with you, being careful not to brush against the reefs and watching where you kick with your fins. For more information, visit **www.responsibletravel.com**. Also, consider booking an eco-friendly diving holiday, such as those run by Baobab Travel (**www.baobabtravel.com**, 0121 314 6011).

TOP TIP – TOURISM CONCERN

STOP CHILD SEX TOURISM

Large numbers of children from countries such as China, Cambodia and Burma are being forced to work as prostitutes in China. More than a million children aged 7-17 enter the sex trade each year, and many end up in brothels frequented by sex tourists. You can help by not turning a blind eye – if you see anything suspicious when abroad, tell your hotel or guesthouse manager immediately. For more information on the fight against sex tourism, contact End Child Prostitution, Child Pornography and the Trafficking of Children for Sexual Purposes at **www.ecpat.org.uk** (020 7233 9887) or Tourism Concern at **www.tourismconcern.org.uk**.

SPEND CULTURALLY Local and traditional values are being subsumed by globalisation. When travelling abroad, be sure to eat in local restaurants and buy local produce. You'll support not only the regional economy and culture, but also provide counterweight to the growing influence of the multinationals like Starbucks or McDonald's. You will also get to experience local cultural lifestyles and escape from sometimes crowded tourist areas.

TOP TIP – TOURISM CONCERN
RESPECT THE LOCAL CULTURES

When you travel, give consideration to the fact that you're often going into a culture completely different from your own. If you think carefully about what is appropriate in terms of the clothes you wear and the way you behave, then you'll be more welcomed and respected by the local people. Drug and alcohol laws can vary in different countries, and the effects of travellers taking drugs can be dramatic. For example, if travellers take drugs when visiting the hill tribes of Thailand, it encourages the local people to start selling drugs and then become addicted themselves. This is especially true of the younger people, who are keen to emulate Western tourists. The result can devastate local communities, so think before you act. For more information, contact Tourism Concern at **www.tourismconcern.org.uk** (020 7133 3330).

TOP TIP – WWW.RESPONSIBLETRAVEL.COM
USE LOCAL GUIDES

You will get an amazing insight into local cultures and places, and they will get an income. Agree a fair price *before* you set off, and remember that, in developing countries, what is a little to you might help feed or educate their families.

'TAKE ONLY PHOTOGRAPHS, LEAVE ONLY FOOTPRINTS'

As a tourist, you are directly responsible for the environment in the places that you visit. So, if you notice environmental damage, be sure to report it to local tour operators, and if you booked through an operator in the UK, tell them on your return. Ethical tourism organisations publish their own Travellers' Codes of Conduct for you to follow. Familiarise yourself with them, and try to follow them wherever you go.

TRAVEL TO WORK Want a working holiday? The National Trust organises them and has many other volunteer positions on offer. For more information, visit **www.nationaltrust.org.uk/volunteering**.
And if you want a real cultural experience, consider taking a course in

Teaching English as a Foreign Language (TEFL). With opportunities to teach in places such as Indonesia, China and Turkey, you can really get to know the place and the people. Courses are easily organised through the TEFL website **www.tefl.com**, The British Council at **www.britishcouncil.org/learning-elt-teach-english.htm** and volunteer companies such as **www.i-to-i.com**.

EXCHANGE IT Exchange programmes involve staying with a family in your chosen country, while someone from the exchange family comes to live with yours. Under the ERASMUS scheme, undergraduates from the UK can study in another EU state for three to 12 months, giving them the opportunity to learn a new language, experience a new culture and gain a new perspective on their study course. Have a look at **www.studystay.com/htm/Courses/Exchange_programs.htm** and **www.erasmus.ac.uk** for more information.

PORTERS' RIGHTS When enjoying your adventure holidays abroad, don't neglect the importance of fair trade in tourism. Porters are an essential part of trekking in the Himalayas, Peru and Pakistan, but their working conditions are often appalling. Nepalese porters suffer four times as many accidents and illnesses as Western trekkers, and in the UK the majority of operators are not addressing the issues of porters' rights. They are not superhuman, and cannot carry heavy loads improperly dressed and shod. So, if you're going on holiday, check that your tour operator has policies on porters. Find out more at **www.tourismconcern.org.uk/index.php?page=trekking-wrongs**.

MALARIA CONTROL When you travel to malarial areas, don't rely solely on insect repellent. Use it in combination with other less environmentally harmful methods to gain better overall protection. Cover up in the morning and evenings when mosquitoes bite, and wear dark clothes. Sleep under a mosquito net during the night, and if you're roughing it, make sure you aren't sleeping near stagnant water or banana trees, where mosquitoes like to breed. Get natural insect repellent plus more tips and advice from **www.alfresco.uk.com**.

TOP TIP – TOURISM CONCERN
MINIMISE YOUR ENVIRONMENTAL IMPACT

When you're abroad, give extra thought to what happens to your rubbish. Try to take biodegradable products and a water filter bottle with you when you go out. Some places can often have limited water, fuel and electricity resources, so be sensitive and restrict your use of these. Protect the local wildlife and habitats by respecting local rules and codes of conduct, such as keeping to footpaths, not touching coral and not buying products made from endangered species. By following these simple rules, you can reduce your ecological footprint and your negative impact on the areas you visit. For more information, contact Tourism Concern at **www.tourismconcern.org.uk** (020 7133 3330).

TOP TIP – BTCV
TAKE A CONSERVATION BREAK

Try a holiday with a difference and have the experience of a lifetime! By taking part in practical hands-on conservation projects either in the UK or around the world, you can do your bit to contribute to a sustainable future. You can also benefit from some stunning scenery, a sense of achievement and a new bunch of friends! BTCV organises holidays from taster conservation weekends in rugged North Yorkshire to six-week bird census and beach survey holidays in the Caribbean. Visit **www.btcv.org** or contact customer services on 01302 388 883.

BE DOLPHIN AND WHALE FRIENDLY Swimming with dolphins is increasing in popularity as a growing number of people want to get close to these beautiful and fascinating animals. Sadly, many dolphins suffer an impoverished and often dramatically shortened existence in captivity and many have been captured from the wild in traumatic and sometimes lethal hunts. Once confined, they are forced to live a life of severe deprivation, suffering lower life expectancy and higher infant mortality than in the wild. Help the Whale and Dolphin Conservation Society (WDCS) campaign for tougher regulations by choosing to see whales and dolphins with a responsible tour operator in the wild. See **www.wdcs.org.uk**.

A wheel effect

With global warming currently the greatest environmental threat, our streets gridlocked, choking pollution and road traffic predicted to increase by up to 50% in 2025, there has never been more reason to abandon your car and walk. Road transport is currently the third-largest source of carbon dioxide emissions in the UK – after industry and domestic use – which is directly contributing to the Earth's increasing temperature. And as if global warming was not enough reason to leave the car in the garage, up to a fifth of all lung cancer deaths in cities are caused by tiny particles of pollution; the majority of which are from vehicle exhausts. The convenience of car travel also means that the population is increasingly suffering from health issues. A 10% increase in the number of people walking regularly would lead to a 4% reduction in the numbers of people with heart disease, saving the NHS £200 million a year. We need to work with the government to try and meet the target of a 60% reduction in emissions by 2050. Plus this may rise to 80% – an incentive to work even harder.

Reversing the trend

CARS AND THE PLANET Current studies show that 71% of road trips by motor car are under five miles and 46% are less than two miles. So, the best thing you can do for the environment – and for yourself – is to leave those car keys at home. However, if you do need to get into your car, there are all sorts of ways to make that journey less damaging.

TAKE PUBLIC TRANSPORT Traffic delays cost the country around £15 billion each year. One litre of fuel can carry a person four miles in a large car, five and a half miles in a small car, 31 miles in a bus with 40 passengers and 34 miles in a train with 300 passengers. A double-decker bus can carry the same number of people as 20 full cars, yet takes up just one seventh of the road space.

TOP TIP – WORLD CARFREE NETWORK
WORLD CAR FREE DAY

Sacrifice your car each 22 September for the European National and World Car Free Day – you might just be surprised at how easy it can be! In 2007, the Car Free Day attracted over 1,500 participating cities and 40 countries across the world, some of whom closed town centre streets to cars and lorries, and opened them up for people to enjoy walking, cycling and dancing. Visit **www.eta.co.uk**, **www.22september.org** and **www.worldcarfree.net/wcfd** for further information on alternative eco-friendly transport solutions.

JOIN A CAR-SHARING POOL Every day, more than 10 million empty car seats clog the roads, with one-person car trips accounting for 60% of all journeys. If just half of all UK motorists received a lift one day a week, congestion and pollution would be reduced by 10% and traffic jams by 20%. Also, the air quality is often poorer inside the car than out, especially in heavy traffic, and car users regularly suffer up to three times as much pollution than pedestrians. Lift-sharing also contributes to social inclusion, helping many socially excluded people access facilities such as healthcare, shops or social activities. Visit **www.carplus.org.uk** (0113 234 9299) and **www.liftshare.org**.

CHOOSE A LOW-IMPACT VEHICLE In a journey of 6,000 miles, the average car produces its own weight in carbon dioxide emissions. And it's not just CO_2 that's the problem – other exhaust emissions, oil and noise also create pollution. You can help by buying a car which has the fewest environmental impacts and is the most fuel-efficient. For a guide to cars, contact the Environmental Transport Association (**www.eta.co.uk** or call 0845 389 1010), and visit **www.vcacarfueldata.org.uk** to help you find out your car's pollution emission and help you to choose a better car in the future.

GET A LIFT If you're heading off on a long journey with space in your car, offer that space to someone who needs it. Freewheelers links drivers and passengers to share the cost of travel. It saves you money, helps other people and reduces pollution. Visit **www.freewheelers.com** to search an online database of people offering or requiring lifts. Hook up with people travelling to work, festivals, gigs and sporting events.

CHOOSE YOUR FUEL WISELY Air pollution as a result of traffic fumes is a serious problem in Britain. Three times as many people in Europe die from the health-damaging effects of vehicle emissions as die in road accidents. Although leaded petrol has now been banned, exhaust fumes still contain carbon monoxide, nitrous oxides, benzene and particulates – minute particles of matter – that can negatively impact on human health. Benzene, which accounts for 5% of the output of a car, is a known cause of leukaemia, while nitrous oxides are respiratory tract irritants that can cause emphysema. You can help by buying ultra-low sulphur petrol where possible, which produces 45% less nitrogen oxide and is lower in benzene. Finally, join *Ethical Consumer* magazine and Greenpeace's campaign to boycott Esso. Esso is the oil company most strongly involved in the Bush administration's anti-environmental policies, and the StopEsso boycott aims to stop the company through consumer action. Visit **www.greenpeace.org.uk/climate/stop-esso**.

FIT A FUEL SAVER – CUT EMISSIONS BY 40% Simply fitting a fuel-saving device into the fuel line that feeds your car engine can reduce harmful emissions by 40%, saving you at least 10% on fuel costs. Devices can be easily fitted to any hydro-carbon-fuelled vehicles or energy-efficient cars, and will last for ever. They can even be transferred from vehicle to vehicle, so there are no excuses! For information on fuel savers, visit **www.powerplus.be** or **www.fuelsaver.co.uk**. And more good news – the less your car pollutes, the less car tax you pay. From April 2010 there will be a new first-year tax rate based on carbon dioxide emissions of the car. Cars that emit less than the proposed 130g/km European standard of CO_2 emissions will pay no car tax at all in the first year. But a higher first-year rate will be introduced on the most polluting cars.

MORE HASTE – LESS SPEED Stick to the speed limit! Rapid acceleration and harsh braking leads to greater fuel consumption; smooth driving can use 30% less fuel and makes for a more pleasant journey. Driving at 50mph uses 25% less fuel than 70mph, so improve your efficiency and decrease your speed.

GO ELECTRIC Become a green driver and make your friends green with envy. It costs from £7,000-10,000 to convert a small local runabout and £20,000-35,000 for a car that needs to travel over 100 miles in one journey. Visit the Electric Car Association on **www.avt.uk.com**, or call 01823 480196. Alternatively, hybrid cars (run on petrol and electricity) produce 75% less pollution than standard ultra-low-emission vehicles, and they can be charged in the comfort of your own home! The Environmental Transport Association has a car buyers' guide at **www.eta.co.uk**.

TOP TIP – EVUK

NO LOCAL EMISSIONS – NO GLOBAL EMISSIONS!

Buy an electric vehicle and power it with renewable power. In London, electric cars are exempt from congestion charges. Lobby your local authority to provide charging bays for electric vehicles. Visit the Campaign for Real, Long-Range Electric Vehicles at **www.evuk.co.uk** or find electric cars, trucks and bikes at **www.nicecarcompany.co.uk**.

RECYCLE USED MOTOR OIL Every year, 13,000 tonnes of car oil are improperly discarded, contaminating the country's rivers, lakes and streams, and threatening aquatic life. The toxic metals contained in oil, such as lead, nickel and cadmium, can poison the soil and lead to infertility and poor crop yields. Used oil which has been properly handled can be easily re-refined into lubricants, processed into fuel oils and used as raw materials for the refining and petrochemical industries. Many petrol stations or recycling depots will recover your oil for you. For details on schemes near you contact the Oil Bank at **www.oilbankline.org.uk**. Find out more from the Environment Agency's Oil Care Code campaign at **www.environment-agency.gov.uk**.

TOP TIP – GREENPEACE

DON'T BUY ESSO!

The StopEsso campaign is calling on the public not to buy any Esso products until the company changes its stand on global warming and stops interfering in international negotiations to tackle climate change. Join over one million people in the UK who are boycotting the world's biggest climate villain. StopEsso is a coalition of Greenpeace, Friends of the Earth, and People and Planet. To find out how you can join the boycott, visit **www.stopesso.com**.

DON'T LEAVE IT IDLING! As well as wasting fuel and costing you money, idling also prevents the catalytic converter from working efficiently and removing pollution in the exhaust. Idling also creates noise pollution; you may not be aware of it, but others most certainly will be! If you're going to be parked for more than 30 seconds turn off the engine.

MORE CAR DON'TS...

Don't use the A/C!

Why use the air conditioning? Open the car's air vents instead.

Don't open windows unless you need to!

Opening windows just increases wind resistance and thus efficiency.

Don't buy enormous cars!

Just buy the smallest car that fits your needs.

Don't neglect your car!

Old plugs, leads on their last legs and clogged cleaners are the main culprits for lost gallons with modern fuel-injected systems.

TOP TIP – FORUM FOR THE FUTURE
RUNNING ON JOJOBA

Most people have heard of jojoba in relation to beauty products such as shampoo, moisturisers and massage oil. But now you could be using jojoba to run your car! Recent research has shown that mixing a small amount of methanol with raw jojoba oil produces a mixture with similar properties to diesel. However, the new product is far more environmentally friendly than diesel, as it's lower in carbon and contains no polluting sulphur. Jojoba is just the latest plant oil, following rapeseed, sunflower and soybean oil, to be successfully tested as a diesel alternative. In Britain there are already biofuel producers up and running, such as Green Spirit. Find out about its work at **www.greenspiritfuels.com**, where you can also download a helpful leaflet called *Making Sense of Biofuels*. You can also find Forum for the Future articles on biofuel at **www.greenfutures.org.uk**.

TOP TIP – CPRE
AIRPORT EXPANSION

The government has forecast that air travel could almost triple by 2030 – from 2000's 180 million to 500 million passengers a year. To provide for this level of activity, the government is considering building new airports and expanding current ones. This would result in an increase in noise pollution, air pollution and greenhouse gases, plus land and special sites would be lost, new roads built, rural economies could be hurt and water supply could be put at risk. For example, the new expansion at Heathrow is providing 173% more flights, forcing 3,000 people from their homes, demolishing 700 houses and putting 150,000 more people under a flight path. See **www.stopheathrowexpansion.com** for more information, then write to your MP with your concerns. Find airport expansion publications at **www.cpre.org.uk**.

RUNNING ON COOKING OIL If you're seriously thinking about recycling cooking oil to use to run your car, the Low Impact Living Initiative can give you all the information you need at **www.lowimpact.org/factsheet_biodiesel.htm**. They run weekend courses on producing bio-diesel, from home-made plant to commercial production, including environment agency and VAT issues. Alternatively, you can buy bio-diesel from Ebony Solutions (**www.ebony-solutions.co.uk**), where it is taxed at source and apparently gives off the pleasant odour of French fries!

BEWARE THE DANGERS INSIDE YOUR CAR A little-known fact is that the interior of a car can give off high levels of toxins. For example, interior plastics can leak an ammonia gas that has been linked with foetal abnormalities, and so pregnant women in America are now advised to drive with their car windows open. Textiles and leathers used inside cars can also emit up to 60,000 different allergens, which may have harmful effects on human health. Write to your car manufacturer to ask them what they're doing to assess these risks, and demand they subject all their car components to rigorous testing.

Pedal power

TIPS FOR CYCLISTS Traffic jams getting you down? It's understandable when we spend on average nine days a year in the car. The UK has the worst traffic congestion in Europe, costing the economy £20 billion each year. A whopping 70% of us choose to travel to work by car, each of which cost on average £2,400 a year to run. Bikes outnumber cars in the UK, yet most of them are unused because of the sheer danger and unpleasantness of cycling in traffic, yet in London, cycling is often twice as fast as cars. Cycling is the most environmentally sound means of transport after walking. So, save your money, time and the environment and get on your bike today.

SET CYCLING GOALS Aim to cycle once a week to work or to see your friends. Start with small achievable journeys and gradually increase the distance, as you become more accustomed to it. The British Medical Association believes that cycling for 30 minutes a day can increase your life expectancy and can even give you a fitness level equivalent to a person 10 years younger. Then get even more inspired with *The Cyclist's Companion.*

KIDS – RIDE YOUR BIKE TO SCHOOL Cycling to school is good for the health of your kids and the environment. If you wish to provide an escort, you might cycle to the school with your kids and then ride the rest of the way to work. But make sure that your children are aware of road safety and wear helmets and reflective strips every time.

KIDS – GO ON A FAMILY BIKE RIDE Parents, arrange annual family cycling trips! Challenge your kids to cycle from an early age and improve their confidence through teaching them a lifelong skill. Cycling can also encourage environmental participation from young children to provide further eco-friendly choices later on in life. Studies have found that obesity figures among children have doubled in the last 10 years. Cycling for just 15 minutes can provide the daily moderate activity needed to promote health in children, and it can be fun!

USE YOUR BIKE FOR SHORT JOURNEYS On short journeys, the catalytic converter that helps cut down a car's carbon monoxide emissions does not become effective until you have driven two miles. Road transport is responsible for 70% of all carbon monoxide emissions. Around 71% of all car journeys are less than five miles long and 46% less

less than two miles. Make a difference by using your bike for all journeys under a mile. If a third of short car journeys were made by bike, national heart disease rates would fall by 5-10%. And when you tire of the roads, try something a bit more challenging and start mountain biking! Log on to **www.mbuk.com** and **www.bikeradar.com**, which are both dedicated to mountain biking for professionals and budding enthusiasts.

RECYCLE YOUR BICYCLE Got a new bike? Don't discard your old one – recycle it. Bike Recycling projects can even find a use for bikes destined for the scrap heap! The schemes are usually community run and help provide jobs for people out of work. Look for your nearest project at **www.wasteconnect.co.uk**. Alternatively, donate your bicycle to ReCycle. This charity helps people in developing countries, who use the bikes to cut water collection journey times by up to three hours in places, and helps travel to towns and farms. It has sent 26,000 bikes out so far. Donate your old bike at **www.re-cycle.org**.

GET AN ELECTRIC BIKE Make cycling a more realistic option with an electric bicycle. Electric bikes are the cleanest motorised vehicles on the road and, costing just 1.5p a mile to run, they're the most affordable solution for yourself and for the environment. Visit **www.powabyke.com** or call 01225 443737.

RECLAIM THE STREETS Use Pedal Power! With 27 million cars on the roads of Britain, cyclists, runners, walkers and other road users are being pushed off the roads to make way for even more cars and even more pollution. Critical Mass is an international protest which uses 'pedal power' to encourage people to stand up and reclaim the streets. Often described as an 'unorganised coincidence', Critical Mass happens when a lot of cyclists happen to be in the same place at the same time and decide to cycle the same way together for a while. For information on rides near you and abroad, see **www.urban75.com/Action/critical.html**.

MAKE CYCLING EASIER Join a campaign. Several organisations are pioneering cyclists' rights – contact them and find out how to get involved: Sustrans (**www.sustrans.org.uk**, 0845 113 00 65); CTC – the UK's national cyclists' organisation (**www.ctc.org.uk**, 0870 873 0060); and the London Cycling Campaign (**www.lcc.org.uk**, 020 7234 9310).

Tread carefully

TYRES AND WHAT TO DO WITH THEM How many tyres will you make use of in a lifetime? Whether it's 20 or 200, consider that those tyres will sit in a landfill for around 400 years before beginning to decompose. Forty million scrap tyres are discarded in the UK each year – in Europe it's 200 million. When you return old tyres to the garage, ask if their tyre collectors are members of the Responsible Recycler Scheme. The scheme ensures the members recycle wherever possible, rather than dumping. It's not a small organisation, either – 80% of all tyres are currently recycled in this way, so there's no excuse for your retailer to be dealing with the remaining 20%. For details of this scheme visit www.tyresafety.co.uk/html/responsible.htm and www.tyredisposal.co.uk.

TYRES IN YOUR GARDEN Tyres are made from rubber, oil, sulphur and zinc oxide, which makes them almost obscenely durable. Put this durability to good use in the garden. Use old tyres to grow potatoes; put a potato seed in the centre of the tyre and cover with 1cm of compost. As the plant grows, add soil to just below the tip of the shoot and add more tyres as required. Similarly, tyres can be used to protect newly-planted trees or make a frame for climber plants. You can also use tyres for garden steps, compost heaps, animal feed containers or raised garden platforms. There are countless uses for tyres, just go mad and use your imagination.

TYRED KIDS Kids – make a tyre swing or playground area. Tie them to secure branches or get your parents to set them securely in a sandpit.

PUMP UP YOUR TYRES For every 6psi that a tyre is under-inflated, fuel consumption can rise by 1%. Michelin has produced special energy-saving tyres which it claims are 20% free rolling over a conventional design and can save 6% in fuel use over 12,000 miles – which equals £70 in your pocket. See **www.etyres.co.uk/michelin**.

BUY RETREADED TYRES Retreading is the most environmentally friendly method of dealing with used tyres. Retreading only uses half the amount of energy needed to replace the whole tyre, and doubles the lifespan of car tyres. Truck tyres can be retread twice further and aeroplane tyres seven times. Find out more at **www.retreaders.org.uk**.

ECO-FRIENDLY TYRES As tyres wear, they release polyaromatic hydrocarbons into the atmosphere, which can cause allergies, breathing problems and may be carcinogenic. Several companies are taking steps to remedy this with more eco-friendly ranges. Goodyear's GT3 uses a substance derived from maize starch instead of chemical compounds, and JK Tyres, India's largest domestic producer and exporter, has a coloured eco-friendly radial tyre range. See **www.jktyre.com**.

BUY PRODUCTS MADE FROM RECYCLED TYRES With a total worldwide production of tyres exceeding 800 million per year, there's some hope for tyres after a life on the road. With hundreds of products, including stationery, mouse mats and coasters, there's no need for tyres to end up on the scrap heap. In fact, from 2006, all tyres and landfill tyres were banned from landfill disposal. Find out more at **www.letsrecycle.com/equipment/tyres.jsp**. Recycled rubber from old tyres can also be used in mats, soles and heels of shoes, bike pedals and tips for walking sticks and crutches, and even conveyor belts and inner tubes for bicycles. A by-product of old tyres is granulated rubber powders or crumb, which can be used for sporting or athletic tracks, playground flooring and general road surfaces. Find out more from the Bureau of International Recycling at **www.bir.org/aboutrecycling/tyres.asp** and REUZE at **www.reuze.co.uk/tyres.shtml**.

SAY NO TO TYRE ENERGY PLANTS Tyres have a high calorific value, and are therefore often burnt to provide energy. The fumes emitted are poisonous and can pollute water supplies. Fires can also become impossible to control, devastating the environment further. These plants also give off toxic dioxins, which are recognised carcinogenics, affecting fertility and the immune system, as well as particulates and toxic emissions. Plants such as these are found in cement kilns and should not be used due to the long-term damage they inflict on the environment. Find out more from Friends of the Earth (**www.foe.org.uk**, 020 7490 1555).

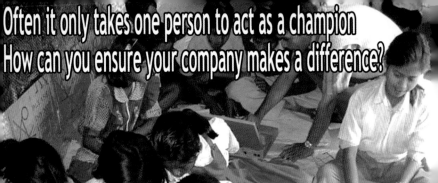

Make it work

Businesses waste resources. Lighting, heating, paper, computers that constantly need updating, refurbishment, office moves… the list of waste-generating activities goes on. But this also means that changing wasteful practices will make a big difference. The government has set a target to reduce greenhouse gas emissions by 60% by 2050 – up to 80% is currently being debated – and increased energy efficiency in homes, businesses, schools and industries was identified as the best way to meet that target. Pioneering businesses have already proved that corporate social responsibility works. Friends Provident was the first company to get virtually all of its electricity from renewable sources at no extra cost to the company or shareholders, helping to reduce energy-related CO_2 emissions by 80%. It has introduced measures to reduce inter-office travel and has a campaign to reduce paper use year on year. Many other companies have followed suit. But no matter where you work, or what kind of business you're in, even one recycling bin will make a difference…

Office efficiency

MAKING YOUR WORK ENVIRONMENT GREENER

For businesses, becoming more energy-efficient and environmentally aware has all sorts of rewards, including financial gain and enhanced reputation. If your company is thinking of relocating or doing building work to its current structure, just stop and think about the materials that'll be used, the building methods that'll be employed and the resulting environment that'll be created. Check out *Make a Difference at Work* by Adharanand Finn for loads of great tips. The Association for Environment Conscious Building (www.aecb.net) and www.greenbuildingstore.co.uk also have plenty of information about how to create a more environmentally friendly working environment. Finally, if you are refurbishing your old office and want to give it a makeover, why not consider recycling your old furniture, computers and phones – you can do this with companies such as www.officegreen.co.uk or find local resources through www.wasteonline.org.uk.

SAVE PAPER! An office worker uses an average of 20,000 A4 sheets a year. Most of this gets thrown away. But every tonne of paper recycled will save approximately 17 trees, 462 gallons of oil, and five cubic metres of landfill. With just a few simple steps you can reduce the amount of paper your office uses. If you print and photocopy on both sides, send emails and faxes rather than letters and memos, circulate documents by intranet, cancel unwanted publications and use transit envelopes, it will all help. You can also reuse paper for notes and sending internal documents. And if you haven't got one, install an office recycling scheme that includes all types of paper – including post-it notes! Finally, by using recycled paper, you will strengthen the long-term market in recycled paper. Turn scrap paper into notepads, and use both sides of the paper when photocopying or producing reports. Plus, ask do you need that copy and are the settings correct? Recycling bins beside photocopiers are full of wrong-size copies.

PUT A SPIDER PLANT ON YOUR DESK Indoor plants are a natural air conditioner and can remove up to 87% of indoor pollution in 24 hours. Find out about other healthy plants from the Flowers and Plants Association at **www.flowers.org.uk/plants/health/health.htm**.

DON'T PRINT YOUR EMAILS Avoid printing out your emails if you can. And when you send an email, include a reminder at the top, such as: 'Don't print! Save trees!'

RECYCLE OR REFILL YOUR INK CARTRIDGES Over 7.5 million toner cartridges and 12 million ink jet cartridges end up in landfills each year – almost 90% of them could be recycled. Cartridge World reports that a total of 47 million printer cartridges go into landfills each year – and that 12 months of cartridge recycling could save up to 15 million litres of oil each year in the UK. The company now has more than 280 stores in the UK where you can refill your cartridge instead of buying a new one. Find a retailer at **www.cartridgeworld.org** or call 0800 18 33 800.

USE GREEN STATIONERY In the UK, six billion disposable plastic cups are thrown away each year. If you are one of the guilty drinkers you can redeem yourself by using pencils made from recycled plastic cups. Or use a mug and buy them anyway! You can also use colouring pencils made from sustainable wood or mouse mats, pencil cases made from recycled tyres, and pens made from plastic bottles. See **www.wow-wow.co.uk/shop/office/stationery.html**. You could also encourage your office to buy recycled stationery. For more information, visit the Green Stationery Company website at **www.greenstat.co.uk**, or call 01225 480556. Alternatively, try Recycled Paper Supplies at **www.recycled-paper.co.uk**.

THINK DURABLE Try to avoid buying disposable products, such as pens and pencils. Make sure your company buys refillable pens and propelling pencils in preference. Where disposable pens are necessary, ensure that their barrels are made from recycled material. Use solvent-free correction fluids and paints in the office, and choose locally produced goods and materials to reduce the energy and pollution involved in their transportation. For green office equipment, ranging from eco-friendly marker pens to stapleless staples, visit **www.naturalcollection.com**.

FAIR TEA BREAKS Make a stir in your office by asking for Fairtrade tea and coffee. The world price of raw coffee has fallen and the market price of commodities has frequently dropped below the price of producing them, forcing farmers to work harder and longer for less. Since the prices of tea and coffee haven't been reduced by the same amount, where's the money going? Fairtrade buys direct from farmers at higher prices. Visit **www.coffee.uk.com** to buy a range of Fairtrade coffees, teas, herb teas and cocoas. Also see **www.cafedirect.co.uk** or **www.fairtrade.org.uk**.

SAVE ENERGY IN THE OFFICE With a bit of planning you can save energy, too. Position desks and workstations to exploit natural light. Check the plumbing regularly and repair leaks and dripping taps quickly. Only heat work areas that are being used and fit controls to radiators to regulate individual room temperatures. Be sure to switch off lights and machines when not in use! For advice on reducing carbon emissions and moving towards a low-carbon future, contact the Carbon Trust at **www.thecarbontrust.co.uk** or The CarbonNeutral Company at **www.carbonneutral.com**.

DON'T DUMP THE FURNITURE Don't throw out your old office furniture into the landfill – it can be recycled! Green Works is a not-for-profit organisation that recycles unwanted office furniture to schools, charitable organisations and businesses in need. Apart from reducing landfill, it supports projects based in deprived inner-city areas and provides employment and training to disadvantaged and disabled people. For more information, visit **www.green-works.co.uk** or call 0845 230 2231.

TOP TIP – RETHINK RUBBISH

DON'T BE A MUG!

Rediscover the real taste of tea and coffee by drinking your cuppa out of a real mug. It will taste better than if it were in plastic, you won't burn your hands and you'll cut down on the use of plastic cups. If your office does use a vending machine, however, and there isn't a viable alternative, contact Save-A-Cup on 01494 510 167 or visit **www.save-a-cup.co.uk**, which offers a collection and recycling service. Your used plastic cups can be made into a whole range of products, such as pens, rulers and cup coasters.

SHARE FACILITIES AND REDUCE OVERHEAD COSTS

If your company shares an open-plan office space with another company, think about setting up a sharing scheme. By sharing equipment such as printers and copiers, you could help reduce their energy consumption and reduce overhead costs.

COMPANIES – RETHINK YOUR ROLE IN THE FUTURE

How does your company's products and the way they are produced impact on the environment and the people who live in it? Are they

contributing to society or functioning at society's expense? Key questions to ask yourself – are the materials sourced and the production methods used sustainable? Does it follow Fairtrade principles? Are its investments ethical? Does it invest in its workforce – both at home and overseas? Does it support its local community or charities? And what, apart from its products, does it do to contribute to society? Get advice from the book *Make a Difference at Work*, **www.businessgreen.com** and the business section of The CarbonNeutral Company at **www.carbonneutral.com**.

TOP TIP – WWW.GREENCHOICES.ORG

REDUCE WATER WASTE

Water bills could be costing your company over 1% of business turnover, and many organisations are paying more in water and associated costs than they need to. Investing a little time and money in implementing a simple water management plan could reduce water consumption, releasing money to be invested in other parts of your business. As part of its commitment to 'greening the business world' the Environment Agency (**www.environment-agency.gov.uk**) has produced a series of free publications to help your organisation become more water efficient. It also offers up-to-date information on all aspects of businesses and their impact on the environment.

ASK YOUR BUSINESS TO SEND AN ENERGY MANAGEMENT EMAIL TO EVERY EMPLOYEE If every company sent out an energy management newsletter to its employees detailing energy-saving tips, substantial energy savings could be made in a relatively short space of time. Visit **www.resourcefutures.co.uk** – set up in 2006 after the merger of Network Recycling, SWAP and The Recycling Consortium. They can help your company with communications, technical consultancy, research, monitoring and evaluation, and community engagement. Do it today!

MAKE YOUR COMPANY SUSTAINABLE Get advice on making your workplace practices more sustainable and environmentally friendly.

Contact Business in the Environment at **www.bitc.org.uk** or call 020 7566 8650, or the National Centre for Business and Sustainability at **www.thencbs.co.uk** (0161 247 7979). Make sure the advice reaches the right people and is acted on. Friends of the Earth also publishes a *Green Office Action Plan.* Get your copy from **www.green-office.org.uk**.

PUBLISH ENVIRONMENTAL AND SOCIAL ACCOUNTS

Encourage your company to publish its environmental and social accounts – to take a detailed audit not only of its financial progress, but also of its effect on the environment and society. A number of high-profile companies have already done this, including The Body Shop, Camelot, Traidcraft and Ben & Jerry's. To find out more, visit the New Economics Foundation (NEF) at **www.neweconomics.org** or the Institute for Social and Ethical Accountability at **www.accountability21.net**.

KEEP AN EYE ON THE WORLD'S MULTINATIONALS

Your office may have a glowing social environmental record, but what about those that don't? Find out why Indians are accusing Coca-Cola® of polluting their water supply, or what happens in Nike sweatshops in China – visit **www.corporatewatch.org.uk** and **www.corpwatch.org**.

TOP TIP – THE NATURAL COLLECTION

DON'T USE POISON PENS

Conventional marker pens are filled with chemicals. But there are pens that don't intoxicate – Friendly Markers have a barrel made of waxed recycled paper and inks that contain no heavy metals or xylene or toluene solvents. For whiteboard or flipchart – water-based or permanent – they are effective and eco-friendly. Go to **www.naturalcollection.com** for the full range of natural and environmentally friendly pens and office stationery.

Technology bytes

COMPUTERS, PHONES AND MORE We can now link up across the planet, so let's try to link *with* the planet. Computers are all around us, and we're upgrading and replacing them all the time. But it takes a lot of natural resources to make a computer. Seven litres of crude oil are used to make the plastic inside just one system. So what can you do?

DONATE YOUR OLD COMPUTERS Each year over 100 million computers are sold and one million computers end up in landfill sites – in 2000, one billion computers were estimated to have been sold, with another billion due by the beginning of 2008! If your computer has ended its life in one situation, it can still work in another. Finding a new home will extend its life and provide someone with a computer who can't afford a new one. Sell it on eBay on **www.ebay.co.uk** or donate it to Computer Aid International, who will pass it on to an organisation in need – visit **www.computeraid.org** or call 020 8361 5540. And if you are buying a computer for the kids, think about buying a recycled computer rather than a new one.

USE MOBILE PHONES CAREFULLY Computers and mobile communications have promised, and provided, an incredible technological revolution, but while they have become a part of daily life, they have also become another environmental problem. Mobile phones made in the UK emit a low level of radio waves that are considered safe for us. However, there is evidence that phones can stimulate changes in brain activity, but the reason for this is not clear and not enough research has been done. In the absence of further research, use your phone cautiously – keep calls short, use a hands-free kit and when buying a new phone take account of its SAR values which monitor radio waves. Get more information from the Health Protection Agency at **www.hpa.org.uk**.

sustrans
JOIN THE MOVEMENT

IF INDOORS, USE YOUR MOBILE BY A WINDOW Signal strengths can be up to 10 times greater by a window, so standing near one means the handset needs less power to connect with the mast. Make sure you have the handset on the window-side, too, so that less of the signal passes through your head.

SAY NO TO MASTHEADS BY SCHOOLS Over 5.5 million UK schoolchildren, aged under 16 years, own a mobile phone. And there are now over 50,300 base stations in the UK, which permanently emit signals that may be harmful – 2% are mounted on schools. Some evidence suggests that the radio waves emitted from mastheads may provoke headaches, disrupt sleep and cause short-term memory loss. Find out more at **www.mastaction.co.uk**, or write to Mast Action, PO Box 312, Hertfordshire EN7 5ZE.

CHANGE YOUR CHARGER Here are some phone rechargers that are good for both you and the environment. The Green Shop (**www.greenshop.co.uk**) sells solar-powered mobile phone chargers. They're a convenient power supply for charging your mobile phone at no cost when you have no access to a power point. Alternatively, you could charge up your phone using pedal power. For more information on this nifty little gadget that attaches to your bicycle, visit **www.edirectory.co.uk**. And if cycle charging sounds a bit too active, get a wind-up charger for a more leisurely way of generating power to talk. Three minutes of wind-up provides eight minutes of conversation – also available from The Green Shop.

RECYCLE YOUR OLD MOBILE There are over 52 million potentially toxic redundant mobile phones lying abandoned around our houses – with around 15 million handsets replaced in the UK each year! Donate your old phone to a charity so that someone else can make use of it. Ask your phone provider how you can swap your old handset for a new one or contact **www.recycleyourmobile.co.uk** for more advice – they manage over 30 schemes, including partnerships with Great Ormond Street Children's Hospital and Comic Relief.

LOOK FOR THE ENERGY STAR The Energy Star System is a US-developed rating system that also applies to goods sold in the UK. When you buy a printer, modem, scanner or monitor with the Energy Star sign on it you know it will be one of the most efficient models. If you use Energy Star Computer equipment you could save up to £25 per year per computer. Find out more about Energy Star products at **www.energystar.gov**.

SCREENSAVERS DON'T SAVE ENERGY In fact, sometimes they use more energy than when the computer is in use. If you are going to be away from your computer for over an hour, switch it to sleep mode or turn it off. A computer monitor left on overnight wastes enough energy to laser print 800 A4 pages.

TURN OFF YOUR COMPUTER WHEN YOU LEAVE WORK Employees who didn't turn their computers off when they went home at night cost their companies £90 million in 2002. Worse, throughout the night, those computers pumped a staggering 2.8 million tonnes of CO_2 into the environment. Always turn your computer off when you go home, and if you work at home, turn it off when you're not working. Get more helpful energy-saving tips from **www.green-pc.blogspot.com**.

RECYCLE YOUR COMPACT DISCS Don't throw away old CDs. Donate them to a charity shop or a local school so they can be reused. Or string them up in fruit trees if you wish to keep birds away from your fruit.

RECHARGE YOUR BATTERIES Every year over 15 billion batteries are produced and sold worldwide. The majority are non-rechargeable alkaline or lithium batteries. No battery is biodegradable, so all wasted batteries will simply gather in the rubbish dumps around the world. Rechargeable batteries can be used up to 1,000 times, and the technology is always improving. Some rechargeable batteries are even recyclable – that's good news for the landfill. For more information, visit **www.greenbatteries.com**.

DO YOU REALLY NEED THAT NEW GADGET? Gadgets make useful small presents, they're ingenious and fun to use. But when we lead such busy lives, how often are they really used after the novelty has worn off? For example, sales of Apple's hot new iPhone were more than 70,000 in their first week of issue in 2007 in the UK! Many people who bought them would already have had a perfectly good mobile phone, handheld computer or MP3 player – many of which are probably still lying around and could be recycled. Try to limit the amount of gadgets you buy, or make sure they benefit the environment. Visit **www.greenchoices.org** or **www.naturalcollection.com** for solar-powered and wind-up devices, energy- and water-saving products for the home.

shared
interes
Invest with Shared Interes
Invest in fair trade

Wise investments

If you invest your money in a savings scheme, pension or insurance policy, that company has your money to do what it will with for the duration of the scheme. Most large UK fund managers, for example, include BAE Systems in the stock market portfolio of their ISAs or PEPs. This British company is among the top suppliers of military equipment to the developing world. Do you want your hard-earned cash to finance a war? Or drug-testing on animals? Or child labour? In fact, most of the companies listed in the FTSE 100 are off-limits, but you can make a profit and be ethical, as many companies have found. So think before you invest, borrow or buy. Ask questions, read the small print – a small investment of your time could save an awful lot of pain in a lab, sweatshop or distant country.

Banking on the future

ETHICAL MONEY Switch your money to an ethical bank. The Co-operative Bank (www.co-operativebank.co.uk, 0845 721 2212) and the Triodos Bank (www.triodos.co.uk, 0117 973 9339) provide a wide range of accounts, loans and savings schemes, as does the Ecology Building Society at www.ecology.co.uk, which offers savings schemes as well as mortgages. Ethical banks don't encourage trade with oppressive regimes or support the distribution of arms. They discriminate in favour of companies with sound environmental policies, so your money is working for – not against – the world. When you close existing accounts, banks usually ask why. Make sure you tell them.

LEARN THE LINGO Investment is traditionally filled with phrases that are designed solely so that bankers and traders are kept in a job, otherwise there would be no need for the middleman, and ethical investment is no different. However, it does help to know the criteria that investment companies use to decide whether a company is ethical or not. They have the best of sector, where investments are made in companies that, although not 100% environmentally friendly, are leading the field in their area and are still striving to improve. Similarly, there is thematic investment, which invests directly in companies that are believed to be improving the world, such as health or education organisations. Another method is positive and negative screening, in which a company is compared to a positive or negative list of ethical standards, and if it fulfils enough positive criteria, or too many negative criteria, then it will pass or fail respectively.

RENOVATE WHEN YOU RELOCATE If you're looking to move house, consider renovating a derelict building. These can traditionally be hard to get mortgages for as most building societies and lenders tend to shy away from such an investment, but the Ecology Building Society actively encourages such borrowers. It only gives mortgages to buyers purchasing derelict buildings, energy-efficient homes or people looking to build new homes from reclaimed or sustainable materials. That way you can create your own energy-efficient dream home from scratch. Visit **www.ecology.co.uk** or call 0845 674 5566.

INSURE IN THE FUTURE Car insurance is essential, but when you join the AA or the RAC you are indirectly supporting the despoilment of the countryside, as these organisations lobby the government to increase the number of roads being built. But there is an alternative. The Environmental Transport Association – an organisation that campaigns for alternative methods of transport and a reduction in car use, while fully recognising our need for cars – provides insurance and breakdown services at competitive rates. Visit **www.eta.co.uk** or call 0845 389 1010 for details. Or see **www.greeninsurancecompany.co.uk** for car insurance, car leasing, mobile phone recycling and green gas and electricity. To insure your home and your travels ethically, contact Naturesave Policies Ltd on 01803 864390 or visit **www.naturesave.co.uk**.

COOL COMMUNICATIONS The Phone Co-op is making communication greener. Owned and controlled by its customers, it offsets all the carbon dioxide generated by its activities and the telecoms services it supplies through payment of a voluntary levy to Climate Care which, in turn, invests in renewable energy and reforestation projects. It purchases its electricity from a green source, and has a strong recycling policy. It offers a good low-cost phone service, plus flat rate internet services and a low-cost pay-as-you-go service. Visit **www.phonecoop.org.uk**, or call 0845 458 9000 for more details (and a human being at the end of the line!).

TAKE OUT A GREEN MORTGAGE Borrowing money ethically is just as important as investing ethically. Before you take out a mortgage with any of the big players, check out the policies of the Co-operative Bank (**www.co-operativebank.co.uk**, 08457 212 212). It also offers a free energy survey. The Norwich and Peterborough Building Society (**www.norwichandpeterborough.co.uk**, 0845 300 2511) offers mortgage products linked to reforestation schemes. The Ecology Building Society (**www.ecology.co.uk**, 0845 674 5566) grants mortgages on properties which give an ecological payback, encouraging energy-efficient housing and ecological renovation. Find more green mortgages at **www.mortgages.co.uk/green-mortgages.html**.

RETIRE ETHICALLY! Pension funds control more than a third of the shares in the UK stock market – so everybody who has a pension can do their bit. Make the effort and read the small print – notably your pension fund's Statement of Investment principles. If you don't have this, ask to be sent a copy. Research by the Campaign Against the Arms Trade (CAAT) (**www.caat.org.uk**, 020 7281 0297) shows that the pension funds of many local authorities, trades unions, NHS Trusts and even charities are being invested in the arms trade. What contributes to a long and happy retirement in one part of the world could be causing misery in another. Find a range of ethical pensions and other financial advice at **www.ethicalinvestors.co.uk**.

PROOF OF THE PUDDING The organisation Friends Provident (**www.friendsprovident.co.uk**, 0870 607 1352) has been providing ethical investment schemes since 1984, proving you can make a profit with sound ideals. Take a look at what it has to offer – the company will be only too glad to tell you what your money would be used for.

USE YOUR INVESTOR POWER The Ethical Investment Research Service (EIRIS) provides the independent research needed by investors to make responsible investment decisions. With research covering over 2,800 companies across the globe, EIRIS can tailor-make 'acceptable lists' of the companies that most fit an individual investor's social, environmental and ethical priorities. EIRIS has also produced a number of guides on ethical investment, including ones on funds, banks, pensions and charities. Visit **www.eiris.org** or call 020 7840 5700. You can also invest ethically at **www.norwichunion.com**.

GREEN CREDIT CARDS Affinity – or charity – credit cards give a small percentage of your spending (usually around 0.25%) to charity. There is an enormous range to choose from, including The Wildlife Trusts, the Woodland Trust, Dogs Trust, The National Trust and NSPCC among others. They are an easy, popular way to make a difference, and although they may attract a higher rate of interest on spending, customers think it's worth it. Visit **www.charitycard.co.uk** for a full list of charity credit cards available. A standard credit card – the Smile credit card (**www.smile.co.uk**) – is available from the Co-operative Bank. The Co-op also recently issued its new Think Credit Card. It's made out of more environmentally friendly plastic, automatically purchases and protects half an acre of Brazilian rainforest upon your first purchase and offers a special rate on products bought from ethical partners – see **www.co-operativebank.co.uk**. Barclaycard has also issued a similar 'green' card, called Breathe, that donates 50% of net profits to tackle climate change – see **www.barclaycardbreathe.co.uk**.

AND FINALLY, FORGET MONEY ALTOGETHER...

The New Civilisation Network Alternative Money System team (**www.newciv.org/ncn/moneyteam.html**) was founded to discuss the prospects of doing away with money systems and using a resource-based system instead. It might sound Utopian, but its website features information on schemes and ideas, including Letslink UK, the umbrella organisation for Local Exchange Trading Schemes (LETS). LETS promotes the exchange of goods and services, so individuals, groups and businesses can function in the community without money. Visit **www.letslinkuk.org**.

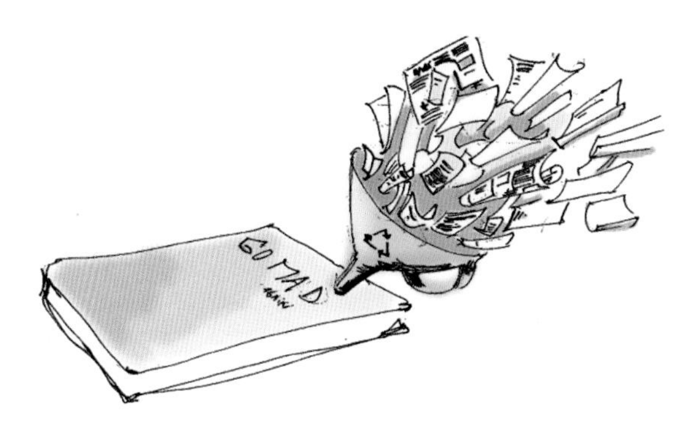

Find out more!

All the organisations mentioned in *Go Make a Difference* are listed here – so make that phone call, send that email or write that letter!

Go Make a Difference is all about interaction, so please let us know of any organisations or initiatives you feel should be mentioned in the book, as well as any new environmental tips. Send your idea by post or email and if we use your suggestion, we'll send you a free copy of the next edition of *Go Make a Difference*!

Go Make a Difference Tips
Think Publishing Ltd
The Pall Mall Deposit
124-128 Barlby Road
London W10 6BL

Email editorial@thinkpublishing.co.uk.
Don't forget to include your address.

ABOUT ORGANICS
Organic food, wine, skin care, clothing, holidays, gardening and more.
• 01789 491610
www.aboutorganics.co.uk

ADBUSTERS
Campaign to topple existing power structures and forge a shift in the way we live. 1243 West 7th Avenue, Vancouver, BC V6H 1B7, Canada • +1 800 663 1243
www.adbusters.org

ADNAMS
Brewers of traditional cask beer since 1872.
• 01502 727200
www.beerfromthecoast.co.uk

THE ADVENTURE TRAVEL COMPANY
Responsible travel tour operators.
• 0845 450 5316
www.adventurecompany.co.uk

AGGIE HORTICULTURE
Site offering ideas on how children can start a garden in their school.
http://aggie-horticulture.tamu.edu

ALBION CANVAS
Environmentally friendly tents.
• 0845 456 9290
www.albioncanvas.co.uk

ALTERNATIVE CEREMONIES
Offers alternatives to traditional wedding, baby-naming and funeral ceremonies.
www.alternative-ceremonies.org.uk

ALTERNATIVE VEHICLES TECHNOLOGY
Electric cars, conversions and components. • 01823 480196
www.avt.uk.com

AMAZING RECYCLED PRODUCTS
An American company specialising in innovative products made from a wide variety of recycled materials.
www.amazingrecycled.com

AMNESTY INTERNATIONAL
Worldwide movement of people campaigning for internationally recognised human rights. 1 Easton Street, London WC1X 0DW • 020 7413 5500
www.amnesty.org

ANITARODDICK.COM
Body Shop founder campaigns on environmental and humanitarian issues.
www.anitaroddick.com

ARCANIA GREEN TECHNOLOGY SPECIALISTS
The first UK company to offer services powered by 100% solar power.
www.arcania.co.uk

ASSOCIATION FOR ENVIRONMENT CONSCIOUS BUILDING
UK's leading independent environmental building trade organisation.
PO Box 32, Llandysul SA44 5ZA
• 0845 4569773
www.aecb.net

AURO UK
Organic paints. Cheltenham Road, Bisley, Nr Stroud, Gloucestershire GL6 7BX
• 01452 772020
www.auro.co.uk

AUTO-CHLOR SYSTEM
Auto-Chlor System is the national leader in the production and installation of low-energy dishmachines.
www.autochlor.com

AVEDA
For environmentally friendly hair, skin, make-up and lifestyle products.
www.aveda.com

AVIAN ADVENTURES
Birdwatching and wildlife holidays organised worldwide.
• 01384 372013
www.avianadventures.co.uk

BABY CATALOGUE
Baby equipment and supplies, including environmentally friendly products. Perfectly Happy People Ltd, 93 Bollo Lane, Chiswick, London W4 5LU
• 0870 1202 018
www.thebabycatalogue.com

BABY MILK ACTION
A non-profit organisation to promote safe and appropriate infant feeding.
34 Trumpington Street,
Cambridge CB2 1QY
• 01223 464420
www.babymilkaction.org

BABY ORGANIX
Manufacturers of organic baby food.
Freepost BH1 336, Christchurch,
Dorset BH23 2ZZ
• 0800 393 511
www.organix.com

BABY THINGS
A website for buying and selling used or unwanted babies' and children's goods free of charge.
www.baby-things.com

BAG IT AND BIN IT
National water industry-led campaign promoting responsible disposal of discarded personal products.
www.bagandbin.org

BAN LINDANE CAMPAIGN
see Pesticide Action Network
www.pan-uk.org

BANANA LINK
Supporting sustainable production and trade in bananas. 8a Guildhall Hill, Norwich,
Norfolk NR2 1JG
• 01603 765670
www.bananalink.org.uk

BAOBAB TRAVEL
Eco-tours specialising in Africa.
• 0121 314 6011
www.baobabtravel.com

BARN OWL TRUST
A charity dedicated to conserving the barn owl and its natural habitat in the UK.
Waterleat, Ashburton, Devon TQ13 7HU
• 01364 653026
www.barnowltrust.org.uk

BAT CONSERVATION TRUST
A UK organisation devoted to the conservation of bats and their habitats.
• 020 7627 2629
www.bats.org.uk

BATTERSEA DOGS & CATS HOME
An organisation that rescues and rehomes stray and ill-treated dogs and cats.
4 Battersea Park Road, Battersea,
London SW8 4AA
• 020 7622 3626
www.dogshome.org

BEANIES WHOLEFOODS
Specialists in quality organic foods.
205-207 Crookes Valley Road,
Sheffield S10 1BA
• 0114 268 1662
www.beanieswholefoods.co.uk

BEAUTIFUL BRITAIN
A website dedicated to outdoor living, with tips on introducing wildlife to ponds, gardens, canals, etc.
www.beautifulbritain.co.uk

BEAUTY NATURALS
Natural health and beauty products.
• 0845 094 0400
www.beautynaturals.com

BEAUTY WITHOUT CRUELTY
An international educational charitable trust for animal rights.
4 Prince of Wales Drive, Wanowrie,
Pune 411 040
• 020 2686 1166
www.bwcindia.org

BENFIELD ATT
Information, help and materials for self-build kit-houses and DIY homes.
• 01291 437050
www.adtimtec.com

BEST FOOT FORWARD
A company set up to assist individuals and organisations to become environmentally sustainable.
9 Newtec Place, Oxford OX4 1RE
• 01865 250818
www.bestfootforward.com

BHOPAL MEDICAL APPEAL
A campaign site providing information about the chemical leak in Bhopal and its ongoing consequences.
Development House, 56-64 Leonard Street,
London EC2A 4LT
• 020 7065 0909
www.bhopal.org

BICYCLE BEANO
Offers cycling tours of the Welsh countryside, combined with quality accommodation and vegetarian cuisine.
• 01982 560471
www.bicycle-beano.co.uk

BIO REGIONAL DEVELOPMENT GROUP
A group founded on the ideal of local production for local needs, that promotes sustainable development. BedZED Centre, Helios Road, Wallington, Surrey SM6 7BZ • 020 8404 4880
www.bioregional.com

BIOREGIONAL CHARCOAL
All BioRegional Charcoal is made from timber from well-managed woodlands certified by the Forest Stewardship Council (FSC).
www.fsc-info.org

BLUE PETER MAKES
A website with ideas and instructions to accompany the *Blue Peter* TV programme.
www.bbc.co.uk/cbbc/bluepeter/active/makes

BODY SHOP INTERNATIONAL PLC
International retail chain renowned for its environmentally friendly and naturally inspired beauty products.
www.thebodyshop.com

BORN
Provides information and alternative products, enabling parents to make informed choices about their babies' welfare. 64 Gloucester Road, Bishopston, Bristol BS7 8BH
• 0845 130 2676
www.borndirect.com

BORNEO TRAVEL
Provides travel information on Sarawak, the larger of the two Malaysian states on the island of Borneo.
• 01492 650 225
www.borneotravel.com

BOYCOTTBUSH
This site is where *Ethical Consumer* charts the campaigners' progress and lists the brands for consumers to avoid.
www.boycottbush.net

BREAD MATTERS
Works with other individuals and groups to promote healthier eating and lifestyles.
• 01768 881899
www.breadmatters.com

BRITISH ASSOCIATION FOR FAIR TRADE SHOPS
A network of independent Fair Trade or World Shops, aiming to promote Fairtrade retail in the UK. Unit 7, 8-13 New Inn Street, London EC2A 3PY • 07796 050045
www.bafts.org.uk

BRITISH ASSOCIATION OF HOMEOPATHIC VETERINARY SURGEONS
Provides advice on animal remedies.
• 01367 718115

BRITISH COMPLEMENTARY MEDICINE ASSOCIATION
Provides information on complementary therapies, for practitioners, clients and students, aiming to promote high standards throughout the country.
PO Box 5122, Bournemouth BH8 0WG
• 0845 345 5977
www.bcma.co.uk

BRITISH FILM INSTITUTE (BFI)
A registered charity that promotes film, television and the moving image.
Stephen Street Office/bfi National Library, British Film Institute, 21 Stephen Street, London W1T 1LN • 020 7255 1444
www.bfi.org.uk

BRITISH GLASS MANUFACTURERS CONFEDERATION
Promotes glass as the leading choice for containers. • 0114 290 1850
www.britglass.org.uk/Index.html

BRITISH HEDGEHOG PRESERVATION SOCIETY
A UK charity dedicated to helping and protecting hedgehogs. Hedgehog House, Dhustone, Ludlow, Shropshire SY8 3PL
• 01584 890801
www.britishhedgehogs.org.uk

BRITISH KITE SURFING ASSOCIATION (BKSA)
An association providing information on this radical sport and other extreme activities. Thames Street, Charlbury, Oxford OX7 3QL
• 07882 680113
www.kitesurfing.org

BRITISH RED CROSS
For your nearest British Red Cross shop.
UK Office, 44 Moorfields,
London EC2Y 9AL
• 0844 8711 111
www.redcross.org.uk

BRITISH TOY AND HOBBY ASSOCIATION
Represents the interests of British toy manufacturers and works to raise standards of practice in the industry.
• 020 7701 7271
www.btha.co.uk

BRITISH TOY MAKERS GUILD
Promotes British craft toys for children and grown-ups.
www.toymakersguild.co.uk

BRITISH TRUST FOR CONSERVATION VOLUNTEERS
An organisation that works with volunteers to bring about positive environmental change. BTCV, Sedum House, Mallard Way, Doncaster DN4 8DB
• 01302 388 883
www.btcv.org

BRITISH UNION FOR THE ABOLITION OF VIVISECTION
Britain's anti-vivisection organisation that campaigns to end all animal experimentation. 16A Crane Grove, London N7 8NN
• 020 7700 4888
www.buav.org

BRITISH WATERWAYS
Promotes, manages and conserves Britain's inland waterways.
www.britishwaterways.co.uk

BRITISH WIND ENERGY ASSOCIATION
Aims to promote wind energy in the UK.
• 020 7689 1960
www.bwea.com/about/index.html

BROCKWOOD PARK SCHOOL
Committed to educating young people to give them an awareness of the environment and the world around them.
• 01962 771744
www.brockwood.org.uk

BURNS PET NUTRITION
Holistic dog food and cat food recipes, without additives or colourings.
• 01554 890482
www.burns-pet-nutrition.co.uk

BUSINESS IN THE COMMUNITY
Movement of over 700 UK companies to improve their positive impact on society.
137 Shepherdess Walk, London N1 7RQ
• 020 7566 8650
www.bitc.org.uk

BUTTERFLY CONSERVATION
Protects native butterflies, moths and their habitats from a range of threats.
Manor Yard, East Lulworth, Wareham, Dorset BH20 5QP
• 01929 400209
www.butterfly-conservation.org

BUY NOTHING DAY
A day celebrating simple living and no spending.
www.buynothingday.co.uk

BUY RECYCLED
Guide to products available in the UK containing recycled materials.
www.recycledproducts.org.uk

BY NATURE
Online organic and ethical living products.
• 0845 456 7689
www.bynature.co.uk

CAFÉDIRECT
Sells fairly traded tea, coffee and cocoa that provides producer partners with a living wage.
• 020 7490 9520
www.cafedirect.co.uk

CAMPAIGN AGAINST ARMS TRADE
Campaigns for the reduction and ultimate abolition of the international arms trade.
11 Goodwin St, London N4 3HQ
• 020 7281 0297
www.caat.org.uk

CAMPAIGN FOR DARK SKIES
Highlights the problem of light pollution.
38 The Vineries, Colehill, Wimborne, Dorset BH21 2PX
www.dark-skies.org

CAMPAIGN FOR REAL ALE (CAMRA)
Helps safeguard the future of British beer. 230 Hatfield Road, St Albans, Hertfordshire AL1 4LW
• 01727 867201
www.camra.org.uk

CAMPAIGN TO PROTECT RURAL ENGLAND
Campaigns for the protection and enhancement of the countryside. CPRE national office: 128 Southwark Street, London SE1 0SW
• 020 7981 2800
www.cpre.org.uk

CANBY
Provides jute bags and environmentally friendly packaging.
27 Park End Street, Oxford OX1 1HU
• 0845 277 0122
www.canby.co.uk

CARBON TRUST
Promotes the development of low-carbon technologies to support the transition to a low-carbon technology in the UK.
Carbon Trust, 8th Floor, 3 Clement's Inn, London WC2A 2AZ
• 0800 085 2005
www.thecarbontrust.co.uk

CARBONNEUTRAL COMPANY
Plants trees to help neutralise carbon dioxide emissions. Bravington House, 2 Bravington Walk, Regent Quarter, Kings Cross, London N1 9AF
• 020 7833 6000
www.carbonneutral.com

CARE, REHABILITATION AND AID FOR SICK HEDGEHOGS
A charity dedicated to care for sick and injured hedgehogs, with the aim of returning them to the wild.
• 01202 699358
www.hedgehogs.org.uk

CARIBBEAN CONSERVATION CORPORATION
Campaigns for research into and preservation of sea turtles. Caribbean Conservation Corporation, 4424 NW 13th Street, Suite A-1 Gainesville, FL 32609, USA
www.cccturtle.org

CAR PLUS
Car-sharing projects. • 0113 234 9299
www.carplus.org.uk

CARTRIDGE WORLD
Recycles and refills cartridges.
• 0800 18 33 800
www.cartridgeworld.org

CARTRIDGES 4 CHARITY
Funds small charities by recycling printer cartridges and mobile phones.
www.cartridges4charity.co.uk

CASH FOR CANS
Promotes local-level aluminium recycling in the UK and abroad, offering incentives to individuals and organisations.
www.thinkcans.net

CATS PROTECTION
A feline welfare charity that rescues and rehomes cats and promotes responsible cat ownership. • 08702 099099
www.cats.org.uk

CENTRE FOR ALTERNATIVE TECHNOLOGY
Environmental charity that aims to inspire, inform and enable people to live more sustainably.
• 01654 705950
www.cat.org.uk

CENTRE FOR SUSTAINABLE URBAN AND REGIONAL FEATURES
Promotes urban regeneration and renewal.
• 0161 295 4018
www.surf.salford.ac.uk

CHANGENAPPY
Listing nappy-related websites, including suppliers and environmentally friendly options.
www.changenappy.co.uk

CHANGING PLACES
Tackles the legacy of post-industrial decay to breathe new life into derelict and neglected land.
www.changingplaces.org.uk

CHARITY CARDS
Provides a selection of charity cards.
• 0191 261 6263
www.charitycards.co.uk
www.christmas-cards.org.uk

CHARITY COMMISSION
A government organisation aiming to increase public confidence in the integrity of charities in England and Wales.
• 0845 3000 218
www.charity-commission.gov.uk

CHEETAH CONSERVATION FUND (CCF)
Research into and preservation of cheetahs in their natural habitat.
711 Quail Ridge Road, Aledo, TX 76008-2870, USA
www.cheetah.org

CHEMICAL BODY BURDEN
Provides information on synthetic chemicals that build up in our bodies.
PO Box 8743, Missoula, MT 59807, USA
www.chemicalbodyburden.org

CHILD
Information on all aspects of pregnancy, childcare and parenting.
www.child.com

CHILDREN'S SCRAPSTORE
Recycles clean and safe waste products to create resources for children's art and play activities. The Proving House, Sevier Street, St Werburgh, Bristol BS2 9LB
• 0117 908 5644
www.childrensscrapstore.co.uk

CHOOSE CLIMATE
Calculates the cost of your flight to the environment.
www.chooseclimate.org

CLIMATE ARK
Offers news and information on climate change and renewable energy.
www.climateark.org

COALITION TO STOP THE USE OF CHILD SOLDIERS
Works to prevent the recruitment and use of children as soldiers.
www.child-soldiers.org

COMMUNITY COMPOSTING NETWORK
Provides advice and supports community composting projects across the UK.
• 0114 258 0483
www.communitycompost.org

COMMUNITY RECYCLING NETWORK
A membership organisation promoting community-based sustainable waste management. • 0117 942 0142
www.crn.org.uk

COMMUNITY REPAINT
A scheme to collect and distribute paint to people who can't afford it.
www.communityrepaint.org.uk

COMPASSION IN WORLD FARMING
Campaigns to end factory farming and improve transport of animals. River Court, Mill Lane, Godalming, Surrey GU7 1EZ
www.ciwf.org.uk

THE COMPOSTING ASSOCIATION
Promotes good practice in composting and the use of composted materials.
Avon House, Tithe Barn Road, Wellingborough, Northamptonshire NN8 1DH • 0870 160 3270
www.compost.org.uk

COMPUTER AID INTERNATIONAL
Charity that refurbishes computers from the UK for reuse in developing countries.
• 020 8361 5540
www.computeraid.org

COMPUTERS FOR CHARITY
A voluntary organisation that campaigns to improve access to IT for community groups, through the recycling of computers.
• 01288 361199
www.computersforcharity.org.uk

CONFRONTING COMPANIES USING SHAREHOLDER POWER
Handbook for socially conscious investors.
www.foe.org/international/shareholder

CONSERVATION CORPORATION AFRICA
For information on holidays to Africa that help rather than harm the continent.
www.ccafrica.com

CONSERVATREE
Promotes recycled paper products within the paper industry.
www.conservatree.com

CONVENTION ON INTERNATIONAL TRADE IN ENDANGERED SPECIES (CITES) SECRETARIAT
The United Nations secretariat that monitors the trade in endangered animals and plants.
www.cites.org

CO-OPERATIVE BANK
Ethically guided banking facilities, encouraging business customers to invest in environmentally conscious companies.
Head Office, PO Box 101, 1 Balloon Street, Manchester M60 4EP
• 08457 212212
www.cooperativebank.co.uk

CORAL CAY CONSERVATION
Not-for-profit organisation that sends volunteers to survey endangered coral reefs and tropical forests.
• 020 7620 1411
www.coralcay.org

CORPORATE WATCH
Investigates corporate crime, and monitors corporate power.
16B Cherwell Street, Oxford OX4 1BG
• 01865 791391
www.corporatewatch.org.uk

CORPWATCH
Counters corporate-led globalisation through education, networking and activism.
www.corpwatch.org

COUNTRY LOVERS
Information on visiting, living or working in Britain's countryside.
www.countrylovers.co.uk

COUNTRYSIDE ACCESS
For the Countryside Code.
www.countrysideaccess.gov.uk

COUNTRYSIDE AGENCY
Statutory body working to improve the quality of countryside life.
20th Floor, Portland House, Stag Place, London SW1E 5RS
• 020 7932 5800
www.naturalengland.org.uk/default.htm

COUNTRYSIDE FOUNDATION FOR EDUCATION
An educational charity that works to bring the countryside into the classroom.
• 01422 885566
www.countrysidefoundation.org.uk

CRITICAL MASS RIDES WORLDWIDE
Organised worldwide group of cyclists who resist the problem of car culture.
www.urban75.com/Action/critical.html

CTC
A one-stop shop for cyclists. PO Box 868, Crawley, RH10 9WW
• 0870 873 0060
www.ctc.org.uk

CULPEPER HERBALISTS
Manufacturers of herbal medicines, aromatherapy products and fine foods.
• 01451 822 681
www.culpeper.co.uk

CULTIVATING COMMUNITIES
Provides information on supporting local agricultural communities.
www.cuco.org.uk

CURTAIN EXCHANGE
For recycling and buying curtains.
www.thecurtainexchange.net

CYCLISTS' TOURING CLUB HQ
Technical advice and information on insurance, organised tours and events.
CTC, Parklands, Railton Rd, Guildford, Surrey GU2 9JX
• 0870 873 0060
www.ctc.org.uk

DAILY BREAD
Organic Fairtrade produce.
• 01604 621531
www.ecofair.co.uk

DAY CHOCOLATE COMPANY
Manufacturers of Fairtrade chocolates produced from Ghanaian cocoa.
• 020 7378 6550
www.divinechocolate.com

DEFENDERS OF THE OUSE VALLEY AND ESTUARY
Zero-waste-strategy policy group in the UK, created to address major environmental interests in the area.
www.dove2000.org

DELFLAND NURSERIES
Organic plants for gardens and allotments.
• 01354 740553
www.organicplants.co.uk

DEODORANT STONE (UK)
Range of natural body deodorants that do not contain aluminium chlorohydrate and are not tested on animals. Caerdelyn, Dolgran, Pencader, Carmarthenshire SA39 9BX • 01559 384856
www.deodorant-stone.co.uk

DISCOVER THE WORLD
An environmentally responsible travel company that specialises in Arctic holidays. • 01737 218800
www.discover-the-world.co.uk

DISCOVERING FOSSILS
An educational resource dedicated to British fossils, fossil-collecting locations and the geology of the UK.
www.discoveringfossils.co.uk

DISCOVERY INITIATIVES
Travel company that supports conservation worldwide.
• 01285 643333
www.discoveryinitiatives.com

DO-IT-YOURSELF NETWORK
A site dedicated to DIY information, including tips on personal recycling projects and composting.
www.diynet.com

DOGS TRUST
Dog-welfare-related issues.
17 Wakley Street, London EC1V 7RQ
• 020 7837 0006
www.dogstrust.org.uk

DOVES FARM FOODS
Gluten-free organic food manufacturer.
Salisbury Road, Hungerford, Berkshire RG17 0RF
• 01488 684880
www.dovesfarm.co.uk

DRIVE ELECTRIC
The electric vehicle specialists.
• 0844 884 4787
www.drivelectric.com

DUKE OF EDINBURGH'S AWARD SCHEME
National award scheme open to young people aged 14-17, with a focus on physical activities, learning skills and community service.
• 01753 727400
www.theaward.org

EARTHSCAN
Publishers of books on the environment and sustainable development.
• 020 7387 8558
www.earthscan.co.uk

EBAY
Online auction for second-hand goods.
www.ebay.co.uk

EBONY SOLUTIONS
Sells fuel made from cooking oil.
www.ebony-solutions.co.uk

ECO-LOGIC BOOKS
Specialises in books that provide practical solutions to environmental problems.
www.eco-logicbooks.com

ECO SALVAGE
Removes abandoned cars and derelictequipment.
www.ecosalvage.com

ECO-SCHOOLS
Aims to get everyone in a school community involved in improving the school environment.
www.ecoschools.org.uk

ECO SOLUTIONS LTD
Environmentally friendly DIY products.
Summerleaze House, Church Road, Winscombe BS25 1BH
• 01934 844484
www.ecosolutions.co.uk

THE ECOLOGIST
The world's longest-running environmental magazine.
www.theecologist.org

ECOLOGY BUILDING SOCIETY
A building society dedicated to improving the environment by promoting sustainable housing and communities.
• 0845 674 5566
www.ecology.co.uk

ECOS ORGANIC PAINTS
Makers of odourless, solvent-free gloss and emulsion paints.
• 01524 852 371
www.ecospaints..com

ECOTEC
Products aimed at improving car fuel consumption. Priestley House, 28-34 Albert Street, Birmingham B4 7UD
• 01844 212939
www.ecotekplc.com

ECOTOPIA
Supplies a great range of eco-friendly, ethical, sustainable and natural products.
www.ecotopia.co.uk

ECOTRICITY
The world's first green energy company.
• 01453 756 111
www.ecotricity.com

ECOVER UK LTD
Manufactures environmentally friendly detergents and cleaning products.
• 0845 130 2230
www.ecover.com

ECOZONE
A range of eco-friendly products for use in and around the home. • 0845 230 4200
www.ecozone.co.uk

EDEN PROJECT
A permanent outdoor exhibition with over 100,000 plants from all over the world, that highlights our relationship with plants. Bodelva, St Austell, Cornwall PL24 2SG
• 01726 811911
www.edenproject.co.uk

EDIRECTORY
Wide range of goods that can be bought using secure online shopping.
www.edirectory.co.uk

EDUCATION INTERNATIONAL
Information on education and the General Agreement on Trade in Services (GATS).
www.ei-ie.org

EFESTIVALS
For music festival listings and reviews.
www.efestivals.co.uk

ELLIE POO PAPER COMPANY
Makes paper from the dung of the Sri Lankan elephant.
• 01761 233818
www.elliepoopaper.com

EMAGAZINE
A magazine on environmental issues.
www.emagazine.com

EMPTY HOMES AGENCY, THE
Highlighting the problems of empty properties in England, and bringing them back into use.
• 020 7022 1870
www.emptyhomes.com

ENERGY SAVING TRUST
Promoting sustainable and efficient uses of energy.
• 0800 512 012
www.est.org.uk

ENERGY STAR
Provides information on energy saving and the energy-saving star rating.
www.energystar.gov

ENMAX
Canadian energy company providing useful energy tips for home and business.
www.enmax.com

ENVIRONMENT AGENCY
Information on energy rating schemes.
• 0800 80 70 60
www.environment-agency.gov.uk

ENVIRONMENTAL DISCOVERY HOLIDAYS
Environmental holidays for young people aged 6-16 during the summer in Dorset.
• 01460 271717
www.yptenc.org.uk/docs/residential_hols.html

ENVIRONMENTAL INVESTIGATION AGENCY (EIA)
An international organisation committed to investigating and exposing environmental crime. 62/63 Upper Street, London N1 0NY • 08708 506 506
www.eia-international.org

ENVIRONMENTAL MOBILE CONTROL
Provides recycling solutions for surplus mobile phone equipment. • 01283 516259
www.emc-recycle.com

ENVIRONMENTAL TRANSPORT ASSOCIATION (ETA)
Motoring organisation campaigning for a sustainable transport system • 0800 212810
www.eta.co.uk

EOSTA
Distributes organic and biodynamic fruit and vegetables from around the world.
www.eosta.com

ERASMUS SCHEME
Opportunities for undergraduates to learn new languages, experience new cultures and gain new perspectives.
www.erasmus.ac.uk

ESSEX COUNTY COUNCIL
An excellent recycling/waste products and services page with an A-Z directory of recycling tips.
• 0845 743 0430
www.essexcc.gov.uk

ETHICAL CONSUMER
Alternative consumer organisation researching the environmental and social records of the companies behind the brand names. Unit 21, 41 Old Birley Street, Manchester M15 5RF
• 0161 226 2929
www.ethicalconsumer.org

ETHICAL INVESTMENT RESEARCH SERVICE (EIRIS)
Provides research into corporate behaviour for ethical investors. 80-84 Bondway, London SW8 1SF • 020 7840 5700
www.eiris.org

ETHICAL JUNCTION
Information on ethical organisations and ethically made products. 112 Lyndhurst Road, Ashurst, Southampton, Hampshire SO40 7AU
• 02380 293763
www.ethicaljunction.org

ETHICAL NETWORK
Non-profit organisation bringing together environmentalists, intellectuals and activists to campaign for positive change.
www.ethicalnetwork.org

ETHICAL TRADING INITIATIVE
An alliance of companies, NGOs and trade union organisations working together to promote ethical trade.
www.ethicaltrade.org

ETHICAL WARES
Ethical mail order company run by vegans who trade without exploiting animals, humans or the wider environment.
www.ethicalwares.com

ETHICAL WILLS
Promoting the use of ethical wills.
www.ethicalwill.com

EUROPA
Website of the European Union.
www.europa.eu.int

EVERGREEN
Dating agency for the 'green' and ethically minded. • 0845 456 1274
www.evergreenagency.co.uk

EXODUS
Walking, adventure, biking, wildlife and cultural holidays worldwide.
• 0845 863 9600
www.exodus.co.uk

EXPERIENCE CORPS
Encourages volunteering in local communities.
www.experiencecorps.co.uk

EXPLORE WORLDWIDE
Adventure holidays around the world.
• 0844 499 0901
www.exploreworldwide.com

EXTRA LARGE REAL NAPPY NETWORK
Information on eco-friendly incontinence pads and incontinence laundries.
• 01386 700293

FACE OF FLOWERS
• 01570 4236523
www.faceofflowers.com

FACSIMILE PREFERENCE SERVICE
Opt out of receiving unsolicited sales and marketing faxes at home.
• 020 7291 3330
www.fpsonline.org.uk

FAIRTRADE FOUNDATION
Promotes Fairtrade and campaigns to encourage the growth of global Fairtrade.
www.fairtrade.org.uk

FARM AROUND
Box scheme delivering seasonal organic food to your door. The Old Bakery, Mercury Road, Gallowfields Trading Estate, Richmond, North Yorkshire DL10 4TQ
• 020 7627 8066
www.farmaround.co.uk

FEDERATION OF CITY FARMS AND COMMUNITY GARDENS
Sustainable and community-led projects working with people, animals and plants.
• 0117 923 1800
www.farmgarden.org.uk

FEMCARE PLUS
Healthier, safer and environmentally friendly feminine hygiene products.
www.femininehygiene.com

FESTIVAL EYE
Listings of camps, festivals and other outdoor events in the UK.
BCM 2002, London WC1 N3XX
www.festivaleye.com

FIELD STUDIES COUNCIL
An educational charity committed to teaching environmental issues. Montford Bridge, Preston Montford, Shrewsbury, Shropshire SY4 1HW • 01743 852100
www.field-studies-council.org

FIRST GIVING
Processes charity donations online.
www.firstgiving.com

FOOD DOCTOR
Independent professional advice on nutrition and health.
• 020 7792 6700
www.thefooddoctor.com

FOOD FOR THOUGHT
Vegetarian London restaurant.
31 Neal Street, Covent Garden, London WC2H 9PR
• 020 7836 0239

FOOD STANDARDS AGENCY
Valuable information on food labelling, organic food, food safety and GM crops.
• 020 7276 8000
www.foodstandards.gov.uk

FOREST STEWARDSHIP COUNCIL
An international NGO dedicated to promoting responsible management of the world's forests. FSC UK, 11-13 Great Oak Street, Llanidloes, Powys SY18 6BU
• 01686 413916
www.fsc-uk.info

FREERANGERS
Animal-free footwear.
• 01207 565957
www.freerangers.co.uk

FREE WHEELERS
Campaigns to reduce pollution by reducing car usage.
www.freewheelers.com

FRESH WATER FILTER COMPANY
Water filters for the home.
• 020 8558 7495
www.freshwaterfilter.com

FRIENDS OF CONSERVATION
Funds international community conservation projects and works with the travel industry to promote sustainable tourism.
• 020 7603 5024
www.foc-uk.com

FRIENDS OF THE EARTH
A national environmental pressure group with local groups who campaign on environmental issues.
• 020 7490 1555 (information service: Freephone 0800 581 051)
www.foe.org.uk

FRIENDS OF THE EARTH – SCOTLAND
www.foe-scotland.org.uk

FRIENDS OF THE EARTH – WALES
www.foe.co.uk/cymru

FRIENDS PROVIDENT
Ethical financial products and services.
• 0870 608 3678
www.friendsprovident.co.uk

FULLER'S ORGANIC
Brewery specialising in organic beer.
• 01908 562412
www.fullers.co.uk

THE FUNERAL COMPANY LIMITED
Provides green funerals and other alternative interments for all denominations.
• 01908 225222
www.thefuneralcompanyltd.com

FUNKY GANDHI
Ethical and green design house that uses sustainable materials and supports Fairtrade.
• 07766 506269
www.funkygandhi.com

FURNITURE RE-USE NETWORK
Promotes the reuse of furniture and household effects for the alleviation of hardship. 48-54 West Street, St Philips, Bristol BS2 0BL
• 0117 954 3571
www.frn.org.uk

FUTURE HEATING LTD
All types of heating installation, including solar. 208 Chase Side, Enfield, Middlesex EN2 0QX
• 020 8351 9360
www.future-heating.co.uk

GARTHENOR ORGANIC PURE WOOL
100% organic, eco-friendly wool.
• 0845 408 2437
www.organicpurewool.co.uk

GET ETHICAL
Shopping portal that promotes ethical shopping and supports social enterprises in the UK.
www.getethical.com

GLOBAL WITNESS
Campaigns to end the links between natural resource exploitation and conflict and corruption.
PO Box 6042, London N19 5WP
• 020 7272 6731
www.globalwitness.org

GOOD ENERGY
Supplies renewable energy products to homes and businesses.
Good Energy, Monkton Reach, Monkton Hill, Chippenham, Wiltshire SN15 1EE
• 0845 601 1410
www.good-energy.co.uk

GOSSYPIUM
An ethical eco-cotton store that manufactures fairly traded clothing.
Unit 1 Shepherd Industrial Estate, I Brooks Road, Lewes BN7 2BY
• 01273 481027
www.gossypium.co.uk

GRAIG FARM
Organic food specialists, home delivery and online.
• 01597 851655
www.graigfarm.co.uk

GREEN BATTERIES
Promotes the use of rechargeable batteries.
www.greenbatteries.com

GREEN BOARD GAMES
Ethical games for all ages.
Unit 112a, Cressex Business Park, Coronation Road, High Wycombe, Bucks HP12 3RP
• 01494 538999
www.greenboardgames.com

GREEN BOOKS
Environmentally inspired books on a range of subjects.
Foxhole, Dartington, Totnes TQ9 6EB
• 01803 863260
www.greenbooks.co.uk

GREEN BUILDING STORE
Safe, sustainable building products.
Heath House Mill, Heath House Lane, Bolster Moor, West Yorkshire HD7 4JW
• 01484 461705
www.greenbuildingstore.co.uk

GREEN CHOICES
A guide to greener living. PO Box 56, Saffron Walden, Essex CB10 1WG
www.greenchoices.org

GREEN CHRONICLE
Information on growing, buying, eating and living organically.
www.greenchronicle.com

GREEN CONE LTD
Compost bins for food and garden waste.
• 020 7499 4344
www.greencone.com

GREEN CUISINE LIMITED
Healthy organic cooking, with recipes and courses on cooking, food and health.
• 01544 230720
www.greencuisine.org

GREEN ENERGY
Encourages sustainable and green sourcesof energy. The National Energy Foundation, Davy Avenue, Knowlhill, Milton Keynes MK5 8NG
• 01908 665577
www.nef.org.uk/greenernergy

GREEN FIBRES
Organic clothing and home products made from organic cotton, linen, hemp, wool and silk, with a wedding list service.
• 0845 330 3440
www.greenfibres.com

GREENFORCE
Non-profit adventure specialists.
• 020 7470 8888
www.greenforce.org

GREEN FUTURES
A magazine on environmental solutions and sustainable futures published by Forum for the Future.
www.greenfutures.org.uk

GREEN GLOBE ACCREDITATIONS
Worldwide certification scheme for sustainable travel and tourism for consumers, companies and communities.
www.ec3global.com

GREEN GUIDES
Database of organic, eco-friendly and ethical businesses and organisations. Markham Publishing, 31 Regal Road, Weasenham Lane Industrial Estate, Wisbech, Cambridgeshire PE13 2RQ
• 01945 461 452
www.greenguide.co.uk

GREEN ISP
Green-friendly internet service provider.
• 0845 058 0659
www.greenisp.net

GREEN LANES ENVIRONMENTAL ACTION MOVEMENT (GLEAM)
Campaigns to prevent damage caused by recreational motor vehicles.
• 0118 971 2103

GREENMATTERS
Site designed to help busy people live a greener life.
www.greenmatters.com

GREEN METROPOLIS
Online bookstore for buying and selling second-hand books, with contributions to the Woodland Trust from every sale.
www.greenmetropolis.com

GREENPEACE
Campaigns to expose global environmental problems and their causes.
• 020 7865 8100
www.greenpeace.org

GREEN PEOPLE
Organic skin and hair care.
• 01403 740350
www.greenpeople.co.uk

GREEN PRICES
Compares products and prices of green energy suppliers in Europe.
www.greenprices.com

GREEN SHOES
Sells environmentally friendly shoes.
www.greenshoes.co.uk

GREEN SHOP
Sustainable and low-impact products for the home. Cheltenham Road, Bisley, Gloucestershire GL6 7BX
• 01452 770629
www.greenshop.co.uk

GREEN STATIONERY COMPANY
Environmentally friendly stationery products. Studio 1, 114 Walcot Street, Bath BA1 5BG
• 01225 480556
www.greenstat.co.uk

GREENWAYS
An offshoot of the Countryside Agency that works for quieter lanes.
• 0845 600 3078
www.countryside.gov.uk

GREEN WORKS
Redundant office equipment for schools,charities, community groups and start-up businesses.
• 0845 230 2231
www.green-works.co.uk

GROUNDWORK
Environmental regeneration charity working for sustainable development in some of the UK's poorest communities.
Lockside, 5 Scotland Street, Birmingham B1 2RR • 0121 236 8565
www.groundwork.org.uk

HAWK AND OWL TRUST
Working to protect birds of prey, and their habitats, from human pressures. The Hawk and Owl Trust, PO Box 100, Taunton TA4 2WX
• 0870 990 3889
www.hawkandowl.org

HEALTHY HOUSE
Products for a healthy environment, at home and in the office. The Old Co-Op, Lower Street, Ruscombe, Stroud, Gloucestershire GL6 6BU
• 01453 752216
www.healthy-house.co.uk

HEJHOG
Organic and eco-friendly products.
• 0845 606 6487
www.hejhog.co.uk

HEMP SHOP
Farms, processes and distributes hemp products across the country. PO Box 396, Brighton BN1 1SX
• 0845 123 5869
www.thehempshop.net

HENRY DOUBLEDAY RESEARCH ASSOCIATION (HDRA)
Dedicated to researching and promoting organic gardening, farming and food. HDRA, Ryton Organic Gardens, Coventry, Warwickshire CV8 3LG
• 0247 630 3517
www.hdra.org.uk

HERBATINT
Natural permanent hair colouring, free from chemicals.
• 020 8960 7968
www.herbatint.co.uk

HIGH & WILD
Responsible Adventure travel specialists.
• 01749 671777
www.highandwild.co.uk

HIKING WEBSITE
Helps make the most of hiking experiences, with gear, trails and more.
www.hikingwebsite.com or
www.campingresource.co.uk

HIPP ORGANIC
Producers of organic baby food.
www.hipp.co.uk

HIPPO THE WATER SAVER
Water-saving device for toilet cisterns.
• 01989 766667 (order line)
www.hippo-the-watersaver.co.uk

HOMECHECK
Guide to flooding, subsidence, crime and more in your neighbourhood.
www.homecheck.co.uk

HONESTY COSMETICS
Wide range of skin and hair products, suitable for vegetarians and vegans.
• 01629 814888
www.honestycosmetics.co.uk

HORSE DIRECTORY
Services, products and information on horses and horse-riding.
www.horse-directory.co.uk

HOSTELS.COM
Huge selection of hostels worldwide.
www.hostels.com

H2OUSE
Information and advice on how to use water efficiently.
www.h2ouse.org

IMPACT INITIATIVES
Information on how to do your bit for your community.
www.impact-initiatives.org.uk

IMPROVEMENT AND DEVELOPMENT AGENCY (IDEA)
An agency promoting the involvement of local authorities in Local Agenda 21. Layden House, 76-78 Turnmill Street, London EC1M 5LG • 020 7296 6880
www.idea.gov.uk or ww.scream.co.uk/la21

INBI HEMP
Clothing company specialising in clothes made from hemp.
• 0870 333 1858
www.inbi-hemp.co.uk

INSTITUTE OF SOCIAL AND ETHNIC ACCOUNTABILITY
Enhancing the performance of companies' sustainable development records.
• 020 7549 0400
www.accountability.org.uk

INTERMEDIATE TECHNOLOGY DEVELOPMENT GROUP (ITDG)
Advocates sustainable use of technology to reduce poverty in developing countries.
• 01926 634400
www.itdg.org

INTERNATIONAL DARK SKY ASSOCIATION
Campaigns to protect the night-time environment and ensure stars are visible.
www.darksky.org

I-TO-I
Promotes voluntary travel.
www.i-to-i.com

IVILLAGE
The website for women.
www.ivillage.co.uk

IWANTONEOFTHOSE.COM
Suppliers of the solar torch.
• 0844 573 7070
www.iwantoneofthose.com

JE GILLMAN & SONS
Funeral directors that sell chipboard-based veneered coffins using wood from managed sustained-yield forests. • 020 8672 1557
www.funeral.org.uk

JUNIPER GREEN
Provides organic dry gin.
• 01483 894650
www.junipergreen.org

KIMBERLEY PROCESS
Joint government, international diamond industry and civil society initiative to stem the flow of conflict diamonds.
www.kimberleyprocess.com

KINETICS
Huge range of bikes and bike equipment.
• 0141 942 2552
www.kinetics-online.co.uk

KINGFISHER NATURAL TOOTHPASTE
Producing natural toothpaste with no added preservatives or colourings.
• 01603 630484
www.kingfishertoothpaste.com

LA LECHE LEAGUE
Help and advice for breastfeeding mothers.
• 0845 456 1855
www.laleche.org.uk

LANDLIFE
An environmental charity that works to bring people and nature closer together.
• 0151 737 1819
www.wildflower.co.uk

LET'S GO GARDENING
Information about gardening in the UK.
www.letsgogardening.co.uk

LIFTSHARE COMMUNITY SCHEME
Car-sharing scheme.
www.liftshare.org

LINGUAPHONE UK
A global language learning company.
www.linguaphone.co.uk

LITTLE RED HEN NURSERIES
Sells and delivers organic plants grown in peat-free compost. 91 Denholme Road, Oxenhope, Keighley BD22 9SJ
www.redhens.co.uk

LOCAL EXCHANGE TRADING SYSTEM (LETSLINK)
Local community-based networks allowing people to exchange goods and services with each other without the need for money.
• 020 7607 7852
www.letslinkuk.org

LONDON CYCLING CAMPAIGN
Campaigns to make London a world-class cycling city.
• 020 7234 9310
www.lcc.org.uk

LOW IMPACT LIVING INITIATIVE
Promotes harmonious ways of living with the environment.
• 01296 714184
www.lowimpact.org

LP GAS ASSOCIATION
Commercial propane and butane gas.
www.lpga.co.uk

MAILING PREFERENCE SERVICE
A register you can put your name on to stop unsolicited junk mail.
• 020 7291 3310
www.mpsonline.org.uk

MAKING COSMETICS
How to make cosmetics at home from natural and manufactured raw materials.
www.makingcosmetics.com

MAKINGYOURCOSMETICS.COM
For recipes and information on ingredients.
www.makeyourcosmetics.com

MAN IN SEAT 61
Journey advice from a man who has travelled the world by rail and sea.
www.seat61.com

MANY MOONS
Menstruation products produced using either organic or reusable products.
www.manymoonsalternatives.com

MARINE CONSERVATION SOCIETY (MCS)
Provides information on how to get involved with cleaning up Britain's beaches.
• 01989 566017

MARSHMALLOW
Advice and tips on making your own beauty products.
www.marshmallow.co.uk

MAST ACTION UK
Fights the insensitive siting of mobile phone and TETRA masts, and offers advice on how to effectively object. • 0870 432 2377
www.mastaction.co.uk

MCSPOTLIGHT
Anything you need to know about McDonald's or McLibel.
www.mcspotlight.org

MEDIAWISE
Helps families and educators maximise the benefits and minimise the harm of mass media on children.
• +1 888 672 5437 or +1 612 672 5437
www.mediafamily.org

MERCY CORPS
Alleviating suffering and poverty by helping people build secure communities.
www.mercycorps.com

MOUNTAIN BIKING UK
Info on mountain biking in the UK.
• 01225 442244
www.mbuk.com

MUMSNET
A website on parenting run by parents for parents.
www.mumsnet.com

NAPPY LADY
Offers practical advice on how to swap from disposable to cloth nappies.
The Nappy Lady, 15 The Stanley Centre, Kelvin Way, Crawley, West Sussex RH10 9SE
• 0845 652 6532
www.thenappylady.co.uk

NATIONAL ASSOCIATION OF FARMERS' MARKETS
A source of information on farmers' markets, and a list of markets in the UK.
FARMA, Lower Ground Floor, 12 Southgate Street, Winchester, Hampshire SO23 9EF • 0845 45 88 420
www.farmersmarkets.net

NATIONAL ASSOCIATION OF NAPPY SERVICES
Voluntary organisation that promotes the use of cotton nappies and increases public awareness of the environmental and health problems associated with disposable nappies.
• 0121 693 4949
www.changeanappy.co.uk

NATIONAL ASSOCIATION OF PAPER MERCHANTS (NAPM)
The trade association representing the interests of UK paper merchants.
PO Box 2850, Nottingham NG5 2WW
• 0115 8412129
www.napm.org.uk

NATIONAL ASSOCIATION OF TOY & LEISURE LIBRARIES
Body dealing with UK toy libraries, offering advice, support, training and toy appraisal.
• 020 7255 4600
www.natll.org.uk

NATIONAL CHILDBIRTH TRUST (NCT)
Runs a range of antenatal classes, helplines, and educational and social events, to give confidence to new parents.
Alexandra House, Oldham Terrace, Acton, London W3 6NH
• 0870 770 3236
www.nctpregnancyandbabycare.com

NATIONAL ENERGY FOUNDATION
A UK charity that provides free advice on energy efficiency and renewable energy.
The National Centre, Davy Avenue, Knowlhill, Milton Keynes MK5 8NG
• 01908 665555
www.nef.org.uk

NATIONAL FOX WELFARE SOCIETY
Charity committed to preserving fox populations in the UK.
135 Higham Road, Rushden, Northants NN10 6DS • 01933 411996
www.nfws.org.uk

NATIONAL HEDGE LAYING SOCIETY (NHLS)
To encourage the art of hedge laying and keep the local styles in existence.
www.hedgelaying.org.uk

NATIONAL INSTITUTE OF MEDICAL HERBALISTS
A professional association of practitioners of herbal medicine. • 01392 426022
www.nimh.org.uk

NATIONAL PLAYING FIELDS ASSOCIATION
Committed to protecting and improving playing fields. Head Office, 2d Woodstock Studios, 36 Woodstock Grove, London W12 8LE • 020 8735 3380
www.npfa.co.uk

NATIONAL RECYCLING FORUM
A guide to products that contain recycled materials.
www.recycledproducts.org.uk

NATIONAL SKI AREAS ASSOCIATION
Promotes efforts to reduce carbon dioxide and other heat-trapping emissions, using wind-powered ski lifts and car-pooling.
www.nsaa.org

NATIONAL SOCIETY OF ALLOTMENT AND LEISURE GARDENS
Maintaining British heritage by establishing cooperation between agriculturalists and the organisation of smallholdings and allotments.
• 01536 266576
www.nsalg.org.uk

NATURAL CLOTHING
Organic clothing and cotton nappies for babies, adults and children.
• 0845 345 0498
www.naturalclothing.co.uk

NATURAL COLLECTION
Online catalogue with a range of eclectic, unusual, useful and interesting products chosen to contribute to a better world.
• 0845 3677 003
www.naturalcollection.com

NATURAL DEATH CENTRE
Helping people to arrange inexpensive and environmentally friendly funerals.
• 0871 288 2098
www.naturaldeath.org.uk

NATURAL ECO TRADING
Environmentally friendly household cleaning products.
• 01892 616871
www.greenbrands.co.uk

NATURAL ENGLAND
Responsible for conservation of wildlife and geology in England. Northminster House, Peterborough PE1 1UA
• 08708 506 506
www.naturalengland.org.uk/default.htm

NATURAL FRIENDS
Introduction agency for environmentally sensitive people. 15 Benyon Gardens, Culford, Bury St Edmunds, Suffolk IP28 6EA • 01284 728315
www.natural-friends.com

NATURAL HISTORY MUSEUM
Museum whose collections promote an enjoyment and responsible use of the natural world. Cromwell Road, London SW7 5BD
• 020 7942 5000
www.nhm.ac.uk

NATURAL RESOURCES DEFENSE COUNCIL
An environmental action organisation.
40 West 20th Street, New York, NY 10011, USA • +1 212 727 2700
www.nrdc.org

NATUREBOTTS
Eco disposable nappies. • 0845 226 2186
www.naturebotts.co.uk

NATURE'S CALENDAR
Gives a detailed insight into nature's calendar, and information on how to become involved in phenological activities. • 01476 584878
www.naturescalendar.org.uk

NATURE SAVE – POLICIES LIMITED
Provides ethical insurance policies.
58 Fore Street, Totnes TQ9 5RU
• 01803 864390
www.naturesave.co.uk

NEW ECONOMICS FOUNDATION
Promotes solutions to social, environmental and economic problems.
3 Jonathan Street, London SE11 5NH
• 020 7820 6300
www.neweconomics.org

NHBS MAIL ORDER BOOKSTORE
A bookstore specialising in natural history, the environment, science and sustainable development. • 01803 865913
www.nhbs.com

NHS ORGAN DONOR NET
Provides information on organ transplants and how to become an organ donor. UK Transplant, Fox Dean Road, Stoke Gifford, Bristol BS34 8RR • 0117 975 7575
www.uktransplant.org.uk/ukt

NO SWEAT
The UK campaign against sweatshops.
PO Box 36707, London SW9 8YA
• 07904 431959
www.nosweat.org.uk

NORWICH AND PETERBOROUGH BUILDING SOCIETY
A building society in the UK with strong environmental policies. • 0845 300 2511
www.npbs.co.uk

NOT TOO PRETTY
Information on cosmetics and associated products that contain dangerous phthalates.
www.safecosmetics.org

OFFICE OF ENERGY EFFICIENCY AND RENEWABLE ENERGY
Aims to bring a future of clean, affordable and abundant energy.
www.eere.energy.gov

OFFICES OF WATER SERVICES
England and Wales's sewage and water industry's regulator. • 0121 625 1373
www.ofwat.gov.uk

OIL BANK
Find the location of your nearest oil bank to recycle old oil and filters.
• 08708 506 506
www.oilbankline.org.uk

OLLIE RECYCLES
A website for children to learn the 3Rs: reduce, reuse and recycle.
www.ollierecycles.com/uk

ONE TREE HILL ALLOTMENT SOCIETY (OTHAS)
Essential information for cultivating/gardening in the UK.
www.othas.org.uk

ONEWORLD INTERNATIONAL
Dedicated to harnessing the democratic potential of the internet to promote human rights and sustainable development. • 020 7922 7844
www.oneworld.net

ORGANICA J
A company offering a collection of organic, GM-free products, from clothing to healthcare. • 01330 850257
www.organicaj.co.uk

ORGANIC CONSUMERS' ASSOCIATION
A non-profit organisation campaigning for food safety, organic agriculture, Fairtrade and environmental sustainability. • +1 218 226 4164
www.organicconsumers.org

ORGANIC DELIVERY COMPANY
An organic food delivery service especially for Londoners. 70 Rivington Street, London EC2A 3AY • 020 7739 8181
www.organicdelivery.co.uk

ORGANIC DIRECTORY
A comprehensive guide for the organic movement, listing organic retailers, box schemes, farm shops, restaurants etc.
www.theorganicdirectory.co.uk
www.whyorganic.org/page4_5.asp?main=4&sub=5

ORGANIC FOOD, UK
Anything and everything you want to know about organic food.
www.organicfood.co.uk

ORGANIC HOLIDAYS
Information about holiday accommodation on organic farms and smallholdings. Organic Holidays, Tranfield House, Tranfield Gardens, Guiseley, Leeds LS20 8PZ • 01943 871468
www.organic-holidays.com

ORGANICO
Importers of high-quality organic food at fair prices. • 01189 238767
www.organico.co.uk

OVER THE GARDEN GATE
A community site dedicated to wildlife in the garden and surrounding countryside.
www.overthegardengate.co.uk

OXFAM
A relief and campaign organisation committed to finding lasting solutions to poverty and suffering around the world. • 0870 333 2700
www.oxfam.org.uk

PAPER BACK
Paper merchant specialising in recycled paper. • 020 8980 5580
www.paperback.coop

PARROTFISH COMPANY
Provides educational resources about issues around the world. • 01473 655007
www.parrotfish.co.uk

PATAGONIA
Outdoor clothing and equipment manufacturer that places an emphasis on environmentally friendly manufacturing.
www.patagonia.com

PEOPLE & PLANET
UK Student Action on world poverty, human rights and the environment. • 01865 245678
www.peopleandplanet.org

PESTICIDE ACTION NETWORK UK
An independent, non-profit organisation that aims to reduce our dependence on toxic chemicals and pesticides. • 020 7065 0905
www.pan-uk.org

PHONE CO-OP
A telecommunications provider that takes an ethical and environmentally responsible approach to business. • 0845 458 9000
www.phonecoop.org.uk

PLANTLIFE
A national membership charity dedicatedto conserving plant life in its natural habitat. • 01722 342730
www.plantlife.org.uk

POLYMER RECYCLING LIMITED
Developing recycling techniques in the plastics industry. • 0151 707 3684
www.polymerrecycling.co.uk

POWABYKE
A company offering electric bikes as an eco-friendly alternative to cars.
• 01225 443737
www.powabyke.com

POWERPLUS
A company specialising in fuel-saving and emission-reduction technology.
www.powerplus.be

PRELOVED
A website allowing you to buy and sell second-hand items.
www.preloved.co.uk

PUMPKIN CARVING
For information on celebrating Halloween and growing pumpkins.
www.pumpkin-carving.com

PURE H2O
A water purification company that provides water systems.
• 01784 221188
www.pureh2o.co.uk

PURE NUFF STUFF
Completely natural skin care products, toiletries and cosmetics.
• 01736 366008
www.purenuffstuff.co.uk

PURE ORGANICS LIMITED
Producers of organic food.
• 01980 626263
www.organics.org

PUREWINE COMPANY
Provides over 175 different organic, vegetarian and vegan wines.
• 0844 800 9157
www.purewine.co.uk

QUADRIS ENVIRONMENTAL INVESTMENTS
Runs socially responsible investment funds.
• 01483 756800
www.quadris.co.uk

RAINFOREST ACTION NETWORK
Protects tropical rainforests and human rights of those living in and around them.
• +1 415 398 4404
www.ran.org

RAINFOREST CONCERN
Charity that protects threatened natural habitats, their wildlife and indigenous people.
• 020 7229 2093
www.rainforestconcern.org

RAMBLERS' ASSOCIATION
Works for walkers across England, Scotland and Wales. • 020 7339 8500
www.ramblers.org.uk

RECLAIM THE STREETS
For information on street-reclaiming action around the world.
www.rts.gn.apc.org

RECOUP
Specialists in plastic recycling.
• 01733 390021
www.recoup.org

RE-CYCLE
Collects and donates second-hand bicycles to communities in developing countries.
• 01206 863111
www.re-cycle.org

RECYCLE MORE
Provides information on recycling in the UK, in homes, businesses and schools.
• 0845 068 2572
www.recycle-more.co.uk

RECYCLE NOW
Provides information on how to recycle rubbish around the UK.
www.recyclenow.com

RECYCLED PAPER SUPPLIES
Provides stationery products, including recycled paper, card and envelopes.
• 01676 533832
www.recycled-paper.co.uk
www.rps.gn.apc.org

RECYCLING HELPLINE
Find out about your local council's recycling department.
• 0800 435576

RECYCLING OF USED PLASTICS
Promotes plastic recycling in the UK.
• 01733 390021
www.recoup.org

RED LETTER DAYS
A choice of over 300 experiences you can give as exciting and unforgettable gifts.
• 0845 640 8000
www.redletterdays.co.uk

REED DESIGN
For information about making and flying your own kites.
• 020 7738 8373
www.reeddesign.co.uk

REEL FURNITURE
Eco-friendly wooden furniture for home, garden and conservatory.
• 01953 457247
www.reelfurniture.co.uk

RE-FORM FURNITURE
Furniture made from 100% recycled materials. • 01209 890084
www.re-formfurniture.co.uk

REMARKABLE
Everyday items produced from recycled or sustainable sources.
• 01905 769999
www.remarkable.co.uk

RESCUE PET
An internet database with details of animal shelters and pets in need of a home.
www.rescuepet.org.uk

RESPONSIBLETRAVEL.COM
Promotes eco-tourism holidays in over 110 countries, designed to benefit tourists, hosts and the environment.
www.responsibletravel.com

RETIRED GREYHOUND TRUST
An organisation set up to find homes for greyhounds retired from racing in the UK.
• 0844 826 8424
www.retiredgreyhounds.co.uk
www.adopt-a-greyhound.org

REUZE
A site about where, what and how to recycle in the UK.
www.reuze.co.uk

ROYAL BOTANIC GARDENS, KEW
Botanical garden and educational resource housing the largest living plant collection in the world. • 020 8332 5000
www.kew.org

ROYAL SOCIETY FOR THE PREVENTION OF CRUELTY TO ANIMALS (RSPCA)
A charity working to rescue and rehome animals suffering from distress or cruelty.
• 0300 1234 999
www.rspca.org.uk

THE ROYAL SOCIETY FOR THE PROTECTION OF BIRDS (RSPB)
A charity working for a healthy environment rich in birds and wildlife.
• 01767 680551
www.rspb.org.uk

SAFEWASH
Supplies the T-wave laundry disc, an environmentally friendly and money-saving alternative to detergents.
• +1 877 233 9274
www.safewash.com

SALVO
Suppliers of vintage or antique building materials.
www.salvo.co.uk

SAMARITAN'S PURSE INTERNATIONAL
Runs operation Christmas Child – sending your gift-filled shoeboxes to needy children around the world.
• (828) 262 1980
www.samaritanspurse.org

SAVAWATT
Promotes the sensible use of electricity.
www.savawatt.com

SAVE-A-CUP
Offers a recycling service.
• 01494 510167
www.save-a-cup.co.uk

SAVE OUR SEEDS (SOS)
An EU-wide campaign to keep conventional and organic seeds free of genetically modified plants.
www.saveourseeds.org

SAVE THE CHILDREN
A UK children's charity working to create a better future for children.
• 020 7012 6400
www.savethechildren.org.uk

SAWDAYS SPECIAL PLACES TO STAY
Publishes books with intriguing alternatives to corporate and five-star accommodation in the UK, France, Spain, Portugal, Italy, Morocco and India.
• 01275 395430
www.sawdays.co.uk

SCOPE
Campaigns to achieve equality for people with cerebral palsy. • 0808 800 3333
www.scope.org.uk

SCOTTISH WILDLIFE TRUST
Protecting Scotland's Wildlife.
Cramond House, Kirk Cramond, Cramond Glebe Road, Edinburgh EH4 6NS
• 0131 312 7765
www.swt.org.uk

SCRIB
Steel Can Recycling Information Bureau. Everything you need to know about can recycling. c/o Corus Steel Packaging Recycling, Trostre Works, Llanelli, Carmarthenshire SA14 9SD
• 01554 712632
www.scrib.org

SEA SALT ORGANIC
Company that produces organic cotton clothing and eco-friendly stationery and toys.
www.seasaltorganic.co.uk

SEEDS OF CHANGE
Offers organic seeds and food.
www.seedsofchange.com

SELECT SOLAR
Specialists in solar panels.
• 01793 752032
www.selectsolar.co.uk

SHARED INTEREST SOCIETY
A cooperative lending society, offering ethical investment in Fairtrade with developing countries.
• 0191 233 9100
www.shared-interest.com

SILVER CHILLI
A company offering Fairtrade silver jewellery manufactured by Mexican craftsmen.
www.silverchilli.com

SILVERTREK
Stockists of outdoor gear company VauDe's Ecolog range.
• 0118 958 2211

SIMPLY ORGANIC
Organic soups, sauces, ready meals and baby food. c/o Serious Food, Llantrisant, Mid Glamorgan CF72 8LF
• 01443 237 222
www.simplyorganic.co.uk

SIMPLY SOAPS
Producers of herbal soaps that use organic ingredients suitable for vegetarians and vegans. Brilling, Rackheath Path, Norwich NR13 6LP • 01603 720869
www.simplysoaps.com

SLOW FOOD MOVEMENT
An international movement helping people rediscover the importance of careful food production and preparation, and thus banish the degrading effects of fast food.
• 01584 879599
www.slowfood.com

SMARTWOOD
Provides information about recycled wood products and runs a wood certification scheme.
• +1 212 677 1900
www.smartwood.org

SMILE.CO.UK
Online banking.
www.smile.co.uk

SOAP KITCHEN
Provides a selection of handmade natural toiletries and soaps.
• 01805 622944
www.thesoapkitchen.co.uk

SOCIETY OF HOMEOPATHS
Registers professional homeopaths in the UK and provides practice information and advice.
• 0845 450 6611
www.homeopathy-soh.org

SOCIETY OF INDEPENDENT BREWERS (SIBA)
Provides information about Britain's micro-brewers.
www.siba.co.uk

SOIL ASSOCIATION
A campaigning and certification organisation for organic food and farming.
• 0117 314 5000
www.soilassociation.org

SOLA LIGHTING LTD
Providers of energy-efficient daylight solutions for new or existing homes and businesses. • 0845 458 0101
www.solalighting.com

SOLAR ENERGY ALLIANCE
Information and advice on solar-powered energy. • 01502 515532
www.gosolar.u-net.com

SOLARTWIN
Solar panels and water-heating systems.
• 0845 1300 137
www.solartwin.com

SOSLYNX.ORG
A site dedicated to saving the Iberian lynx.
www.soslynx.org

SPIEZIA
Organic skin care and natural products.
• 0870 850 8851
www.spieziaorganics.com

SPIRIT OF NATURE LTD
Offers natural and environmentally friendly products, including organic clothing, natural skin care, and eco-household products.
• 0870 725 9885
www.spiritofnature.co.uk

SPRINTS
A scheme enabling you to swap empty print cartridges and old mobile phones for new school equipment.
• 0845 130 2050

STUDY STAY
Committed to providing free and impartial information about UK study to prospective international students.
www.studystay.com/htm/courses/exchange_programs.htm

SUMA
Independent wholefood wholesaler-distributor. Specialising in vegetarian, fairly traded, organic, ethical and natural products. • 01422 313845
www.suma.coop

SURFERS AGAINST SEWAGE (SAS)
A campaign for clean and safe recreational waters in the UK.
• 0845 458 3001
www.sas.org.uk

SUSTAIN: THE ALLIANCE FOR BETTER FOOD AND FARMING
An alliance that promotes food and farming policies and practices to benefit people, animals and the environment.
• 020 7837 1228
www.sustainweb.org

SUSTAINABLE COTTON PROJECT
Builds bridges between farmers, manufacturers and consumers to initiate markets for organic cotton.
www.sustainablecotton.org

SUSTRANS (SAFE ROUTES TO SCHOOLS INFORMATION TEAM)
A sustainable transport charity that campaigns for a reduction in motor traffic and its adverse effects.
• 0117 927 7555
www.sustrans.org.uk

SWADDLES
An online organic food home delivery service. Swaddles Green Farm, Chard TA20 3JR
• 0845 456 1768
www.swaddles.co.uk

SWEATSHOP WATCH
A coalition of groups committed to eliminating the exploitation that occurs in sweatshops.
• +1 213 748 5945
www.sweatshopwatch.org

TALKING BALLOONS
A website that specialises in screen-print biodegradable balloons for parties and celebrations. McGregor's Way, Turnoaks Business Park, Chesterfield, S40 2WB
• 01246 270555
www.talking-balloons.co.uk

TATTY BUMPKIN
Natural organic lifestyle for children – clothes, accessories, educational material.
www.tattybumpkin.com

TEACHING ENGLISH AS A FOREIGN LANGUAGE (TEFL)

For information on working as a foreign language teacher. 72 Pentyla Baglan Road, Port Talbot SA12 8AD

www.tefl.com

TEARFUND

Works for the elimnation of global poverty – including campaigns on injustice, unfair trade and landmines.
• 0845 355 8355

www.tearfund.org

TELEPHONE PREFERENCE SERVICE

A service set up by the Direct Marketing Association Ltd to allow consumers to opt out of receiving unsolicited sales and marketing calls.
• 020 7291 3320

www.tpsonline.org.uk

TIMBER RESEARCH DEVELOPMENT ASSOCIATION

An internationally recognised body dealing with the specification and use of timber and wood products. TRADA, Stocking Lane, Hughenden Valley, High Wycombe HP14 4ND
• 01494 569600

www.trada.co.uk

TIMEBANK

A national organisation campaigning to raise awareness of the importance of giving time and volunteering. 2nd Floor, Downstream Building, 1 London Bridge, London SE1 9BG
• 0845 456 1668

www.timebank.org.uk

TLIO (THE LAND IS OURS)

A group campaigning for ordinary people to access the land and be involved in any decision-making processes that affect it.
• 01460 249204

www.tlio.org.uk

TOMS OF MAINE

Creates natural toothpaste and other products using ingredients from nature. Tom's of Maine UK Ltd, PO Box 1873, Salisbury SP4 6WZ
• 020 7985 2944

www.tomsofmaine.com

TOOLS FOR SELF RELIANCE

Works with local organisations in Africa to provide tools and training. TFSR, Netley Marsh, Southampton SO40 7GY
• 02380 869697

www.tfsr.org.uk

TOTNES GENETIX GROUP

Campaigns against genetically modified farming and promotes locally grown food that maximises nutritional value and minimises environmental damage.

www.togg.org.uk

TOURISM CONCERN

A membership organisation campaigning for ethical and fair-traded tourism. Stapleton House, 277-281 Holloway Road, London N7 8HN • 020 7133 3330

www.tourismconcern.org.uk

TRAFFIC INTERNATIONAL

Works to ensure that trade in wild plants and animals is not a threat to nature conservation. Traffic International, 219a Huntingdon Road, Cambridge CB3 0DL • 01223 277427

www.traffic.org

TRAIDCRAFT PLC

A Fairtrade organisation that campaigns to help poor communities work their own way out of poverty. • 0191 491 0591

www.traidcraft.co.uk

THE TRAVELLING NATURALIST

Provides guided wildlife holidays with a special emphasis on birds.
• 01305 267994

www.naturalist.co.uk

TREES FOR CITIES

Works to improve London's urban communities through tree-planting schemes.
• 020 7587 1320

www.treesforcitiesorg.site.securepod.com

TRIBES

Organises holidays run on Fairtrade principles. • 01728 685971

www.tribes.co.uk

TRIODOS BANK

A European ethical bank, financing initiatives that deliver social, environmental and cultural benefits. • 0117 973 9339

www.triodos.co.uk

TYRE DISPOSAL
Campaigns to raise awareness on tyre disposal and recycling tyres.
www.tyredisposal.co.uk

U REFILL TONER LTD
Provides DIY toner refill kits.
• 0121 693 2644
www.refilltoner.com

UK ATTRACTIONS
A wealth of information on attractions across the UK.
www.ukattraction.com

UNITED NATIONS ENVIRONMENT PROGRAMME (UNEP)
UNEP DTIE, Tourism Programme. United Nations Avenue, Gigiri, PO Box 30552, 00100, Nairobi, Kenya
• (254-20) 7621234
www.uneptie.org/en/index.asp

UNICEF
United Nations programme to promote health, education, equality and protection for every child. Africa House, 64-78 Kingsway WC2B 6NB
• 0870 606 3377
www.unicef.org

URL BARON
For a selection of email cards.
www.urlbaron.com

USHOPUGIVE
An online retail outlet that donates a percentage of what you spend to a charity of your choice, without you paying extra.
www.ushopugive.com

USWITCH
A company that helps customers take advantage of the lowest prices on gas, electricity, home phones and digital TVs from a range of suppliers.
111 Buckingham Palace Road, London SW1W 0SR
• 0800 404 7908
www.uswitch.com

VAUDE
Stocks VauDe outdoor gear – tents, sleeping bags, rucksacks and clothing.
• 01665 510660
www.vaude.co.uk

VEGAN SOCIETY
A society for vegans with information on ethical, compassionate lifestyles that benefit humans, animals and the environment.
• 0121 523 1730
www.vegansociety.com

VEGETARIAN SHOES
Sells environmentally friendly shoes.
www.vegetarian-shoes.co.uk

VEGETARIAN SOCIETY
Working towards a future where vegetarianism is accepted as normal.
Parkdale, Dunham Road, Altrincham, Cheshire WA14 4QG • 0161 925 2000
www.vegsoc.org

VINCEREMOS WINES AND SPIRITS
Suppliers of organic alcohol.
• 0800 107 3086
www.vinceremos.co.uk

VINTAGE ROOTS
Suppliers of organic wine.
• 0800 980 4992
www.vintageroots.co.uk

VIRIDIAN
Organic vitamin company.
• 01327 878050
www.viridian-nutrition.com

VISION AID OVERSEAS
A charity dedicated to improving the vision of poorly-sighted people in developing countries. Recycles spectacles and optical instruments. Unit 12 The Bell Centre, Newton Road, Manor Royal, Crawley, West Sussex RH10 9FZ
• 01293 535016
www.vao.org.uk

VIVA!
Vegetarians International Voice for Animals.
• 0117 944 1000
www.viva.org.uk

VOLUNTEER DEVELOPMENT NORTHERN IRELAND
A Northern Ireland charity providing support and advice to local volunteer agencies. 129 Ormeau Road, Belfast BT7 1SH
• 02890 236100
www.volunteering-ni.org

VOLUNTEER DEVELOPMENT SCOTLAND
A Scottish charity providing support and advice to local volunteer agencies. Volunteer Development Scotland, Stirling Enterprise Park, Stirling FK7 7RP
• 01786 479593
www.vds.org.uk

VOLUNTEER DEVELOPMENT WALES
A Welsh charity providing support and advice to local volunteer agencies.
• 0800 2888 329
www.wcva.org.uk

VOLUNTEERING ENGLAND
A UK charity providing support and advice to local volunteer agencies.
• 0845 305 6979
www.volunteering.org.uk

VOLUNTEERING IRELAND
An Irish Charity providing support and advice to local volunteer agencies. Coleraine House, Coleraine Street, Dublin 7, Republic of Ireland
• +353 1 872 2622
www.volunteeringireland.com

WASTEAWARE
Household waste and recycling information.
www.wasteaware.org.uk

WASTECONNECT
An online database for searching local recycling points in the UK.
• 0905 535 0940
www.wasteconnect.co.uk

WASTE EXCHANGE DIRECTORY
Telephone directory recycling scheme.
www.integra.org.uk/wastedirectory

WASTE ONLINE
For information on how to dispose of batteries and other waste.
www.wasteonline.org.uk

WASTE WATCH
An organisation that promotes and encourages waste reduction, reuse and recycling. 56-64 Leonard Street, London EC2A 4LT
• 020 7549 0300
www.wastewatch.org.uk

WATER AID
A charity working in Africa and Asia to improve water infrastructure, and provide sanitation and hygiene education. Prince Consort House, 27-29 Albert Embankment, London SE1 7UB
• 020 7793 4500
www.wateraid.org/uk

WATER IS COOL IN SCHOOL CAMPAIGN
Aims to improve the quality of provision and access to fresh drinking water for schools in the UK. Contact via ERIC: 34 Old School House Britannia Rd, Kingswood, Bristol BS15 8DB
www.wateriscoolinschool.org

THE WAVENDON ALLOTMENT AND GARDEN SOCIETY (WAGS)
Promotes allotments and vegetable gardening in Milton Keynes and the surrounding area.
http://dir.gardenweb.com/directory/wags

WHALE AND DOLPHIN CONSERVATION SOCIETY (WDCS)
Working for the protection of whales, dolphins and their environment worldwide.
• 0870 870 5001
www.wdcs.org

WHITEDOT
An organisation that campaigns to reduce the amount of TV we watch.
www.whitedot.org

WIGGLY WIGGLERS
Supplies wormeries, gardening accessories, and wildlife products.
• 01981 500391
www.wigglywigglers.co.uk

WILDFOWL AND WETLANDS TRUST
An organisation to research and protect wildfowl and their habitats. WWT Slimbridge, Glos GL2 7BT
• 01453 891900
www.wwt.org.uk

WILDLIFE AID
Caring for wild animals.
• 01372 377332
www.wildlifeaid.com

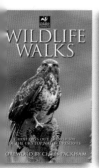

WILDLIFE & COUNTRYSIDE LINK
Provides a list of wildlife and countryside charities. 89 Albert Embankment, London SE1 7TP
www.wcl.org.uk

THE WILDLIFE TRUSTS
A wealth of information about wildlife and our environment.
The Kiln, Waterside, Mather Road, Newark, Nottinghamshire NG24 1WT
• 01636 677711
www.wildlifetrusts.org

WILDWINGS
Runs wildlife eco-tours.
• 01179 658333
www.wildwings.co.uk

WILLING WORKERS ON ORGANIC FARMS (WWOOF)
Provides information about volunteering on organic farms around the world.
www.wwoof.org

WOMAD
World of Music, Arts and Dance.
www.womad.org

WOMENEXCEL.COM
For tips on natural face masks.
www.womenexcel.com/ecowatch/ecobeautytips.htm

WOMEN'S ENVIRONMENTAL NETWORK
Campaigns on issues which link women, environment and health. PO Box 30626, London E1 1TZ
• 020 7481 9004
www.wen.org.uk

WOODCRAFT FOLK
Provides a programme of games, drama, craftwork and education for young people. 13 Ritherdon Road, London SW17 8QE • 020 8672 6031
www.woodcraft.org.uk

WOODLAND TRUST
Working for the protection of Britain's native woodland heritage.
Autumn Park, Dysart Road, Grantham, Lincolnshire NG31 6LL
• 01476 581111
www.woodland-trust.org.uk

WOODLAND TRUST – NORTHERN IRELAND
The Woodland Trust in Northern Ireland, 1 Dufferin Court, Dufferin Avenue, Bangor, County Down BT20 3BX
• 028 91275787
www.woodland-trust.org.uk

WOODLAND TRUST – SCOTLAND
The Woodland Trust Scotland, South Inch Business Centre, Shore Road, Perth PH2 8BW
• 01738 635829
www.woodland-trust.org.uk

WOODLAND TRUST – WALES
The Woodland Trust Wales (Coed Cadw), Yr Hen Orsaf, Llanidloes, Powys SY18 6EB
• 01686 412508
www.woodland-trust.org.uk

WWF-UK
An international conservation organisation working to protect species and their natural habitats.
Panda House, Weyside Park, Godalming, Surrey GU7 1XR
• 01483 426444
www.wwf.org.uk

YOUNG PEOPLES TRUST FOR THE ENVIRONMENT (YPENTC)
Encourages young people's understanding of the environment. YPTE, 3A Market Square, Crewkerne, Somerset TA18 7LE
• 01460 271717
www.yptenc.org.uk

ZEROWASTE
A trust encouraging us to work towards zero waste production. PO Box 33, 1695 Takapuna, Auckland, New Zealand
www.zerowaste.co.nz